Victorian Decorative Glass
British Designs 1850-1914

Mervyn Gulliver

Schiffer Publishing Ltd

4880 Lower Valley Road, Atglen, PA 19310 USA

Dedication
To my wife, Lynn

Library of Congress Cataloging-in-Publication Data

Gulliver, Mervyn.
  Victorian decorative glass: British designs, 1850-1914/
Mervyn Gulliver.
      p. cm.
  ISBN 0-7643-1597-8
1. Decoration and ornament--Victorian style--Collectors and
collecting. 2. Victoriana-Collectors and collecting. I. Title.
  NK1378 .G85 2002
  748'.0941'09034-dc21
                              2002003078
Copyright © 2002 by Mervyn Gulliver

Designed by "Sue"
Type set in Geometr231 Hv BT /ZapfHumnst BT
ISBN: 0-7643-1597-8
Printed in China
1 2 3 4

Published by Schiffer Publishing Ltd.
4880 Lower Valley Road
Atglen, PA 19310
Phone: (610) 593-1777; Fax: (610) 593-2002
E-mail: Schifferbk@aol.com
Please visit our web site catalog at
www.schifferbooks.com
We are always looking for people to write books on new
and related subjects. If you have an idea for a book,
please contact us at the above address.

This book may be purchased from the publisher.
Include $3.95 for shipping.
Please try your bookstore first.
You may write for a free catalog.

In Europe, Schiffer books are distributed by
Bushwood Books
6 Marksbury Ave. Kew Gardens
Surrey TW9 4JF England
Phone: 44 (0)20 8392-8585; Fax: 44 (0)20 8392-9876
E-mail: Bushwd@aol.com
Free postage in the UK. Europe: air mail at cost.
Please try your bookstore first.

Acknowledgements

I would like to offer my sincere thanks to the following companies and public services for their invaluable assistance in my research for this project:

To The Edinburgh Crystal Glass Company Limited, Eastfield, Penicuik, Midlothian, Scotland, for their kind permission to access and reproduce designs from the surviving pattern books of Thomas Webb & Sons Limited and those of the Richardson family businesses of which they are the copyright owners.

To Stuart & Sons Limited at Redhouse Glassworks, Stourbridge, West Midlands, for their kind permission to access their various surviving pattern books and to reproduce designs from them as I require for this project. I acknowledge that they are the copyright owners of the drawings that I may select to use from their archives.

To Broadfield House Glass Museum, Kingswinford, for their kind permission to access and reproduce selected information from their archives.

To Royal Brierley Crystal and Broadfield House Glass Museum, Kingswinford, for their kind permission to access and reproduce selected information from the surviving archive material of Stevens & Williams Limited.

To Dudley Libraries, Archives and Local History Service at Cosely, West Midlands, for the efficient and friendly service that they have afforded me in my research into the glass pattern books currently in their custody.

To the Public Record Office at Kew, England, for the efficient and friendly way in which they gave me access to the Design Registers and books of Representations in their custody.

I would like to thank Eric Reynolds for his kind advice on matters appertaining to the glass of John Walsh Walsh, and for his permission to photograph items in his collection and reproduce them in this book.

I would also like to offer my thanks to Margaret Gulliver and June Jeffery for allowing me to photograph items in their respective collections and to reproduce them in this book.

Finally, and most importantly, I would like to thank my wife, Lynn, without whose continuous patience, help, and support this book would never have become a reality.

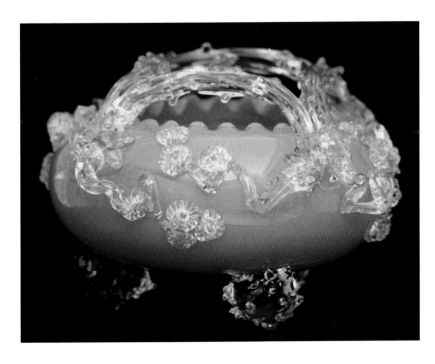

Introduction

The period 1850-1914 was an exceptionally dynamic period for the glass making industry in Britain, Europe, and America. Manufacturers competed with each other to create innovative and cost effective manufacturing techniques and designs to satisfy the changing fashions of the Victorian and Edwardian eras.

A vast range of new glass mixes were invented, creating all sorts of innovative internal and external decorative effects. Surface reduction techniques such as acid etching, intaglio cutting, and sand blasting were developed alongside the traditional cutting and engraving techniques. Cost effective mass production for the cheaper domestic market was achieved with the invention of machines to make press molded glass. The inspection of even a few of the surviving pattern books and trade catalogues confirms that the range of glass designs created was simply phenomenal. It is fortunate that a large amount of the decorative glass manufactured in this period has survived, and that the very finest examples can be seen in museums and reference sources published to date.

This book has been conceived as the first stage of a major project which will concentrate primarily on recording designs created for hand formed, functional, and decorative glassware manufactured for the wider general domestic market of the time. Although the emphasis in this book is on glass items produced by British manufacturers, some American and European glass items of the period will be found illustrating a particular technique or design. Similarly, illustrations of some items from the more expensive ranges are also included to complement those published to date. The format for this volume comprises a series of schedules and illustrations which are set within the following five chapters:

Chapter One commences with designs created for the component parts of glass items, i.e. rims, bodies (including applied motifs), and feet. The Chapter finishes with descriptions of the five basic techniques that were used to decorate glass items: applied texture, applied decoration, internal decoration, surface reduction techniques, and surface tooling techniques.

Chapters Two, Three, and Four present designs created for Flower Holders, Food Related Items, and Drink Related Items. Each of these chapters is divided into their respective item types which are then further classified according to the specific decorative technique used in their design. In instances where multiple techniques have been used on an item, the most prominent technique used determines its location in the chapter.

Dimensions of each item are provided, first in inches and then in centimetres, and they represent the height x width respectively, measured to the nearest 0.25 of an inch or 0.5 of a centimetre.

A price guide for each item is also included in each caption. However, all prices quoted in this book are approximate and are based on 2001, United Kingdom values for items in good condition. The author and the publisher accept no responsibility for items that may sell for more or less than the values suggested in this book.

Attribution of Designs

It is often difficult to attribute glass designs of this period to specific manufacturers because:
- very little of the glass produced was given an identification mark
- manufacturers often closely copied each other's designs
- some of the respective designs shown in the Registered Design books of Representations, and surviving manufacturer's pattern books, are sometimes only drawn in a diagrammatic format left open for final interpretation by the glass workers making the items
- pattern books have not survived, which makes it impossible to substantiate hearsay comments passed down through the generations.

However, some of the items illustrated in Chapters Two, Three, and Four have identifying marks, and some without marks have been attributed by reference to one or more of the following surviving documents:
- manufacturers pattern books
- Registered Design records
- publications of the era such as *The Pottery Gazette*
- associated retail trade and exhibition catalogues. The remaining items have still to be attributed.

Chapter Five contains sketch illustrations of Registered Designs recorded between 1850-1914 by seven major glass manufacturers who operated in the Birmingham, Manchester, and Stourbridge areas.

The book concludes with a brief glossary of glass making terms and a bibliography for further reference.

Contents

Chapter One
Component Designs & Decorative Techniques

1. Materials and Color

The basic ingredients of a glass mixture comprised silica (fine sand), potash (alkaline flux) and lead oxide (to provide stability and improved appearance). Impurities in the form of iron in the silica, were neutralized by the addition of a small amount of manganese. The proportions of the ingredients and the range of additional ingredients employed, varied from manufacturer to manufacturer depending on the visual effects they were each intending to achieve.

The mixture of silica, potash and metallic oxides, known as frit, was heated in a separate furnace at a temperature low enough for the mixture to oxidise but not fuse. This was then added to pieces of broken glass, known as cullet, in a clay pot in the working furnace, and eventually vitrified into glass.

Colored glass was obtained by adding suitable amounts of finely ground metal oxides or other substances as follows :

Amethyst was produced from manganese and cobalt
Black came from manganese and iron
Blue came from copper or cobalt
Green came from iron, or iron and copper.
Green /Yellow came from Uranium
White was produced from Bone Ash (calcium phosphate), or tin oxide, or arsenic. The use of any of these created an opaque white glass, a semi-transparent opal glass, or a milk glass.
Red (ruby) was produced from gold chloride (made by dissolving pure gold in a mixture of hydrochloric and nitric acids). Alternatively it was produced from copper oxide. Use of either of these created a color-less glass that developed to ruby red on being reheated.

2. Introductory Remarks

A glass item was brought to its final shape by either (a) being blown and hand shaped on the pontil rod, (b) being blown into a mold, either with or without further hand working, (c) being formed in a press mold, or (d) being formed by the hand modelling processes of Pate de Verre and Cire Perdue.

The aesthetic success achieved by using any of these techniques can sometimes depend on the respective attention paid to the design of the three basic component parts of any object, (a) the rim, (b) the body, and (c) the base.

When items do not have an identification mark, the design of any one or more of these components can sometimes offer an indication of the likely source(s) of manufacture.

The variety of designs both functional and decorative, created for these components was quite extraordinary, and therefore a separate database has been formulated in Section 3 below to record the components of some of the items illustrated in Chapters 2, 3, and 4.

The decoration of an item of glass was achieved by any one, or combination of the following methods :
By using transparent or opaque color, internally or externally applied, or both
By modelling the profile of the item by hand or mold
By applying a texture to a surface
By applying additional material to a surface
By using visible decorative techniques beneath the surface
By reducing the surface by a cutting technique
By tooling the surface without loss of material.

The illustrations show the application of color in various formats and also the use of hand and mold modelling. The remainder of the decorative techniques noted above are described in Sections 4 to 8, and examples are illustrated in Chapters 2, 3, and 4.

3. Component Designs

18 DESIGNS FOR RIMS
1: Plain edge
Ground off, and polished
Fire polished
Folded
Folded, with oval pattern cutting
Multi-way deep crimp

Rim with fire polished edge. Item made by
Thomas Webb & Sons Limited, c.1888.

Top of rim ground off and polished.

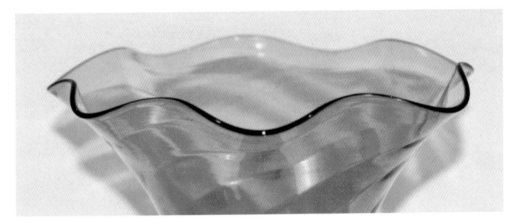

Rim with fire polished edge.

Rim with fire polished edge. Item made by Stuart & Sons Limited, c.1900.

Fire polished edge to star shaped rim of cased glass item.

Five-way, deep crimped rim with plain, fire polished edge.

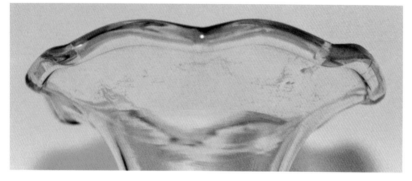

Rim with plain edge folded under.

Rim with plain, folded edge decorated with oval cut pattern.

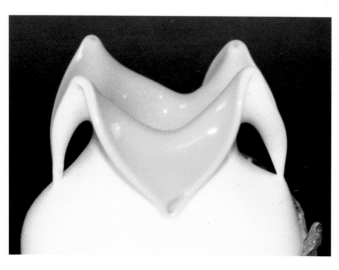

Plain, fire polished edge to rim, which is finished with a four way deep crimp.

Four-way, deep crimped rim with plain, fire polished edge, on item formed in cased glass.

2: Applied trail to edge of rim
Clear or colored glass trail - plain pattern
Clear or colored glass trail - rustic pattern
Opalescent trail

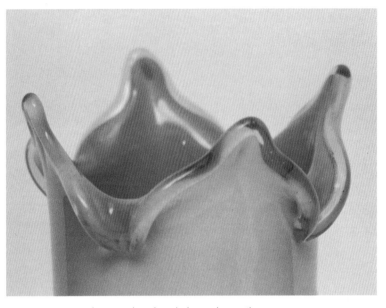

Four-way crimped rim with colored glass edge trail.

Four-way crimped rim with plain profile, clear glass edge trail.

Rim decorated with applied colored glass edge trail set out in a vertical saw tooth pattern.

Vertical, irregular profile crimped rim with colored glass edge trail.

Vertical scallop profile, eight-way, shallow height crimped rim with colored glass edge trail.

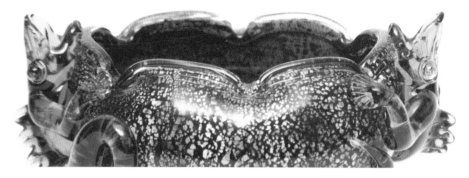

Six-way crimped rim with clear glass edge trail. The profile of the crimp is an example of Registered Design No.390104, as recorded by Thomas Webb & Sons Limited on November17, 1882.

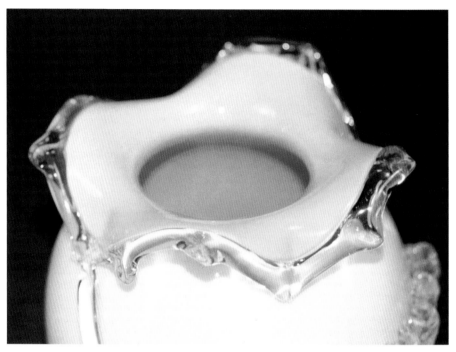

Four-way shallow crimped rim with rustic pull out effect, clear glass edge trail.

Three-way crimped rim with rustic pull out effect, clear glass edge trail.

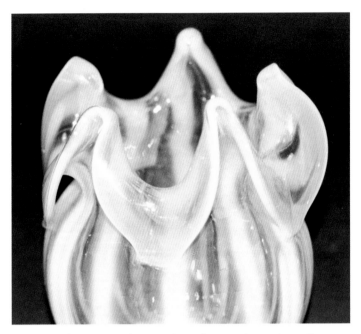

Five-way deep crimped rim, with opalescent glass, edge trail.

Shallow height, eighteen-way crimped rim of mold blown item formed in opalescent glass.

3: Multi-way crimped edge
Shallow height, U-shaped rounded profile
Shallow height, rounded profile - folded
Shallow height, rectangular profile
Shallow height, extra wide rectangular profile
Shallow height rounded profile crimp set between larger
    half round crimp
Shallow height rounded profile multi-crimp set between
    rectangular crimp
Shallow height U-shaped rounded profile with second,
    deep profile, multi-way crimp
Multi-way crimp pushing rim inwards
Shallow height V-shaped profile

Rim with ten-way, shallow height, "U" shaped, edge crimp.

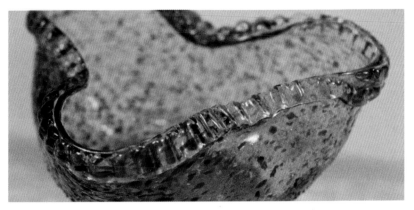

Rim with shallow height, rounded profile multi-way crimped and folded edge.

Rim with eight-way, shallow height, rectangular profile crimped edge.

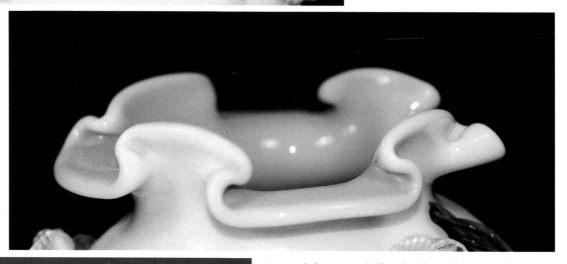

Rim with four-way, shallow height, wide rectangular profile, crimped edge.

Left:
Plan of crimped rim.

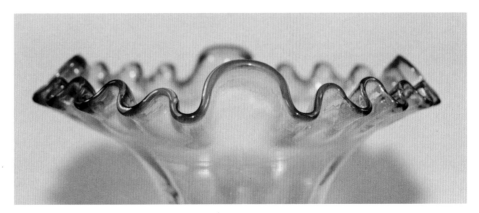

Rim finished with shallow height, rounded profile crimps set between larger half-round crimps.

Rim with an applied clear glass edge trail finished with shallow height, rounded profile crimps set between larger half round crimps.

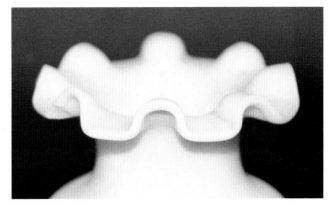

Rim finished with alternate shallow height rounded profile and rectangular profile crimps.

Plan of rim.

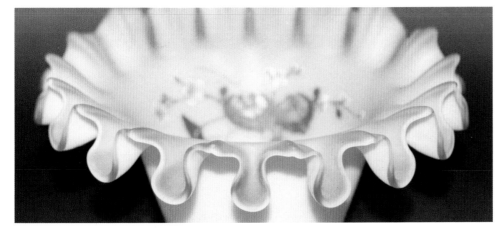

Rim finished with alternate large rectangular profile crimps and narrow rounded profile crimps.

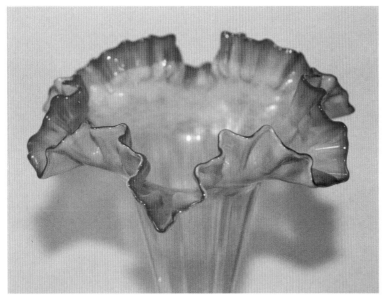

Six-way, deep crimped rim, decorated with shallow height rounded profile multi-way edge crimp. (Plan of rim shown at right)

Plan of rim.

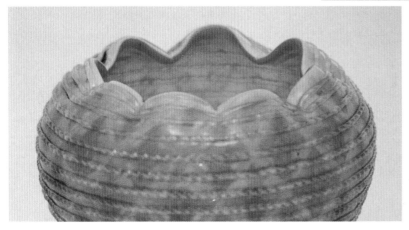

Rim finished with eight-way crimp, pushed inwards.

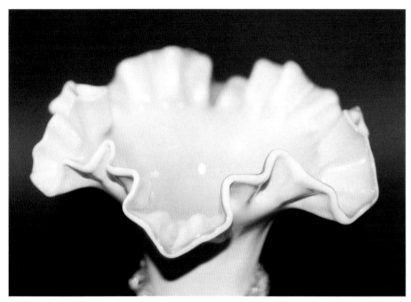

Six-way deep crimped rim, decorated with shallow height rounded profile multi-way edge crimp formed in opaque colored glass.

Rim decorated with applied clear glass trail and finished with a "V" profile multi-crimp.

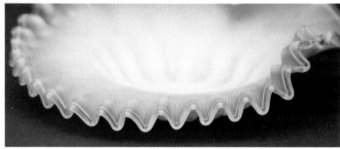

4: Multi-way vertical crimp
Eight-way, rectangular stepped profile
Tightly set, rounded profile
Tightly set, rounded profile, turned inwards
Square / rectangular profile turned inwards
Four-way 'V' shaped crimp forming cross profile at rim level

Vertical eight-way, stepped rectangular profile, crimped rim with colored glass edge trail.

Plan of rim.

Vertical eight-way, stepped rectangular profile, crimped rim with
colored glass edge trail, applied to a single layer glass item.

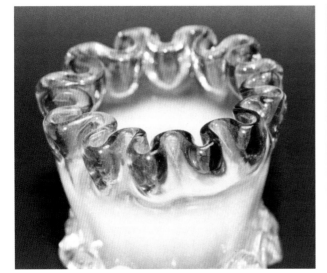

Tightly set, rounded profile vertical crimped rim.

Plan of vertical fourteen-way,
rounded profile, crimped rim.

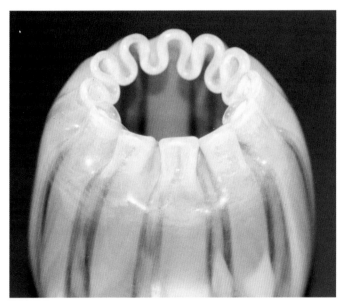

Tightly set, rounded profile crimped rim, turned inwards.

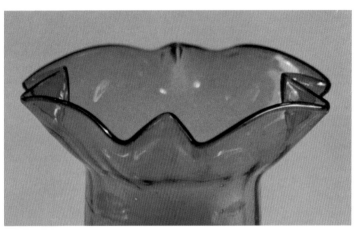

Four-way vertical "V" shaped crimped rim, in the shape of a cross.

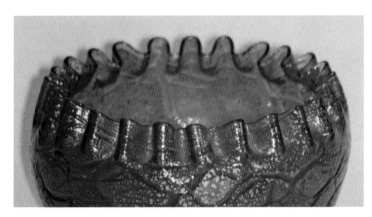

Tightly set, rounded profile crimped rim, turned inwards.

Plan of rim.

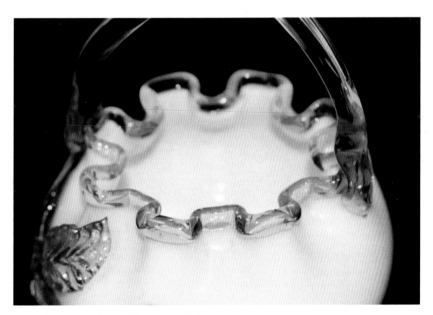

Vertical, rectangular profile crimped rim, pushed inwards.

5: Petal shaped edge
Plain edge
Applied trail

Crimped rim with edge profiled into ten petal shapes.

Plan of crimped rim with edge profiled into six petal shapes.

Crimped rim with edge profiled into eight, petal shapes, with alternate petals turned upwards.

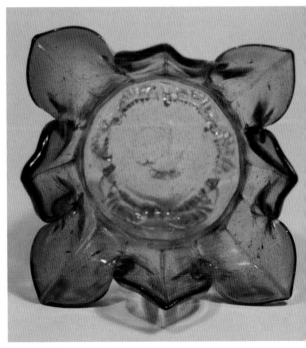

Plan of rim.

Crimped rim with edge profiled into nine petal shapes.

Six-way crimped rim with edge profiled into six petal shapes.

Six-way crimped rim with edge profiled into six petal shapes.

Clear glass ten-way crimped rim with edge profiled into ten petal shapes, and decorated with applied colored trail.

Nine-way crimped rim with edge profiled into nine petal shapes.

Color shaded, ten-way crimped rim with edge profiled into ten petal shapes, and decorated with applied colored trail.

6: Jack-in-the-Pulpit profiled rim
Plain or crimped edge
Plain or folded crimped edge
Applied trail

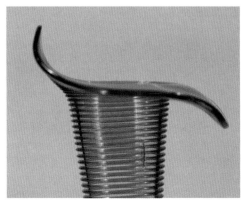

Jack-in-the-Pulpit shaped rim with plain edge.

Jack-in-the-Pulpit shaped rim with plain edge and pincered motif to apex.

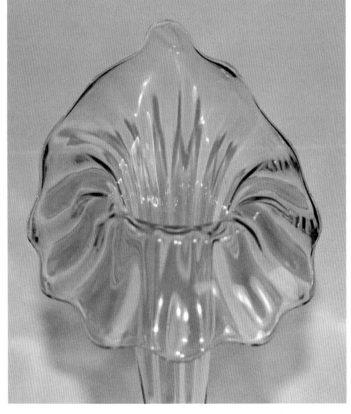

Front view of Jack-in-the-Pulpit shaped rim with plain, shallow crimped edge.

Jack-in-the-Pulpit shaped rim with shallow height, rounded profile edge crimp.

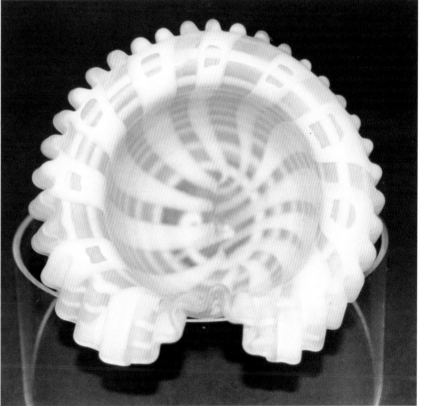

Plan view.

Side view.

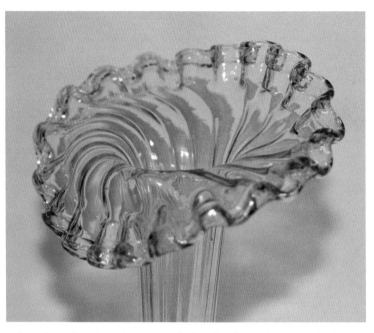

Jack-in-the-Pulpit shaped rim with shallow height, multi-crimped edge folded under.

Jack-in-the-Pulpit shaped rim with shallow height multi-crimped edge, decorated with applied plain trail. This design is on a vase made by Burtles, Tate & Co.

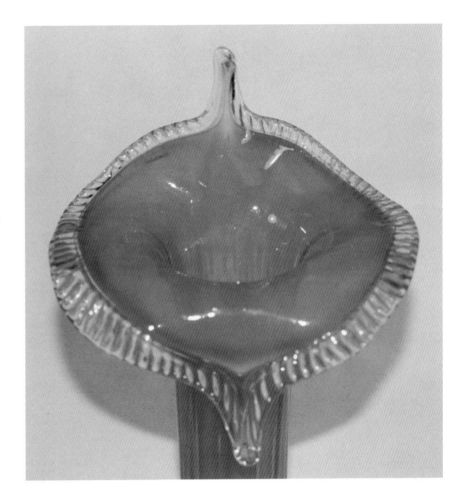

Front view of Jack-in-the-Pulpit shaped rim with shallow height multi-crimped edge, decorated with applied pincered trail.

Side view.

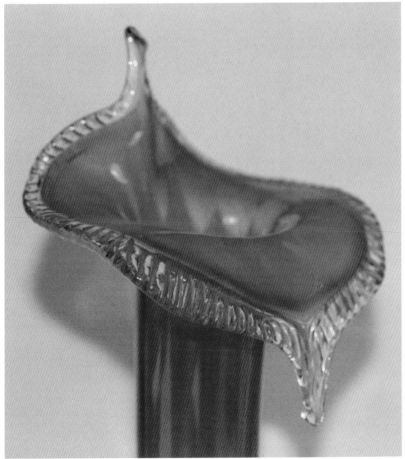

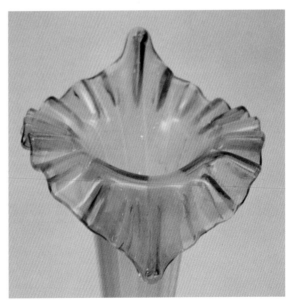

Jack-in-the-Pulpit shaped rim with shallow height multi-crimped edge, decorated with applied plain trail.

7: Rim turned over and down
Plain edge or crimped edge
Threaded plain edge or threaded crimped edge
Threaded with pincered trail to edge
Plain edge, multi-way crimp, with upright, pincered trail
    to top of rim

Projecting turned down rim decorated with a broad band of shallow height, rounded profile, multi-way crimping.

Rim decorated with machine threading, turned over and down, and finished with a multi-way vertical crimp.

View of underside of crimped edge, showing tooled surface to threading.

Upright pincered trail applied to top of turned over rim decorated with multi-way edge crimp.

Rim decorated with machine threading, turned over and down, and finished with an applied pincered trail. This design is on an item manufactured by Stuart & Son Limited.

8: Rim folded inwards or upwards

Plain rim folded inwards on one, two, three, or four
   sides
   Six way crimped rim forming a fan shape
   Threaded rim with shallow profile multi-way edge
crimp
   Shallow profile multi-way edge crimp, with a three
way second crimp turned upwards

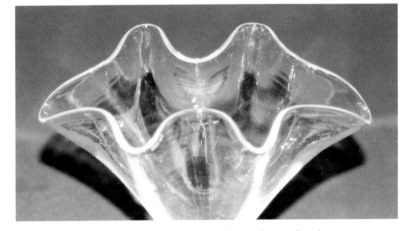

Six-way vertical crimped rim, pinched together to form a fan shape.

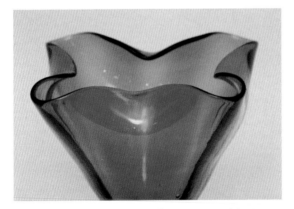

Rim folded inwards between four-way vertical crimp.

Machine threaded rim with multi-way crimped edge, pinched together to form a fan shape. Item made by Stuart & Sons Limited.

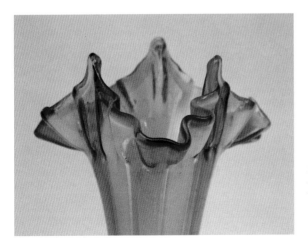

Shallow profile multi-way edge crimp, and
finished with a three-way, deep second crimp.
The rim edge is turned and pulled upwards.

9: Pinched together rim – multiple openings
Plain edge
Crimped edge

Plain edged rim pinched together to form three openings. This is an example of Patent No.24048 – Top for flower vases, as registered by Stevens & Williams Limited in 1909.

Plain edged rim pinched together to form five openings. This is an example of Patent No.24048 – Top for flower vases, as registered by Stevens & Williams Limited in 1909.

This rim profile is another variation of Patent No. 24048.

Plan view.

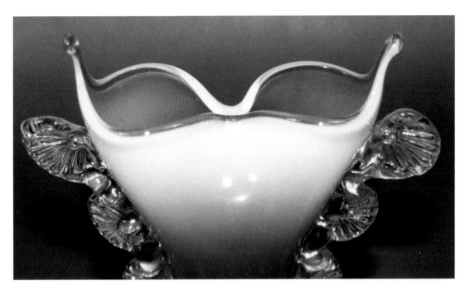

Plain edged rim pinched together to form two openings.

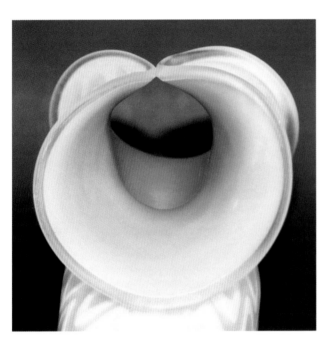

Folded down rim pinched together to form two openings.

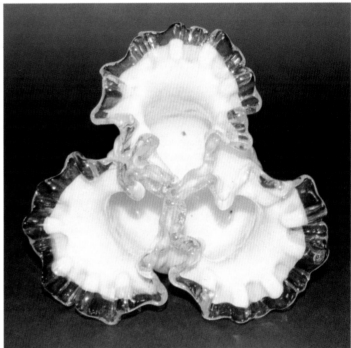

Plan of rim with applied, multi-way crimped edge trail, pinched together in the middle to form three openings.

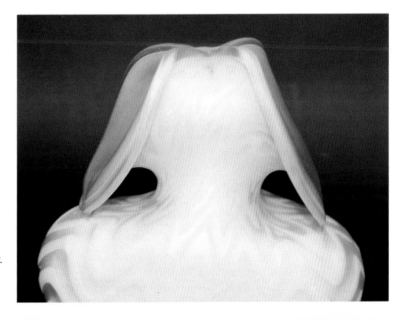

Side view.

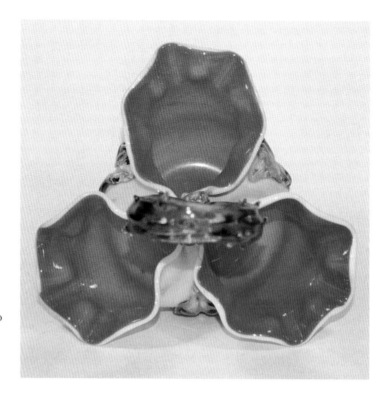

Plan of rim with plain edge, pinched together in the middle to form three openings.

10: Hand formed, free shape rim
Edge vertically cut and sections twisted, turned up or
        down, or curled

Rim edge cut vertically and sections thus created turned up and
down and twisted to create stylised flower head shape.

Plan view.

Rim edge cut vertically and sections thus created turned up and down and twisted to create stylised rustic profile.

Plan view.

Rim edge cut vertically and sections thus created turned up and down to create a decayed flower head shape.

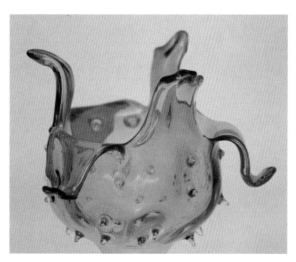

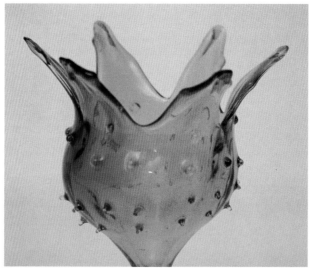

Rim edge cut vertically and sections thus created turned up and down to create a half-decayed flower head shape.

Rim edge cut vertically and sections thus created turned upwards to create an open flower head shape.

11: Vertical edge formed to regular or irregular profile
Saw tooth profile with applied trail and pincered patterning

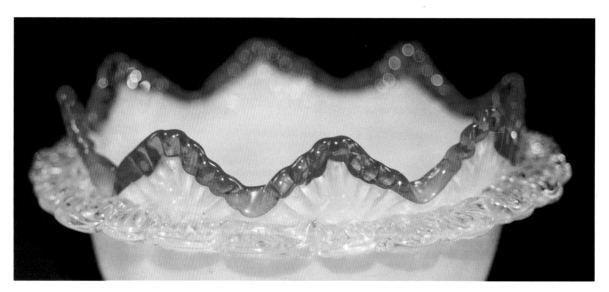

Vertical saw tooth profile rim decorated with applied pincered edge trail with pincered patterning under.

12: Pouring lips
Formed by hand tooling
Formed within mold blown design
Formed with applied shell ribbed decorative profile

Pouring lip formed by hand tooling.

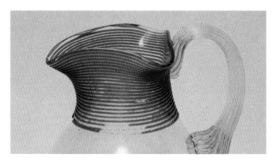

Pouring lip formed as part of a trefoil profile hand shaped rim.

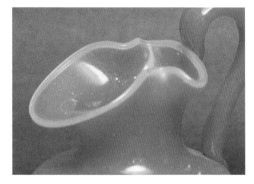

Pouring lip formed as part of a trefoil profile, hand shaped rim.

Pouring lip formed as part of a mold blown design.

Pouring lip formed with applied shell ribbed decorative profile. This lip is an example of Registered Design No.212674, dated October 19, 1867, recorded by Thomas Webb & Son Limited.

13: Metal mounts
Pewter
Silver / silver plated rims

Diamond shaped rim covered over with decorative pewter work.

Typical example of a silver covered rim.

14: Pincered trails
One pattern used all around rim
Two different patterns of trails, one set above
    the other
Profiled with multi-way crimp

Plan of fourteen-way, vertically crimped rim, decorated with applied horizontal half-daisy pattern, pincered trail.

Rim decorated with continuous pincered trail.

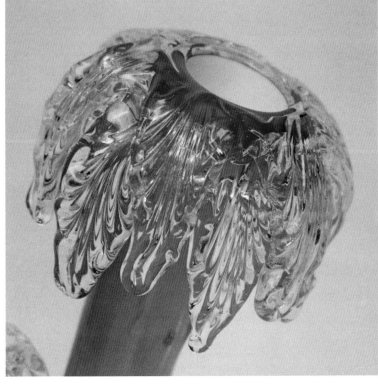

Two rows of stylised palm tree leaves formed in pincered work on an item made by John Walsh Walsh.

Rim decorated with one row of small, stylised palm tree leaves formed in pincered work.

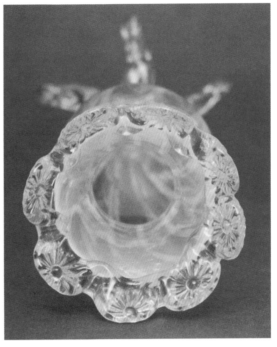

Plan of rim decorated with upright trail of daisy pattern pincered work.

Rim decorated with two rows of abutting, half-daisy pattern, pincered opalescent trails.

Rim decorated with two different patterns of pincered trails.

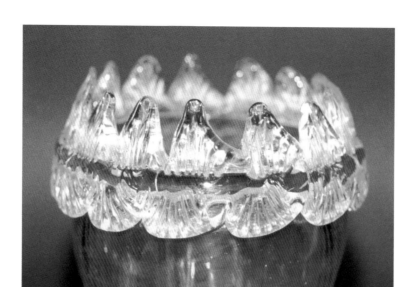

Rim decorated with two different patterns of pincered trails.

Rim decorated with two different patterns of pincered trails.

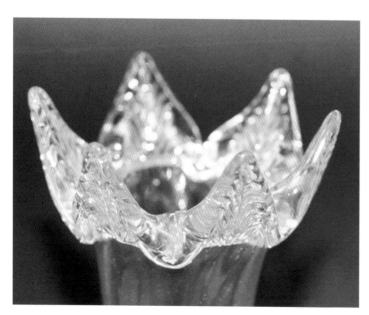

Upright pincered rim trail finished with six-way crimp.

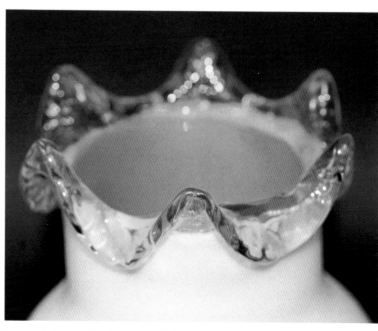

Pincered rim trail finished with shallow height six-way crimp.

Upright pincered rim trail finished with six-way crimp.

Plan of eight-way crimped rim decorated with an applied edge trail finished with a cross ribbed pincered pattern.

15: Rigaree trails
Single rigaree trail
Single rigaree trail - above or below a pincered trail

Rim decorated with one horizontal trail of rigaree. .

Rim decorated with one horizontal trail of rigaree on a vase manufactured by Stuart & Sons Limited.

Rim decorated with single trail of rigaree set above two, overlapping broad bands of pincered drop trails.

Rim decorated with upright pincered trail set above a single trail of rigaree, on an item made by Stuart & Sons Limited.

Rim decorated with single trail of rigaree set above a shell ribbed pincered trail.

16: Inverted wishbone shaped trails
Formed in plain or colored glass

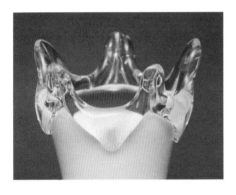

Rim decorated with an applied upright trail finished in an inverted wishbone type profile, similar to that used for feet.

Rim decorated with a stylized crown design formed with colored glass looped trail supported on top of clear glass trail around the rim of the body.

17: Stylised crown shapes
Formed with narrow width clear or colored glass looped trails

Rim decorated with a stylised crown shape formed with a series of looped flat section trails.

18: Open trellis pattern
Formed with clear or colored glass trails

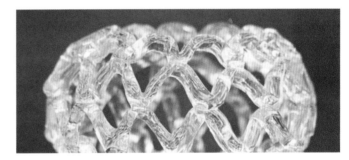

Stylised trellis type pattern formed with narrow clear glass ribbon trails.

Plan view.

SIX DESIGNS FOR BODIES AND APPLIED FUNCTIONAL AND DECORATIVE ELEMENTS
1: Mold blown patterns
The following patterns were often used by glass manufacturers, and examples are shown on various items in Chapters Two, Three and Four:
Diamond patterns
Bold projecting rib patterns
Faint projecting rib patterns
Festoon patterns
Peacock tail patterns
Peacock eye patterns
Circular/oval indented patterns
Stylised floral patterns
Repetitive geometric patterns
Lozenge shaped patterns
Horizontal / vertical wave patterns

2: Typical mold blown / hand formed shapes

The following shapes were often used by glass manu-
facturers for their products, and examples are illustrated
in Chapters Two, Three and Four:
Horn/Cornucopia shapes
Amphora shapes
Trumpet shapes
Stylised flower shapes
Stylised tree shapes
Rustic style, tubular shapes
Geometric and miscellaneous shapes

3: Handle designs

Plain strap handles
Plain dab handle
Strap handle with double rib section
Shell ribbed
Rope twist pattern
Rustic log effect
Plain handle with applied rigaree
Plain handle with applied pincered trailing
Plain handle with cut / engraved / etched pattern
Handle with overlapping connection into rim opening
Plain handle with rustic prunt effect at lower connection
    to body

Plain strap
handle.

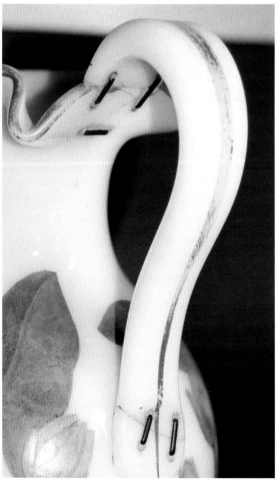

Plain strap handle.

Damaged strap handle
repaired with staples.

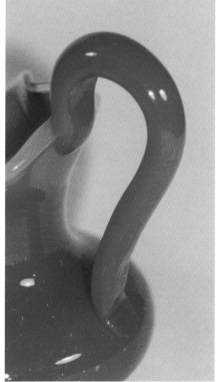

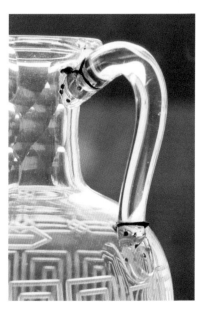

Damaged circular section handle repaired with wire and rivets.

Plain strap handle.

Strap handle formed with double rib section, applied to jug manufactured c.1876 by Hodgetts, Richardson & Son.

Plain dab handle.

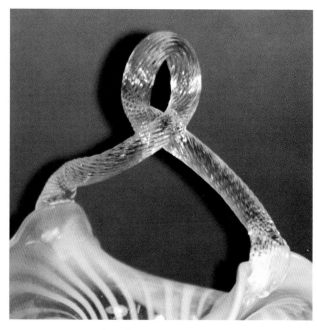

Left:
Example of shell ribbed section handle shown in Registered Design No.212674, dated October 19, 1867, recorded by Thomas Webb & Sons Limited.

Rope twist pattern handle.

Shell ribbed section handle on item manufactured c.1867 by Thomas Webb & Sons Límited.

Shell ribbed section handle with looped attachment at rim level.

Handle formed like rustic briar.

Left:
Handle formed
like rustic briar.

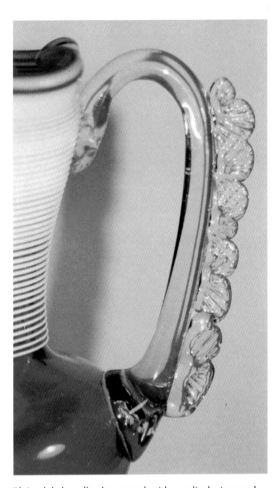

Plain dab handle decorated with applied pincered trail.

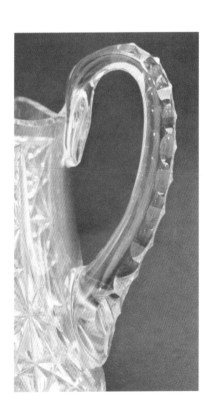

Left:
Plain circular section handle
decorated with applied trail of
rigaree on an item made by
Stuart & Sons Limited.

Right:
Handle decorated with a cut
pattern.

Handle with rustic pattern dab connection to body.

Handle decorated with applied silver deposit design.

Handle with rustic pattern dab connection to body.

Handle with rustic pattern dab connection to body.

4: Decorative motifs applied to body

Single spiral thread / trail
Multiple spiral threads / trails
Multiple vertical trails
Random pattern of threading / trails (See pages 120-122 for examples of the above decorative motifs).
Stylised flower heads with leaf trails.
Leaves formed in two different colored halves
Leaves formed in two different colored halves - daisy head pattern
Stylised fruit, nuts, or acorns with leaf trails
Stylised acanthus leaf motifs – clear glass / single color glass
Stylised fish / reptile motifs
Short lengths of thin glass canes in random pattern (*Peloton*)
Horizontal and / or vertical trails of rigaree
Rigaree trails in festoon patterns with / without prunts
Pincered trails of shell ribbed / daisy head patterns
Pincered trails of ribbed / cross ribbed patterns
Projecting horizontal rounded profile crimped frills
Horizontal / vertical trails with short pincered projecting fins evenly spaced out along its length

Stylised flower head.

Example of stylised daisy head used by Stevens & Williams Limited for their *Mat-Su-No-Ke* Registered Design No.15353, dated October 18, 1884.

Stylised flower head and leaf trail.

Side view.

Stylised flower head and leaf trail.

Stylised flower head and leaf trail.

Stylised flower head and leaf trail.

Stylised flower head and leaf trail.

Stylised flower head and leaf trail.

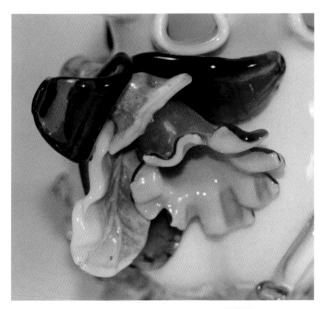

Front view.

Stylised flower head and leaf trail.

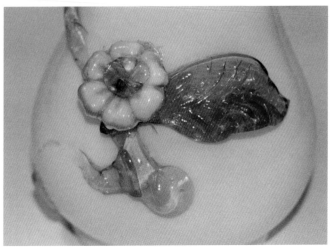

Stylised flower head and leaf trail.

Stylised flower head and leaf trail.

Stylised flower head applied to rustic branch trail.

Side view.

Stylised flower head and leaf trail.

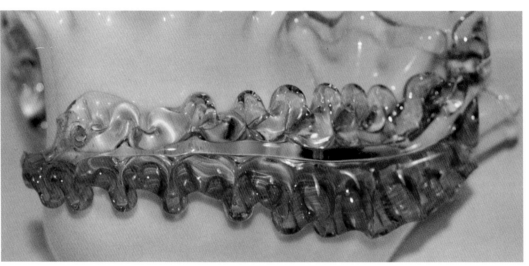

Large stylised leaf formed in two different colored halves.

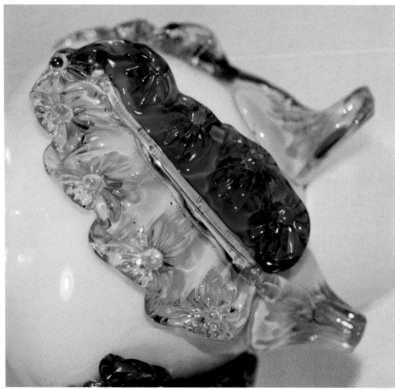

Large stylised leaf formed in two different colored halves and decorated with daisy head pincered pattern.

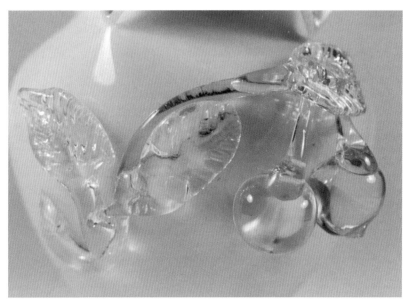

Stylised cherry type fruit and leaf trail.

Stylised horse chestnut casing.

Stylised cherry type fruit and leaf trail.

Stylised cherry type fruit and leaf trail.

Stylised plum type fruit and leaf trail.

Stylised acanthus leaf.

Stylised acanthus leaf.

Stylised acanthus leaf.

Smaller version of stylised acanthus leaf.

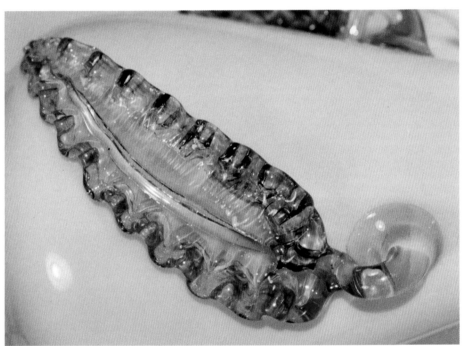

Colored glass acanthus leaf formed with contrasting colored edge trails.

Colored glass acanthus leaf formed with contrasting colored edge trails.

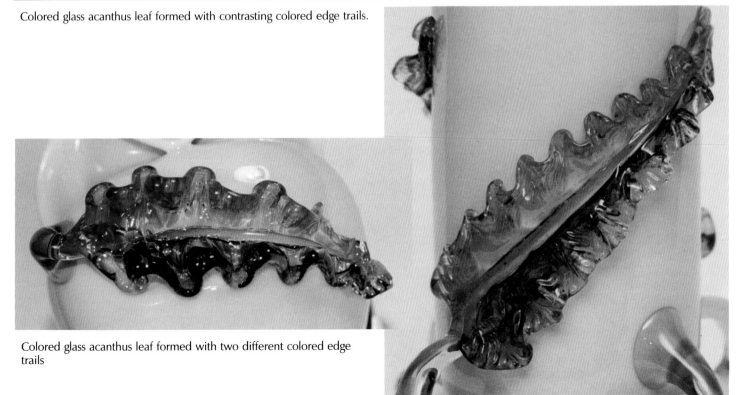

Colored glass acanthus leaf formed with two different colored edge trails

Stylised reptile applied to item made by
Thomas Webb & Sons Limited.

Vertical trails of rigaree.

Stylised reptile motif formed in clear glass.

Festoon trail of rigaree between prunts.

Example of *Peloton* decoration.

Shell rib pattern pincered work trail
set beneath crimped rim.

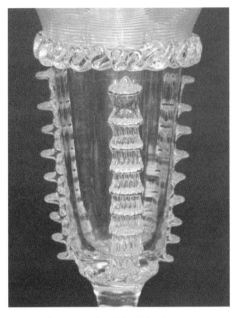

Pincered work trails with ribbed pattern.

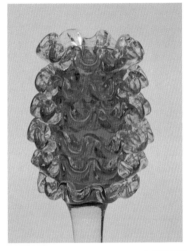

Multiple projecting horizontal rounded profile crimped frill.

Trail with projecting fins decorated with pincered pattern.

Projecting horizontal rounded profile crimped frill.

5: Prunts applied to body and / or underside of feet
Registered Diamond
Stylised flower head
Stylised fruit motif
Stylised lion head motif
Central half dome surrounded by a ring of smaller domes
Ribbed shell pattern
Miscellaneous patterns

Prunt in the form of a stylised flower head applied to base of item.

Registered Diamond prunt applied to base of item
made by Thomas Webb & Sons Limited

Prunt in the form of a stylised flower head applied to base of item.

Prunt in the form of a stylized raspberry, but with large central dome motif.

Stylised raspberry prunt incorporating a circular back pad.

Stylised raspberry prunt applied to item made by John Walsh Walsh.

Prunt in the form of a stylised flower head applied to sides of item made by John Walsh Walsh.

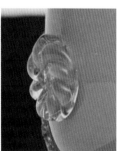

Side view.

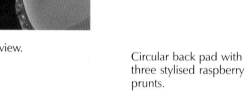

Circular back pad with three stylised raspberry prunts.

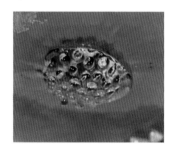

Prunt in the form of a stylised raspberry, applied to base of item made by Stuart & Sons Limited

Right:
Prunt made in the form of a stylised lion head mask on a circular back pad.

Prunt in the form of a stylised raspberry, applied to base of item made by Stuart & Sons Limited

Prunt made with a large center dome surrounded by two rows of smaller domes, applied to the side of an item.

Example of shell ribbed pattern prunt recorded in Registered Design No.212675, dated October 19, 1867, by Thomas Webb & Sons Limited

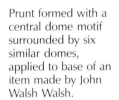

Prunt formed with a central dome motif surrounded by six similar domes, applied to base of an item made by John Walsh Walsh.

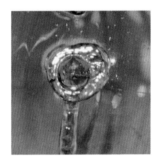

Prunt formed with a central dome applied to a back pad.

6: Finish to underside of a body or foot

The underside of a glass item could be finished off in any of the following ways:

Pontil mark left as snapped off

Pontil mark ground off and polished out

Pontil mark covered by decorative prunt

Base decorated with a cut, multi-point star motif

Base decorated with geometric cut pattern

Base decorated with intaglio cut design

Base left as formed from plain or patterned mold

SEVENTEEN DESIGNS FOR FEET

1: Circular feet

Plain

Plain with folded edge

Deep profile multi-crimp all over

Shallow profile multi-crimp all over

Rib mold blown, ogee profile, with folded edge

Multi-daisy pattern, pincered in clear / colored glass

Shallow profile multi-crimp to edge

Plain circular foot engraved on the underside " Rd 21329". This relates to a Registered Design recorded by Burtles Tate & Co., on February 2, 1885.

Plain pattern, circular applied foot.

Circular foot decorated all over with a deep, rounded profile crimp.

Plain pattern, circular foot with opalescent rim trails, applied to an item made by Stuart & Sons Limited.

Underside of foot, showing snapped off pontil mark.

Circular foot with edge of rim folded under.

Circular foot decorated all over with shallow height multi-crimp.

Underside of foot.

Shallow profile multi-rib, mold blown, circular foot, worked to an ogee profile and finished with a folded under edge.

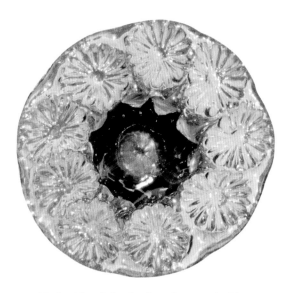

Underside of circular foot decorated with pincered stylised daisy heads.

Underside of foot, showing snapped-off pontil mark.

Underside of circular foot decorated with two different pincered patterns.

Circular foot decorated with a band of shallow height, rounded "V" shaped crimping.

2: Triangular shaped feet
Shallow profile crimp to edge of foot

Triangular shaped foot decorated with shallow height, rounded profile crimped edge.

Underside showing polished off pontil.

3: Leaf and petal shaped feet in clear / colored glass
Stylised, flower head with six petals, formed in clear / colored glass
Five interlinked triangular leaves in clear / colored glass
Six interlinked triangular leaves (3 no. folded up)
Five interlinked circular profile, pincered petal shapes

Pincered work foot made in the form of a six petal stylised flower head.

Underside of foot.

Pincered work foot formed with five, triangular profile stylised leaves.

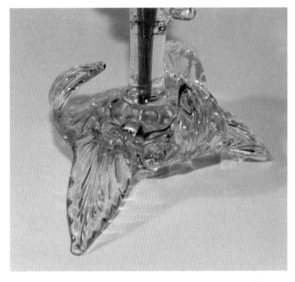

Pincered work foot formed with six, triangular profile stylised leaves, three of which are curled upwards..

Five point, pincered work star shaped foot.

Underside of foot.

Underside of foot formed with five interlinked petal shapes, and decorated with pincered half daisy pattern.

Underside of foot formed with five, pincered work, petal shapes.

Underside of pincered work foot applied to mold blown item, and formed with six, stylised ribbed petals.

View of junction with body.

4: Rustic trails and stylised tree roots
Formed in clear / colored glass with surface pull outs / ribbed patterns

Rustic type foot formed as a series of stylised tree roots.

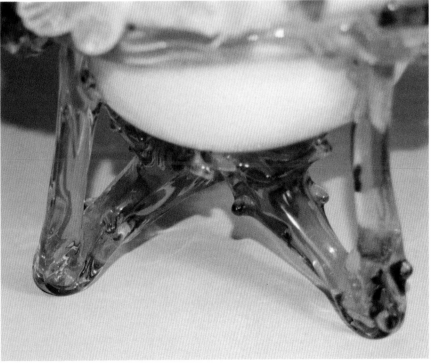

Rustic, stylised tree branch foot, formed with
a rib mold section and surface pull-outs.

Rustic, stylised tree branch foot formed with a relatively smooth section and surface
pull-outs.

5: Open trellis type feet
Formed in clear / colored glass

Foot formed in a stylised
open trellis pattern.

Underside of foot.

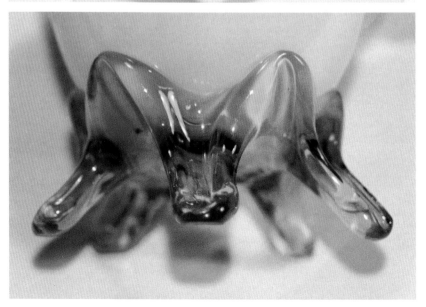

6: Wishbone profile
Shallow height
Tall height

Foot formed with a shallow height,
wishbone pattern trail in colored glass.

Shallow height, opalescent wishbone pattern trail with daisy pattern pincered feet.

Foot formed with a shallow height, wishbone pattern trail in colored glass.

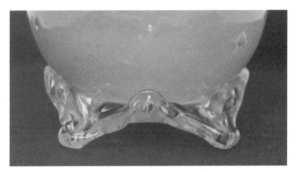

Foot formed with a shallow height, wishbone pattern trail in clear glass.

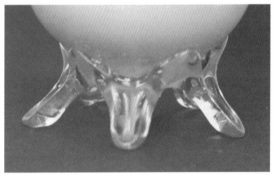

Foot formed with a shallow height, wishbone pattern trail in clear glass.

Shallow height, opalescent wishbone pattern trail with daisy pattern pincered feet.

Foot formed with a shallow height, wishbone pattern trail in clear glass.

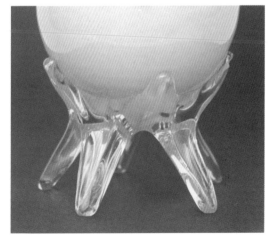

Foot formed with a tall height, wishbone pattern trail in clear glass.

7: Snail shape
Plain surface in clear / colored glass

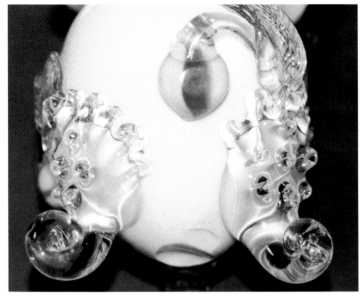

Small, snail shaped foot
formed in clear glass.

Large snail shaped foot
formed in clear glass.

8: Ribbed shell pattern
Fine profile ribs
Bold profile ribs

Fine, shell ribbed foot on an item
made by Stuart & Sons Limited.

Example of foot described in Registered Design 238052, dated
January 12, 1870, as recorded by Hodgetts, Richardson & Son.

Bold, shell ribbed foot on item made by Stuart & Sons Limited.

Pincered work foot in clear glass, formed as a stylised acanthus leaf.

9: Stylised acanthus leaf.
Formed in clear / colored glass

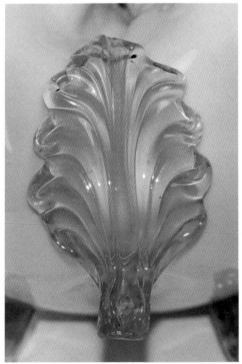

Pincered work foot in colored glass, formed as a stylised acanthus leaf.

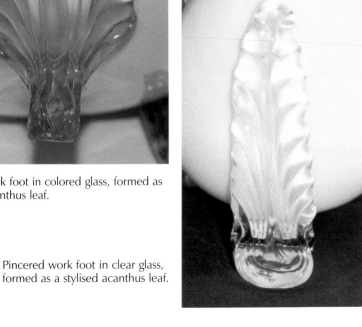

Pincered work foot in clear glass, formed as a stylised acanthus leaf.

Pincered work foot in colored glass, formed as a stylised acanthus leaf.

Stylised clear glass acanthus leaf foot.

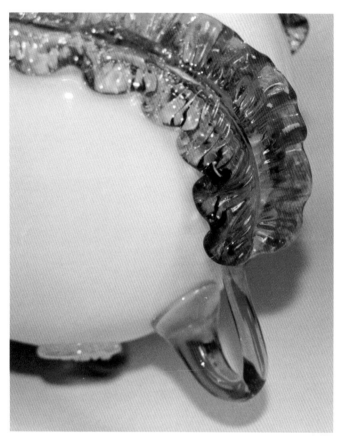

Stalk of stylised acanthus leaf extended to form looped pattern foot.

Clear glass foot, formed out of the stalks of two, pincered work, stylised acanthus leaves.

10: Stylised fish
Formed in clear / colored glass
Gilded finish

Colored glass foot formed as a stylised fish.(Tail is missing from this example) applied to machine threaded body.

Clear glass foot formed as a stylised fish and applied to a crackled glass body with gold foil inclusions.

Left:
Colored glass foot formed as a stylised seal and applied to a colored body of an item made by Thomas Webb & Sons Limited.

Right:
Gilded glass foot formed as a stylised fish, and applied to colored glass body.

11: Stub feet
Plain pattern, formed in   clear / colored glass
Rustic pattern, formed in clear / colored glass
Ribbed pattern, formed in clear / colored glass

Clear glass, faintly ribbed, stub foot.

Rustic pattern stub foot.

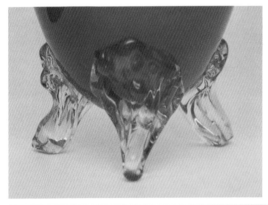

Rustic pattern stub foot.

Rustic pattern stub foot with iridescent finish.

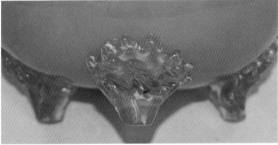

Rustic pattern stub foot on item made by John Walsh Walsh.

Plain pattern, stub foot.

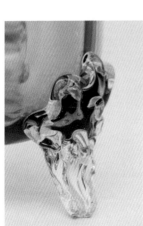

Rustic pattern stub foot.

Ribbed pattern stub foot.

12: Pincered trails
Set vertically / at an angle formed in clear /
    colored glass
Pincered decorative trail around edge of hand
    / mold formed base

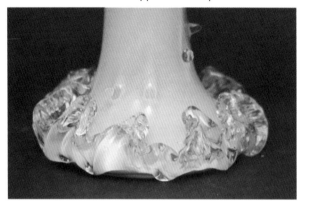

Foot formed with applied pincered trail, set at
slight angle to body.

Foot decorated with applied trail of pincered work.

Foot formed with two different patterns of pincered trails, applied to an item
made by John Walsh Walsh.

Foot formed with applied vertical
pincered trail, on item made by
Stuart & Sons Limited.

13: Hollow conical shapes
Part plain / part threaded
Threaded all over

Inverted, hollow conical shaped foot, formed in clear glass and
decorated with a band of very fine machine threading.

Inverted, hollow conical shaped foot with iridescent finish,
formed in a mold blown diamond pattern, and cased with
applied machine threading.

14: Domed shapes
Hollow profile - plain
Hollow profile - ribbed pattern

Hollow profile domed shape
foot with folded edge.

View of top.

Hollow profile, rib mold blown foot, on item
made by Thomas Webb & Sons Limited.

15: Prong shaped feet

Narrow tapering width prongs with
rounded ends
Broad, parallel sided prongs with
rounded ends

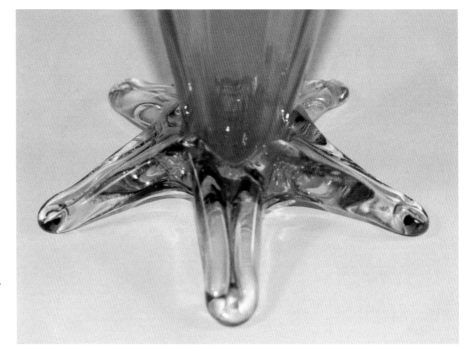

Foot formed with five, narrow
tapering prong shapes.

Underside of foot.

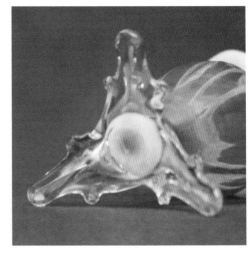

Underside of foot formed with rustic
pattern tapered prong shapes.

Underside of foot formed with five, prong shaped feet decorated with pincered pattern.

View of top.

16: Rustic ball shapes
Formed in clear / colored glass

Clear glass foot formed in the shape of a rustic pattern ball, on an item made by Stevens & Williams Limited.

Colored glass foot formed in the shape of a rustic pattern squashed ball.

17: Miscellaneous designs
Plain designs similar in concept to fish shaped legs

Colored glass foot of similar design to the stylised fish pattern.

4. APPLIED TEXTURE

Fire polishing

In order to remove surface blemishes and obtain a brilliant surface finish, the glass object was held at the furnace mouth so that the surface just melted.

Satin finish

A dull silky textured surface was achieved by dipping the glass item into a bath of white acid. The item would either be left undecorated or be decorated with enamelled and / or gilded designs.

Crackled / Iced / Frosted finishes

A crackled finish was obtained by plunging the red hot glass item into cold water, and then reheating it, and then blowing it to its final shape. The stresses set up within the body as a result of the sudden cooling, created a random pattern of cracks in the external surface, but the internal surface of the item remained smooth.

An iced effect was obtained by rolling an inflated gather over a marver that had been covered with fragments of pounded glass. The gather was then heated slightly and formed into the final shape required.

A frosted effect was achieved by exposing the object to the fumes emitted from white acid, which produced a very fine textured, smooth obscured surface.

5. APPLIED DECORATIVE TECHNIQUES

Transfer printing

This technique involved the transfer of designs engraved on copper plate, via thin paper onto the glass surface. The design was either left as transferred or further decorated with enamelling and / or gilding.

Enamelling

Enamel colors used comprised metallic oxides mixed with a glass frit of finely powdered glass, and suspended in an oily medium for ease of application by brush. The colors were applied to the glass object and fixed by low temperature firing in a muffle kiln, during which time the medium burnt out. A flux mixed with the enamel colours, lowered the firing point to below that of the glass to which they had been applied.

Enamelling was also simply painted straight onto the glass surface and left unfired. This method was cheaper and quicker than the fired process, but was much less durable.

Oil gilding / Fired gilding

Oil gilding comprised gold powder or gold leaf applied over an oil or varnish based size, which was then burnished. This method of gilding was used on plain surfaces or to further decorate engraved decoration. As the fixing medium tended to be water soluble, the gilding easily rubbed off.

Fired gilding comprised gold mixed with any number of fixatives, including honey, white of eggs, mercury, etc. The thick liquid was painted or brushed on, and the glass object was fired again in a low temperature muffle kiln. After receiving two, three or sometimes four firings, the object was removed and burnished, in order to brighten the gold. This was done with brushes made of spun glass and then afterwards with agate and bloodstone. This method was always applied to plain surfaces. Designs using this technique could comprise:
Gilded patterns
Gilded and enamelled patterns

Iridescent finishes

The development of this form of decoration came from a desire to reproduce the iridescence found on old pieces of glass and glazed pottery that had been buried in the ground. Iridescence on such glass is caused by the action of carbonic acid or ammonia salts contained in the earth or air, which in the presence of moisture decompose the glass, forming soluble carbonate of soda or potash.

As this is washed from the glass surface, scales of an acid silicate of lime, alumina or lead, as the case may be, remain, which break up the rays of light into their respective spectrum of colors thereby creating the iridescent effect. These conditions are met when glass is buried in humid earth at high temperatures.

The aim of the nineteenth century glassmakers was to produce a finely ridged metallic film on the surface of an object, that would break up ordinary daylight into its constituent colours, so that it would shimmer and change as the observer changed position.

The research and development of this type of finish appears to have accelerated following the Vienna Exhibition of 1873, where Ludwig Lobmeyr exhibited the first commercially produced iridescent glass of the nineteenth century. He was soon followed by other European, American and British glass manufacturers, who registered patents for their specific techniques for creating an iridescent finish for glass.

The processes used could vary considerably, but the general approach appears to have been to subject a glass object to the fumes of various metallic salts and chemicals being burnt within a muffle type kiln.

An iridescent finish could also be achieved by spraying a mixture of metallic salts onto the items and firing them to achieve a permanent finish. This technique was used for *Carnival Glass.*

Iridescent finishes were applied to translucent / opaque plain or colored glass items.

Machine threading

Prior to 1876, the decoration of glass items with threading was done by hand or by picking up canes of glass from a dip mould, and it was difficult to obtain evenly spaced lines. On May 6, 1876, William J. Hodgetts of Hodgetts, Richardson & Son, registered a patent for the design of a machine to produce regular spaced threading. Other manufacturers in Great Britain, Europe and America soon adopted the respective design principle of this machine, and registered patents for their own machines, taking care not to infringe any of the original patent rights.

Machine threading could be formed with thick or very fine sections which could also be decorated, by partial cutting or tooling, to further enhance a design.

The range of designs on translucent and opaque glass items comprised :

Simple machine threading to all or part of the item
Intaglio cut patterns over machine threading
Threading with tooled surface
Mold blown designs finished with machine threading
Encased machine threading applied to a mold blown body

Trailing

This type of decoration comprised the application to an object's surface of one or more, of any of the following items formed in clear / colored glass:

Single spiral thread / trail
Multiple spiral threads / trails
Multiple vertical trails
Random pattern of threading / trails
Stylised flower heads with leaf trails
Leaves formed in two different colored halves
Leaves formed in two different colored halves- pincered daisy head pattern
Stylised fruit, nuts, or acorns with leaf trails
Stylised acanthus leaf motifs – clear glass / single color glass
Stylised fish / reptile motifs
Short lengths of thin glass canes in random pattern (*Peloton*)
Horizontal or vertical trails of rigaree
Rigaree trails in festoon patterns with / without prunts
Pincered trails of shell ribbed / daisy head patterns
Pincered trails of ribbed or cross ribbed patterns
Projecting horizontal rounded profile crimped frills

Horizontal / vertical trails with short pincered projecting fins evenly spaced out along its length

Glass beads

Beads of clear / coloured glass were used for decoration in any of the following ways:
Individual beads, or groups of beads were fired onto the surface of an object to enhance a particular part of a design.

A technique called *Coralene,* was patented on July 7, 1883, by Arthur Schierholz of Plauen, Thuringia, in the German Empire. This process comprised the application of a design onto a glass object using either clear or colored enamel of a syrupy consistency, and applying small glass beads to its area. The glass was then subjected to enough heat to melt the enamel, and the beads then became bonded to the glass object. This basic design process was soon in use by other manufacturers in Europe, Great Britain and America.

A technique for the application of glass beads, set out in a regular pattern on a glass object, was patented in 1905 by H. Wilkinson of Amblecote. This process involved the application of threads to a ribbed mold blown object, so that the threading only attached to the tips of the ribs. The glass object was then reheated and spun, which had the effect of snapping the threading and making it contract into a bead shape on the tip of each rib.

Silver deposit

The first process was to form a base for the silver by firing a powdered flux containing a large proportion of silver, onto the surface of the glass object. After the flux had set the silver base was scratch buffed with a brush and water. The article was then suspended from a negative copper wire, in a silver plating solution in which pure silver anodes were suspended. A current of 2 volts or 30 amps was used for a period of six hours, and a heavy coating of the silver was deposited upon the silver flux base. The deposit could then be buffed and polished with rouge to a bright finish and then engraved if required.

Metal encased glass

On August 18, 1884, Fritz Heckert of Petersdorf. Germany, patented a process for encasing glass items within an open metalwork frame. The open metal framework which was formed in stamped, cast, pressed or plated metal, was set into a mould. A gather of glass was then put into the framework and blown out to adhere to it. After being released from the mould the surplus material at the rim was removed and it was fire polished to a smooth finish. This basic technique of encasing glass soon came into universal use in Europe, America and Great Britain.

Staining

This process involved the application of a colored stain to the surface of a clear glass body, and firing it to make it permanent. The stained area could, if required, be decorated with a cut or engraved design.

Flashing

This process comprised the application of a very thin layer of colored glass over a clear or colored base layer of glass. This could be achieved by gathering both colors directly onto the blowing iron before blowing the required shape. The finished article could be left plain or further decorated with cut or etched designs.

Casing

This process comprised the formation of a glass object with multi-layers of clear / coloured glass. When fully annealed, the article could then be further decorated with enamelling, gilding or a cutting technique.

6. INTERNAL DECORATIVE TECHNIQUES

Heat reactive glass

Amberina and *Plated Amberina*

On July 24, 1883, Joseph Locke of New England was granted the first patent for a heat reactive glass called *Amberina*.

This type of glass was made with a small amount of gold in solution colloidally dispersed in a transparent amber glass mixture. The glass was allowed to cool below a glowing red heat and then the required areas of the item were then reheated at the glory hole. This rapid cooling and reheating process made the reheated areas strike a ruby red color, and produced a shading effect of amber to red.

Amberina glass was also used in conjunction with opaque colored glass, for example, *Plated Amberina* as patented on June 15, 1886 by Edward D.Libbey. This glass was formed by casing a body of cream colored glass with a gold-ruby *Amberina* glass mixture, which was then reheated to develop a deeper color, blending into the lighter part of the glass which had not been reheated enough to develop any color. This technique was virtually identical to *Peach Glass* produced by Thomas Webb & Sons in 1885.

Peachblow

The *Peachblow* glass made by other American glass manufacturers was identical to the *Plated Amberina* and *Peach Glass,* in that in each case a cream colored glass was cased with a heat reactive glass layer.

Alexandrite

The technique of *Amberina* was further elaborated by Thomas Webb & Sons, c.1900, when they produced a heat reactive glass that they called *Alexandrite*, which shaded from amber to ruby to violet blue at the rim. The article needed to be reheated twice to obtain the change from amber to ruby, and then ruby to violet blue.

Burmese

On December 15, 1885 Frederick Shirley of Mount Washington Glass Company, patented a formula for a heat reactive glass called *Burmese*. The shaded effect was created by adding a small amount of fluorspar, feldspar and oxide of uranium to essentially the same ingredients used for *Amberina* glass.

The uranium oxide made the translucent opal white glass melt to a pale yellow color and the addition of a small amount of gold in a solution of aqua regia and colloidally dispersed throughout the whole batch, made the glass heat reactive. After the article had been formed it was allowed to cool below red heat and then it was reheated at the glory hole. The reheated portions struck a salmon pink color, and shaded into the pale yellow body.

On June 16, 1886 this formula was patented in England and not long afterwards Thomas Webb & Sons Limited were granted a license to produce *Burmese* glass, which they called *Queen's Burmese Ware*.

Items formed in this material were either left in the basic polished finished or given a satin finish, and could also be left plain or decorated with enamelled flower patterns, and sometimes with gilding.

Opalescent glass

A shaded opalescent effect glassware was obtained by using a glass mixture containing bone ash and arsenic. When the glass object had been worked to its finished shape, it was allowed to cool to below red heat, and then the required areas of its surface would be reheated and would strike an opalescent white. If this type of glass was blown into a patterned dip mold, the opalescent effect would appear on the raised portions of the design and the background would remain clear.

Shaded glass

Heat reactive mixes were also created to produce designs with a single color shading into clear glass, such as shaded ruby, and shaded amethyst.

Gold and silver foil inclusions

This process involved encasing a layer of silver foil or gold foil or fragments of them, between two layers of glass.

A gather of glass would be blown and worked by hand (or blown into a mould) to bring it to its final or near final size and shape. The object would then be rolled over the marver on which had been placed the gold or silver foil. The top layer of glass was then applied to the body, either by dipping it into a pot of glass mix, or by blowing the gather into a slightly larger, matching profiled, preformed body.

Internal trailing

Simple vertical trail designs were created with clear and colored canes of glass picked up with a gather of clear or colored glass from a dip mould

Spiral trail designs were formed in a similar manner to vertical trails. The gather with the applied colored canes was twisted to create the spiral effect, prior to being brought to the final shape.

A tartan type pattern was achieved with individual horizontal threads being applied over the vertical canes.

Pulled up festoon patterns were formed by applying single or multiple colored threading by hand or machine, to a partly blown object, and then pulling the threading up with a point at evenly spaced centres around the object. The object was then blown to its final size and shape.

The festoon type of decoration was further refined by John Northwood, the Artistic Director at Stevens & Williams Limited, who patented a machine on February 2, 1885, which could form regularly spaced multi-colored "V" shaped threaded motifs within a glass body.

Air trap patterns

On July 27, 1857, Benjamin Richardson patented a technique of decoration of trapping air bubbles between two layers of glass.

This process involved blowing a gather of glass into a projecting diamond patterned dip mold and then applying a further layer of glass over it by either blowing it into a preformed glass cup, or by dipping it into a pot of molten glass. Both methods gave rows of small round evenly spaced air bubbles.

This process was not developed further until the early 1880s, when a variety of new patterns appeared. The glass body could be formed with three or four layers of glass and its surface could be left plain as formed, or given a satin finish, and /or given enamelled, gilded, and cameo decoration.

Another type of air trap design was created with vertical / spiral hollow ribs. A gather of glass was blown into a dip mold to pick up an arrangement of hollow tubes of glass, which were then marvered into the surface of the body and if required, twisted to give a spiral effect. The item was often given a satin finish, and /or used in conjunction with heat reactive glasses, which could further enhance the respective design with color shading.

The range of air trap designs comprised the following patterns:

Diamond shape
Diamond shape with motif in centre of diamond
Herring bone pattern
Stylised floral designs
Circular / oval patterns
Miscellaneous abstract patterns
Vertical / spiral hollow rib patterns

Imitation stone patterns

In 1830 in Haida, Bohemia, Frederich Egemann produced an imitation stone glass which he called *Lithyalin*.

A black jasper was made by adding forge scales, lava or basalt to the ordinary materials used for glass. A yellowish bronze colored jasper was produced by substituting lead slags for forge scales. A red jasper was formed by the addition of copper oxide etc.

A deficiency of carbon in the process caused the fractured or laminated effects in the glass. The blanks were cut with broad facets to expose the stone like patterning, and then given a polished finish.

Alongside these high quality imitation stone glasses, which were produced throughout the rest of the nineteenth century, could be found more affordable ranges produced in marble patterned cased glass, as well as marbled effect glass items produced in the 1870s onwards by the manufacturers of press moulded glass.

Trapped enamel decoration

On December 16, 1879, Henry Gething Richardson filed a patent for trapping enamelled decoration between two layers of glass.

This process involved blowing a shaped bubble of glass, removing it from the blowpipe, letting it cool, and then applying an enamelled design to its interior surface.

The decorated item was then reattached to a pontil and reheated so that another bubble of glass could be blown inside it and bond to its surface. The new bubble would extend through the mouth of the original exterior one, and would then be finished off to the required shape and design. This process relied heavily on very careful temperature control during the reheating process to avoid differential thermal stress movement between the two skins of glass.

Color splashed glass

A gather of clear or colored glass was rolled over a marver covered with particles of colored glass, and/or mica flakes, or aventurine, to pick them up and then to encase them with another layer of clear or colored glass. This gather would then be blown to the required design by hand forming or in patterned molds.

Imitation tortoiseshell was formed in a similar manner by casing fragments of light and dark amber glass between two layers of clear glass, then forming the final body shape and finishing it with a yellow stain fired onto its surface.

Venetian techniques

The influence of Venetian designs can be seen in some of the designs produced by British glass manufacturers. The following basic Venetian techniques were used direct, or adapted to suit the required designs.
Vetro a retortoli

Circular section canes containing spiralling white or colored canes are laid on a marver and then picked up on the surface of a gather of clear glass. Alternatively the canes could be set upright in a dip mould and the gather of glass blown into it to collect them. In each case, the ends of the canes are joined in the clear glass, and successive marvering and blowing created a regular lacework pattern, commencing radially from the bottom within a thickness of only a few millimetres.

Mezza filigrano

This is a spiral pattern formed by using clear glass canes containing either a white or colored cane. The canes are joined together at each end and twisted to form a spiral pattern.

Vetro a reticello

This comprises the formation of a blown glass *mezza filigrana* item which is opened to form a bowl after it has been detached from the blowpipe, and attached to a pontil.

At the same time as forming this bowl, a similar one is formed but with the canes spiralling in the opposite direction. This latter bowl is then inserted into and bonded by heat to the other bowl, thereby trapping little bubbles of air in the centre of the overlapping canes.

Millefiore

This technique comprises the use of very short lengths of composite colored canes, laid out in a pattern on a marver or from a dip mold, and picked up with a gather of clear or colored glass, and blown to the required design.

Colors used by Venetian glassmakers as far back as the Renaissance were formed as follows:

Blue was formed with cobalt

Violet & Black were formed with manganese

Aquamarine & Red were formed with copper

A pinkish Red was formed with gold

Yellow, Brown, and Green were formed with Silver, Sulphur or Carbon

Towards the end of the nineteenth century, chrome was introduced to obtain green tinges, and during the subsequent thirty years the use of cadmium for yellow, and selenium for pink. When these two materials were blended a vivid blood red was produced.

Aventurine was also incorporated into Venetian designs.

7. SURFACE REDUCTION TECHNIQUES

Acid etching

The basic process involved coating the glass body with an acid resisting material such as a beeswax and resin mixture, scratching the required design into its surface with a sharp metal point, and then dipping it into a bath of hydrofluoric acid. The acid resisting material was then cleaned off , leaving the required pattern etched into the surface. Variations to this technique that were used included the following :

Transfer printing the design from an engraved plate with *acid resisting printers ink* and fixing it to the glass object. The item was then dipped in a bath of hydrofluoric acid.

Painting a design on the glass with a bituminous acid resisting paint and then submerging it in the acid bath. This process was used as the initial stage for the production of commercial cameo glass.

Transfer printing a design from an engraved plate with an *acid paste* containing starch and gum tragacanth, plus a fluoride liquid that attacks glass. The engraved design on the plate was filled with this paste and then transferred by thin paper to the glass surface, left for two minutes and then removed.

Template etching machines were invented to form all manner of designs and patterning.

The effects of the etching process consisted of outlines, so if the areas between were required to be filled in, this had to be carried out by the engraver. John Northwood discovered a method of obscuring such areas with acid.

By mixing hydrofluoric acid with an alkali salt such as potassium carbonate or sodium carbonate, a compound was formed which only attacked the surface, did not eat into the glass, and produced a very fine textured, smooth obscured surface. This liquid became known as *white acid*, and could also be used to form a satin finish for various fancy glassware items being produced at that time.

Sand blasting

The basic technique comprises the application of a design to a glass object by the projection under pressure of a fine stream of abrasive material through a template applied to its surface. Various grades of sand, sharp builder's sand, powdered glass, emery, chilled iron-sand and steel shot could be used for the abrasive medium. Air pressure was achieved by steam, exhaust air, blasts of air, and compressed air.

Cutting

This process involved three processes of roughing out the design, smoothing, and polishing as follows :

Roughing was achieved with iron cutting wheels fed with a steady stream of water and sand.

Smoothing was achieved with cutting wheels of fine grained stones fed only with water.

Polishing out the matt surface left from the cutting wheel was achieved by wooden wheels fed with slurry powder, followed by a brush wheel, fed with pumice or putty powder, followed by wood or cork wheels and putty powder.

Benjamin Richardson had discovered, c.1857, that a mixture of hydrochloric acid and sulphuric acid, diluted with water, would produce a bright polished finish, it was not however until the 1880s that this method of polishing really began to develop. Acid polishing removes more of the glass and the edges of the cutting appear slightly rounded, giving the respective cut designs a softer appearance.

Geometric designs for cut glass items were created by using one or more of the following basic cut patterns:
vertical, diagonal and horizontal V-cuts
concave vertical flute cuts
vertical flat pillar cuts
circular or oval cuts
diagonal flash cuts
flat diamond pattern formed with V-cuts
flat diamond pattern with centre star cut pattern
pyramid diamond pattern
cross cut pyramid diamond pattern
strawberry diamond pattern
hobnail pattern
star patterns
leaf cuts
uneven polygonal cuts creating a hammered effect

Engraving

This process involved cutting designs into a glass surface by means of copper wheels of varying sizes attached to a treadle driven lathe. The edge of the wheel was moistened with a little emery in oil, before being applied to the glass surface.

As well as being used for complex geometric designs, copper wheel engraving was used to create high quality sculptural designs on glass of human figures, animals, plants and trees.

Intaglio

This technique is in effect midway between traditional geometric cutting and engraving, being able to offer greater flexibility in designs, but not of the same quality of copper wheel engraved designs.

Interchangeable small stone wheels on a lathe were used, which produced a V-cut which had a sharp edge at ninety degrees to the surface on one side and gently sloping up to the surface on the other side.

Cameo

This technique involved the following stages:
(a)The formation of the glass blank by the cup casing process, to ensure a uniformly thick top layer for the relief carving
(b) Acid treatment of the blank, to provide a key for the drawing out of the design
(c) Application of a layer of acid resist to those parts of the drawn design, which were to remain
(d) Dipping the item in acid to remove the unwanted areas of glass. This could be done a number of times depending on the thickness required to be removed.
(e) The final modelling of the glass surface left, with hand tools and by copper wheel engraving machine.

Up until the early 1880s, white over blue were used for the blanks, but after then, other combinations of colors were used. It was however, important to ensure that the coefficients of expansion of the respective colored glasses were compatible with each other, to avoid the risk of cracking through differential thermal movements.

8. SURFACE TOOLING TECHNIQUES

Pincered work

Pincer like tools were developed to impress various decorative patterns onto both sides of strips of glass which were applied as decoration to the rim, body, foot, and handles.

Roller type devices were created to impart a milled type pattern to the surface of narrow width applied trails.

Crimping

Devices were created to impart a decorative wavy type profile to the rims and feet of flower holders, bowls, and dishes.

Surface pull-outs

To create a "rustic" type effect, random / regularly spaced out patterns of small projecting knobbles or barbs were pulled out of the surface of the item.

CHAPTER TWO
DESIGNS FOR FLOWER HOLDERS

Vases

Vases with distinctive rim designs:

Rims with petal shaped edge

Jack-in-the Pulpit type rim with plain /crimped edge

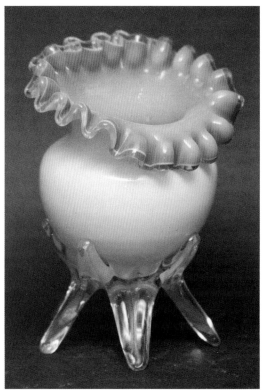

Small vase with petal shaped rim, manufactured c.1890. The edge of the rim is profiled with six petal shapes, and finished with a six-way shallow crimp. The green glass body is formed from a mold with twelve shallow projecting ribs. The clear glass foot has a snapped off pontil mark, and comprises five rounded profile petal shapes decorated with daisy head pattern, pincered work. 6 x 3.25 inches (15.0 x 8.5 cm) $160-180 (£110-125)

A small vase, with Jack-in-the-Pulpit type rim, manufactured c.1885. The twenty-way crimped edge of the rim is finished with a green glass trail. The opal white over shaded ruby glass body has a snapped off pontil, and is supported on five, clear glass, tall wishbone pattern feet. 4.75 x 4.75 inches (12.0 x 12.0 cm) $70-90 (£50-60)

A vase with a Jack-in-the-Pulpit type rim, manufactured c.1885. The rim is finished with a very shallow twelve-way crimp. The tapering, clear glass twisted stem, is formed from a mold with twelve, shallow projecting ribs, and springs from a small knop set on top of the foot. The foot has a snapped off pontil mark, and is formed in a stylised flower head shape, comprising six, pincered work petals. 9.5 x 3.25 inches (24.0 x 8.5 cm) $125-140 (£85-95)

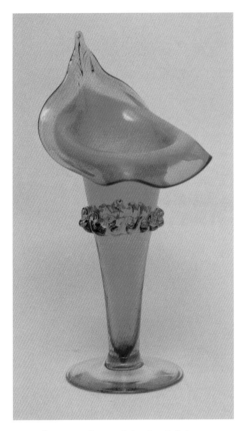

A small vase with a Jack-in-the-Pulpit, type rim, manufactured c.1890. The plain rim is decorated with a pincered motif at the highest point. The tapered, opalescent green glass body is formed from a mold with twelve, very shallow projecting ribs. The circular clear glass foot has a snapped off pontil mark. 7 x 3 inches (18.0 x 7.5 cm) $125-140 (£85-95).

A vase with a Jack-in-the-Pulpit type rim, manufactured c.1890. The rim is finished with a multi-crimped edge. The tapering body is formed with opal white glass, over pale blue glass. The clear glass circular foot, is finished all over with a shallow height, rounded profile multi-crimp, and has a snapped off pontil mark. 9.5 x 5.5 inches (24.0 x 14.0 cm). $220-250 (£150-175)

Side view.

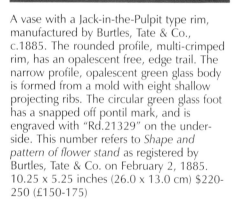

A vase with a Jack-in-the-Pulpit type rim, manufactured by Burtles, Tate & Co., c.1885. The rounded profile, multi-crimped rim, has an opalescent free, edge trail. The narrow profile, opalescent green glass body is formed from a mold with eight shallow projecting ribs. The circular green glass foot has a snapped off pontil mark, and is engraved with "Rd.21329" on the underside. This number refers to *Shape and pattern of flower stand* as registered by Burtles, Tate & Co. on February 2, 1885. 10.25 x 5.25 inches (26.0 x 13.0 cm) $220-250 (£150-175)

Underside of foot.

Right:
A Jack-in the-Pulpit type vase manufactured c.1880. The edge of the rim is finished with a rounded profile, shallow height multi-crimp. The body is formed from a mold with twelve, shallow projecting ribs, and is supported on a circular foot with a ground off pontil mark. 11.0 x 4.25 inches (28.0 x 10.5 cm) $125-140 (£85-95)

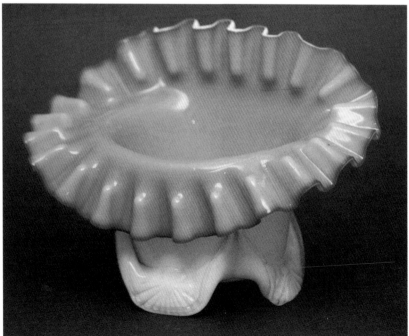

Left:
A small vase, with a Jack-in-the-Pulpit type rim, manufactured c.1890. The edge of the rim is finished with a twenty four-way crimp. The opal white over pale ruby, glass body has a snapped off pontil mark. The base comprises four, wishbone type feet, each of which are decorated with a pincered work daisy pattern. 4 x 6 inches (10.0 x 15.0 cm) $105-125 (£75-85)

Jack-in-the Pulpit type rim with plain / folded crimped edge

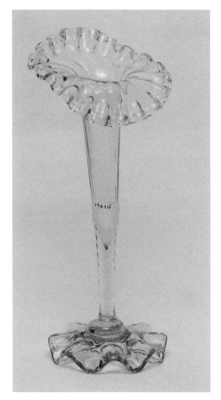

A vase formed with a Jack-in-the-Pulpit type rim, manufactured c.1890. The edge of the multi-crimped rim is folded under. The clear glass body is formed from a mold with sixteen, shallow projecting ribs, and sits on a small circular knop on top of the foot. The circular foot has a snapped off pontil mark, and is formed with a deep profile, eight-way crimp. 8.5 x 4 inches (21.5 x 10.0) $145-175 (£100-120)

Jack-in-the Pulpit type rim with applied trail

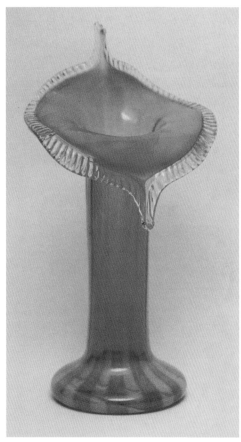

Left:
A vase formed with a Jack-in-the-Pulpit type rim, manufactured c.1890. The edge of the rim is decorated with an applied, clear glass, pincered work trail. The pale ruby glass body is formed from a mold with twenty-four shallow projecting ribs, and is decorated internally with narrow, vertical opalescent striped trails. 9 x 5 inches (23.0 x 12.5 cm) $190-220 (£130-150)

Rims folded inwards or upwards

Small fan shaped vase, manufactured c.1880. The ruby glass body is formed from a mold with fourteen shallow projecting ribs. The base comprises five, stylised tree root feet, formed in green glass. 4 x 3.5 inches (10.0 x 9.0cm) $125-140 (£85-95)

Six-way crimped rim forming a fan shape

Small fan shaped vase, manufactured by Stuart & Sons Limited, c.1900. The rim is finished with a six-way vertical crimp, and pinched inwards to form the fan shape. The clear glass body is formed from a mold with twelve, shallow projecting ribs, and is set on a circular foot with a polished out pontil mark. 5 x 4.75 inches (12.5 x 12.0 cm) $80-95 (£55-65)

Fan shaped vase, manufactured c.1900. The rim is finished with a six-way vertical crimp, and pinched inwards to form the fan shape. The clear glass body has an iridescent finish, and has been formed from a mold with twelve, shallow projecting ribs, and twisted to give a spiral effect. The circular foot has a polished out pontil mark. 6 x 6.75 inches (15.0 x 17.0 cm) $190-220 (£130-150)

Small fan shaped vase, manufactured by Stuart & Sons Limited, c.1900. The rim is finished with a six-way vertical crimp, and pinched inwards to form the fan shape. The pale amber glass body is formed from a mold with twelve, shallow projecting ribs, and decorated with a spiral green glass trail. The circular amber glass foot has a polished out pontil mark. 4.75 x 4.75 inches (12.0 x 12.0 cm) $80-95 (£75-85)

A fan shaped vase, manufactured c.1900. The rim is finished with a six-way vertical crimp, and pinched inwards to form the fan shape. The clear glass body has an iridescent finish, and has been formed from a mold with twelve shallow projecting ribs, and twisted to give a spiral effect. The slender stem supporting the body sits on a circular foot, which has a snapped off pontil mark. 10.5 x 9 inches (27.5 x 23.0 cm) $325-360 (£225-250)

Threaded rim with shallow profile multi-way edge crimp

Pinched together rims, with multiple openings – plain edge

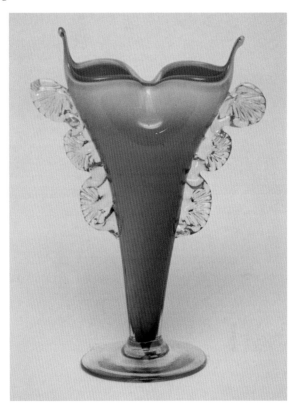

Small vase with fan shaped rim, manufactured c.1890 by Stuart & Sons Limited The flared rim is finished with clear glass machine threading, and pinched inwards to form the fan shape. The clear glass body is formed from a mold with sixteen shallow projecting ribs, and has a polished out pontil mark. 3.25 x 3.25 inches (8.5 x 8.5 cm) $60-70 (£40-50)

A small, trumpet shaped vase with pinched together rim, manufactured c.1880. The edge of the rim is finished with a clear glass, non-opalescent glass trail. The clear over opalescent ruby glass, body is supported on a circular clear glass foot with snapped off pontil. 6 x 4.5 inches (15.0 x 11.5 cm) $145-175 (£100-120)

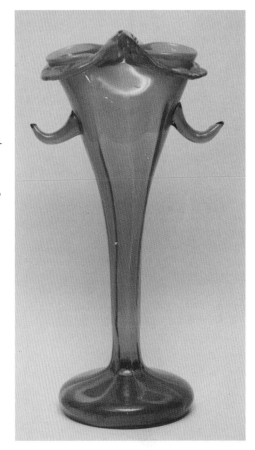

Right:
A tall trumpet shaped vase with pinched together rim, manufactured c.1890. The rim is decorated with an applied trail of pincered work. The opalescent, pale blue body is formed from a mold with nine shallow, projecting ribs. Two hooks are applied to the body to support either hanging baskets or chains to another vase. The circular, squashed profile foot has a snapped off pontil. 12.5 x 5.25 inches (31.5 x 13.0 cm) $180-195 (£125-135)

Small vase with fan shaped rim, manufactured by Stuart & Sons Limited, c.1890. The flared rim is finished with amber/ orange colored machine threading, and pinched inwards to form the fan shape. The amber / orange colored glass body is formed from a mold with sixteen shallow projecting ribs, and has a polished out pontil mark. 3.25 x 3.25 inches (8.5 x 8.5 cm) $60-70 (£40

A small trumpet shaped vase manufactured by Stevens & Williams
Limited, c.1909, and is an example of their Registered Patent
No.24048, for the design of tops for flower vases. The rim is
pinched together to form four small circular openings around a
large central opening. The clear glass body is decorated with four,
applied spiral, green glass trails. The circular, clear glass foot has a
polished out pontil mark engraved with "Pat No.24048 S & W
Limited" 5 x 3.75 inches (12.5 x 9.0 cm) $115-130 (£80-90)

A small trumpet shaped vase manufactured by Stevens & Williams
Limited, c.1909, and is an example of their Registered Patent
No.24048, for the design of tops of flower vases. The rim is
pinched together to form a fan shape and three oval openings. The
clear glass body is formed from a mold with six projecting ribs, and
springs from a small circular knop. The body is decorated with
small oval shaped cuts on the ribs, flash cuts and double intaglio
cuts between the ribs at rim level. The circular clear glass foot has a
polished out pontil mark engraved with "Patent No.24048 S & W
Limited" 6.25 x 4.25 inches (16.0 x 11.0 cm) $110-125 (£75-85)

A small trumpet shaped vase manufactured by Stevens & Williams
Limited, c.1909, and is an example of their Registered Patent
No.24048, for the design of tops of flower vases. The rim is
pinched together to form a fan shape and three oval openings. The
clear glass body is engraved with a bamboo plant pattern, and
springs from a small circular knop. The circular clear glass foot has
a polished out pontil mark engraved with "Patent No.24048 S & W
Limited" 6 x 2.5 inches (15.0 x 6.5 cm) $110-125 (£75-85)

A fan shaped vase manufactured by Stevens & Williams Limited, c.1909, and is an example of their Registered Patent No.24048, for the design of tops of flower vases. The rim is pinched together to form a fan shape and five, oval openings. The clear glass body is engraved with a stylised bamboo plant pattern. The circular clear glass foot has a polished out pontil mark engraved with "Pat No.24048 S & W Limited" 6.5 x 8.0 inches (16.5 x 20.0 cm) $195-220 (£135-150)

Vases with distinctive mold blown patterns:

Diamond patterns

Left:
Mold formed vase manufactured c.1880. The rim is ground off, and polished. The cylindrical, amber glass body is formed from a diamond pattern mold, and has silver foil inclusions, and is decorated with an applied clear glass trail in pincered rib pattern. The foot is formed with a trail of six, clear glass, petal shapes in a pincered rib pattern. 8 x 2.75 inches (20.5 x 7.0 cm) $65-80 (£45-55)

Bold projecting rib patterns

Mold formed vase manufactured c.1880. The rim is ground off and polished. The spherical shaped, pale yellow glass body is formed from a mold with twenty-six bold profile, projecting ribs. The flared neck is decorated with an applied spiral trail of pale ruby machine threading. The base is finished as from the mold. 3.75 x 3.25 inches (9.5 x 8.5cm) $50-65 (£35-45)

Mold formed vase, manufactured c.1900. The oval shaped rim has a fire polished edge. The shallow projecting, large diamond pattern mold formed body is finished with a second, very large, diagonal bold rib pattern. The applied, free shape foot is decorated with a ribbed pincered pattern. 8 x 7.5 inches (20.5 x 19.0 cm) $65-80 (£45-55)

Faint projecting rib patterns

An example of a mold formed vase made to Registered Design No.543290, dated June 5,1909, as recorded by Thomas West Carnie, of 60, Bryanston Street, London W. – Decorative Artist. Manufacturer: Unknown. The rim has a folded over edge. The trumpet shaped, amber glass body is formed from a mold with sixteen shallow projecting ribs. The circular raised hollow foot, has a snapped off pontil, and is engraved on underside with *Rd. 543290*. 7 x 6.5 inches (18.0 x 16.5 cm) $110-125 (£75-85)

A small posy vase manufactured c.1880. The edge of the rim is fire polished. The ruby glass body is formed from a mold with twelve, shallow projecting ribs, and is decorated with an applied trail of clear glass rigaree. The clear glass circular foot has a polished out pontil mark. 3.25 x 2.75 inches (8.0 x 7.0) $65-80 (£45-55)

Underside of foot.

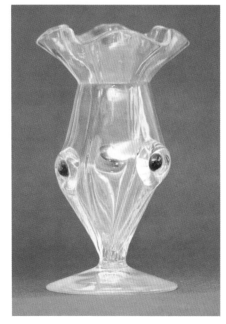

Peacock eye patterns

A small flower vase manufactured c.1900. The flared out rim is finished with a six-way crimp. The clear glass body is formed from a six-sided mold with shallow projecting ribs on the angles, and projecting stylised peacock eye trails in alternate panels. The centers of the eyes are formed with green glass. The applied circular foot has a polished out pontil mark. 5 x 2.25 inches (13.0 x 5.5 cm) $80-90 (£55-65)

A bulb vase manufactured c.1880. The edge of the rim is fire polished. The orange/amber glass body is formed from a mold with twelve, shallow projecting ribs. The base is finished as from the mold. 3.75 x 4.5 inches (9.5 x 11.5 cm) $50-60 (£35-40)

Peacock tail patterns

Right:
A small flower vase manufactured c.1900 by Stuart & Sons Limited The rim is finished with a six-way crimp turned inwards. The circular section, clear glass body is formed from a mold with six, projecting stylised peacock eye trails. The base has a polished out pontil mark. 3.75 x 3.75 inches (9.5 x 9.5cm) $65-80 (£45-55)

Satin finished, pale blue flower vase manufactured c.1890. The edge of the rim is decorated with an applied clear glass edge trail, with a rounded profile multi-crimp, and finished with a second, two way, deep crimp. The body is formed from a mold with a stylised peacock tail pattern, and has an integral circular foot. 8 x 4.5 inches (205 x115 cm) $125 –140 (£85-95)

A small flower vase manufactured c.1900 by Stuart & Sons Limited The rim is finished with a six-way crimp, turned inwards. The circular section, clear glass body is formed from a mold with six, projecting stylised peacock eye trails. The base has a polished out pontil mark. 3.75 x 3.75 inches (9.5 x 9.5cm) $65-80 (£45-55)

Left:
A flower vase manufactured c.1900 by Stuart & Sons Limited
The rim is finished with a five-way crimp, turned inwards.
The conical shaped, clear glass body is formed from a mold
with five, projecting, stylised peacock eye trails, and
decorated with engraved floral patterns. The body is
supported on a short knop type stem, on top of a circular
foot. The underside of the foot has a polished out pontil
mark and is decorated with an intaglio cut floral leaf pattern.
7 x 4.75 inches (17.5 x 12.0 cm) $275-305 (£180 - 210)

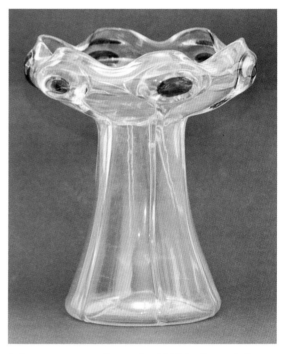

A flower vase manufactured c.1900 by Stuart & Sons
Limited The rim is finished with a six-way shallow
crimp turned inwards. The clear glass body is formed
from a mold with six projecting peacock eye trails
from rim to center of the base, which has a polished
out pontil mark. 9.0 x 7.5 inches (23.0 x 19.0 cm)
$220-255 (£150-175)

Plan view of rim to vase.

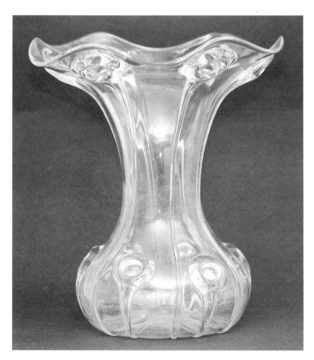

A large flower vase manufactured c.1900 by Stuart & Son Limited
The rim is finished with a six-way shallow crimped rim. The clear
glass body is formed from a mold with twelve peacock eye pattern
projecting trails, six at high level alternating with six at low level.
The base has a polished out pontil mark. 10.0 x 8.75 inches (25.5
x 22.0 cm) $360-400 (£250-275)

Circular/oval indented patterns

A flower vase manufactured c.1900. The trefoil shaped vertical
crimped rim has a fire polished edge. The body is formed from a
mold with an indented, oval shaped pattern, and decorated with
an iridescent finish. The foot is formed in with the body as from
the mold. 6.5 x 3.5 inches (16.5 x 9.0 cm) $50-65 (£35-45)

Plan view of rim to vase.

Stylised floral patterns

View of rim.

Flower vase manufactured c.1900 by John Walsh Walsh. The rim is finished with a nine-way, deep, rounded profile vertical crimp. The opalescent, pale green glass body is formed from a mold, which incorporates their *Brocade* pattern, and is supported on a tall narrow stem. The circular foot is formed with matching opalescent *Brocade* patterning, and has a snapped off pontil mark. 12.25 x 7 inches (31.0 x 18.0 cm) $580-650 (£400-450)

Right:
View of the pattern on the body.

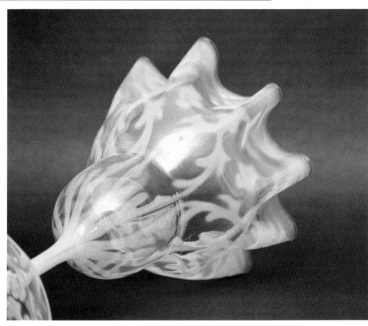

Horizontal / vertical wave patterns

A small mold formed vase, manufactured c.1895. The rim is decorated with an applied trail of green glass. The iridescent, clear glass body is formed from a horizontal, wave patterned mold, and decorated with four, applied green glass drop trails.. The base has a polished out pontil mark. 4.0 x 4.25 inches (10.0 x 10.5 cm) $125-140 (£85-95)

Vases with distinctive mold blown / hand formed shapes:

Horn / Cornucopia shapes

Horn shaped flower holder, manufactured c.1895. The rim is ground off, and polished. The white over pale ruby glass body is formed from a mold with eight bold projecting ribs, and is decorated with an applied trail of amber glass flower head and leaves. The body is supported on a five-way, wishbone pattern, amber glass foot. 5 x 11.25 inches (13.0 x 28.5 cm) $125-140 (£85-95)

Cornucopia shaped vase, manufactured c.1900. The rim is finished with a shallow rectangular crimp. The oval section clear glass body with iridescent finish is formed from a peacock tail, patterned mold. The foot is formed with a group of iridescent, green glass, stylised rustic tree roots. 8 x 6 inches (20.0 x 15.5 cm) $140-160 (£95-110)

Amphora shapes

Amphora shaped vase, manufactured c.1880. The rim is ground off and polished. The amber glass body, is formed from a mold with twelve, shallow projecting ribs, and is decorated with applied trail of clear glass rigaree around the neck. The body is supported on three shell ribbed clear glass feet. 6.25 x 4.0 inches (16.0 x 10.0 cm) $95-110 (£65-75)

Trumpet shapes

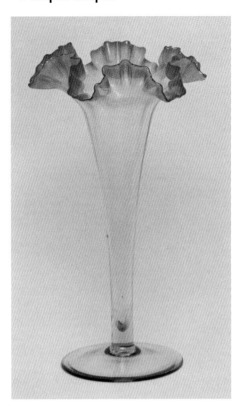

Trumpet shaped vase, manufactured c.1880. The edge of the six-way deep crimped rim is decorated with a rounded profile multi-crimp. The clear glass body is formed from a mold with fourteen, shallow projecting ribs, and shades into pink and ruby around the rim. The applied, circular clear glass foot has a polished out pontil mark. 9.75 x 5.5 inches (25.0 x 14.0cm) $180-200 (£125-135)

Hand formed trumpet shaped vase, manufactured c.1880. The folded edge rim is finished with a shallow, eight-way crimp. The clear glass body changes from a hollow trumpet section to a solid circular section at just below mid-height. The body is decorated with two rows of blue glass rigaree trails. The circular foot has a polished out pontil mark. 9.75 x 4.25 inches (24.5x10.5cm) $140-160 (£95-110)

Small trumpet shaped vase, manufactured c.1880. The rim is decorated with a rounded profile, tightly set, multiple vertical crimp. The body is formed in clear glass shaded to a pale opalescent ruby around the rim, and is decorated with a trail of clear glass rigaree. The circular foot is finished with a shallow, rounded profile, multiple-crimp all over, and has a snapped off pontil mark. 6.5 x 3 inches (16.5 x 7.5 cm) $125-140 (£85-95)

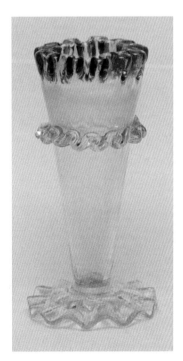

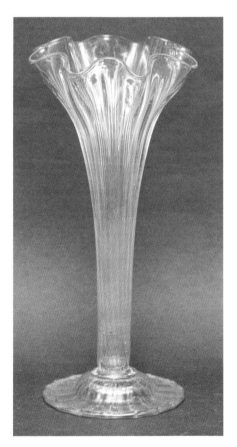

Left:
Small trumpet shaped vase, manufactured c.1880. The rim is decorated with a rounded profile, tightly set, multiple vertical crimp. The body is formed in clear glass shaded to a pale opalescent blue around the rim, and is decorated with a trail of clear glass rigaree. The circular foot is finished with a shallow rounded profile, multi-crimp all over, and has a snapped off pontil mark. 6 x 2.5 inches (15.0 x 6.5 cm) $125-140 (£85-95)

Right:
Trumpet shaped vase, manufactured c.1900. The rim is finished with an eight-way rounded profile vertical crimp. The body is formed in clear glass from a mold with eighteen, shallow projecting ribs. The matching circular, ogee profiled foot has a folded under edge, and a snapped off pontil mark. 10 x 5 inches (25.5 x 12.5 cm) $145-175 (£100-120)

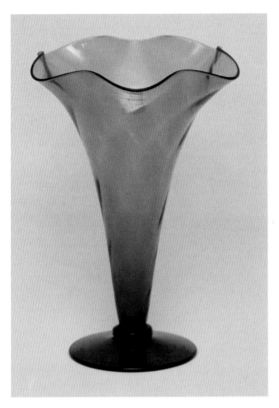

Right:
Small trumpet shaped vase, manufactured c.1900. The rim is finished with an eight-way vertical crimp, which forms alternate narrow and wide, rounded profiles. The green glass body is formed from a mold with eight shallow projecting ribs. The circular clear glass foot is formed with a flat base. 4.5 x 3.0 inches (11.5 x 7.5cm) $50-65 (£35-45)

Trumpet shaped vase, manufactured c.1900 by Stuart & Sons Limited. The rim is finished with a six-way shallow crimp. The green glass body is formed from a mold with eight, shallow projecting ribs, and sits on a small knop set directly on top of the circular green glass foot. 9 x 6.25 inches (23.0 x 16.0cm) $125-140 (£85-95)

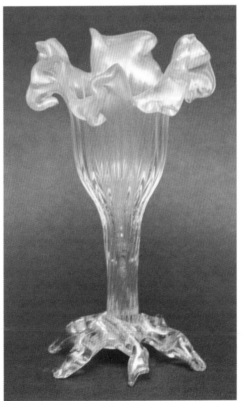

Stylised flower shapes

Left:
A small vase in form of a stylised flower, and possibly a version of the *Gloxinia* pattern as recorded in *The Pottery Gazette* in March 1893, as being manufactured by John Walsh Walsh. The multi-crimped edge of the rim is cut, turned up, down and twisted. The clear glass, tapering shaped body is formed from a mold with twenty projecting ribs, and is decorated with an iridescent finish. The base comprises six, tapering profile, stylised tree roots formed in green iridescent glass. 5.75 x 3.25 inches (14.5 x 8.5 cm) $175-190 (£120-130)

Small trumpet shaped vase, manufactured c.1880. The rim is decorated with a multi-crimped edge and finished with a six-way deep crimp. The white over pale blue glass body, is formed from a mold with fourteen shallow projecting ribs, and is decorated with an applied trail of clear glass rigaree. The applied white glass foot is formed with a flat base. 7 x 4.25 inches (18.0 x 11.5 cm) $125-140 (£85-95)

A small vase made in the stylised form of a tulip. Designs similar to this item, but in different colors and sizes, are recorded in a pattern book of H.G.Richardson in 1894. The rim is finished with a fire polished five-way scalloped profile. The body is formed in pale green glass with six vertical white stripes, and is supported on a slender stem. The foot has a snapped off pontil mark, and comprises five, triangular shaped, pincered leaves, from the top of which spring a further three twisted leaves. 6 x 1.75 inches (15.0 x 4.5 cm) $175-190 (£120-130)

A small vase made in the stylised form of a tulip. Designs similar to this item, but in different colors and sizes, are recorded in a pattern book of H.G.Richardson in 1894. The rim is finished with a fire polished five-way scalloped profile. The body is formed with alternate vertical stripes of pale ruby and opal white glass, and is supported on a slender pale green stem. The foot has a snapped off pontil mark, and comprises five, triangular shaped, pincered leaves, from the top of which spring a further three twisted leaves. 6 x 1.75 inches (15.0 x 4.5 cm) $175-190 (£120-130)

A small vase made in the stylised form of a tulip, similar in design to those made by H. G. Richardson. The rim is edged with a non-opalescent pale green glass trail and finished with an eight way scalloped crimp. The body is formed in pale, opalescent green glass, from a mold with eight shallow projecting ribs, and is supported on a slender green glass stem. The foot has a polished out pontil mark, and comprises five, green glass, stylised pincered leaves. Missing from the top of the foot on this particular item are three vertical pincered leaves.

A small vase made in the stylised form of a decaying flower head. The rim is profiled into six, stepped and tapering petals, and folded over and down. The spherical shaped body with rustic surface pull-outs, is shaded from clear glass at the stem up into an amber/orange color. The foot comprises five, rustic pattern, clear glass, stylised tree root feet. 3.5 x 4.25 inches (9.0 x 10.5 cm) $175-190 (£120-130)

A small vase made in the stylised form of an opened flower head. The rim is profiled into six, stepped and tapering petals, and all set in an upright position. The spherical shaped body with rustic surface pull-outs, is shaded from clear glass at the stem up into an amber/ orange color. The foot comprises five, rustic pattern, clear glass, stylised tree root feet. 4.75 x 4.0 inches (12.0 x 10.0 cm) $175-190 (£120-130)

A small vase made in the stylised form of a half decayed flower head. The rim is profiled into six, stepped and tapering petals, and folded up and down alternately. The spherical shaped body with rustic surface pull-outs, is shaded from clear glass at the stem up into an amber / orange color. The foot comprises five, rustic pattern, clear glass, stylised tree root feet. 4.75 x 3.5 inches (12.0 x 9.0 cm) $175-190 (£120-130)

Right:
A small vase formed in the stylised shape of a hyacinth flower. Designs similar to this item are recorded in the pattern books of H.G.Richardson in 1894. The rim is decorated with one of the six, horizontal frills of projecting clear glass pincered work which is applied all over the ruby glass body which is supported on a slender clear glass stem. The foot comprises a clear glass pincered work trail of rounded profile, petal shapes, mounted on a circular mirror plateau finished with a scallop pattern cut edge pattern. Missing from the top of the foot of this example, are three, upright pincered work leaves. 6.5 x 1.75 inches (16.5 x 4.5 cm) $175-190 (£120-130)

A small, decorative item in the form of a stylised rose bud on a rustic stem. This design bears a strong similarity to Registered Design 155744, dated August 30, 1890, recorded by John Walsh Walsh for a candleholder. However, the Registered Design illustration shows two rose buds on the stem, and they appear to be of a much larger size.
The rose bud illustrated here is formed with three rows of pale green, overlapping pincered work leaves, and has a one inch, (2.5cm) diameter opening in the top.(room for a small candle perhaps). The rustic stem is formed in a darker amber green glass, and is supported on a matching, rustic pattern, free shaped base incorporating seven random edge crimps, and applied stylised leaves, some of which rise up the stem. 8 x 4.5 inches (20.0 x 11.5 cm) $220-250 (£150-175)

Stylised tree shapes

Right:
A small vase formed in the stylised shape of a palm tree. The canopy is formed in clear glass decorated on the underside with pale pink machine threading, and has a perimeter profile of eight, petal shapes. The hollow clear glass section stem is supported on a base which has a snapped off pontil mark, and is formed with five triangular shaped, pincered work leaves. 6.75 x 3 inches (17.0 x 7.5 cm) $145-175 (£100-120)

A small vase formed in the stylised shape of a palm tree. This design bears a strong resemblance to the illustration in Registered Design No. 221354, dated October 27, 1893, as recorded by Boulton & Mills. The canopy of the tree is formed in a light green glass with fine section light green machine threading on the underside, and has a perimeter profile of thirteen petal shapes. The hollow, rustic pattern clear glass stem sits on a base, which has a snapped off pontil mark, and comprises six, triangular shaped, pincered work feet. Three, clear glass pincered leaves rise from the top of the base. 6.0 x 2.75 inches (15.5 x 7.0 cm) $220-250 (£150-175)

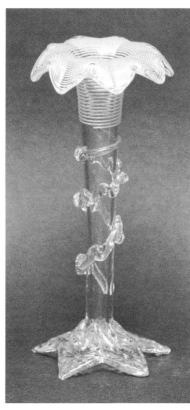

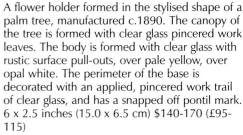

A flower holder formed in the stylised shape of a palm tree, manufactured c.1890. The canopy of the tree is formed with clear glass pincered work leaves. The body is formed with clear glass with rustic surface pull-outs, over pale yellow, over opal white. The perimeter of the base is decorated with an applied, pincered work trail of clear glass, and has a snapped off pontil mark. 6 x 2.5 inches (15.0 x 6.5 cm) $140-170 (£95-115)

Right:
A double flower holder made in the stylised form of two palm trees. This item is an example of Registered Design 100004, recorded May 12, 1888, by John Walsh Walsh. The canopies of each tree are formed with clear glass, pincered work leaves. The body of the small tree is formed in clear glass with rustic surface pull-outs. The body of the large tree is formed with pale pink glass with rustic surface pull-outs, over opal white, and has a snapped off pontil mark. The base is decorated with a pincered work trail of clear glass, triangular shaped leaves, set above another clear glass trail of shell rib pattern pincered work, which forms the foot. 8.75 x 4.25 inches (22.0 x 10.5 cm) $255-290 (£175-200)

Rustic style tubular shapes

Right:
Flower holder, manufactured c.1890, formed with a one inch (2.5cm) diameter pale opalescent green glass tube, with rustic surface pull-outs, and with an opalescent free rim trail. The tube is supported on a base with a snapped off pontil mark, and formed with six, green iridescent rustic, stylised tree root feet. 6 x 1 inches (15.0 x 2.5 cm) $40-50 (£30-35)

Tubular shaped flower holder, formed with 1.75 inches (4.5cm) diameter clear glass tube section with rustic surface pull-outs, and decorated with an applied ribbed glass handle type trail. The body sits on a trail of rigaree set on top of a circular foot finished all over with a twenty four-way shallow rounded profile crimp. The design is very similar to a design produced by H.G Richardson c.1907. 6.75 x 6.25 inches (17.5 x 16.0cm) $125-140 (£85-95)

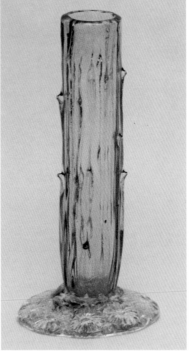

Flower holder, manufactured c.1890, formed with one inch (2.5cm) diameter pale green glass tube, with rustic surface pull-outs, supported on a circular clear glass foot, decorated with daisy head pattern pincered work, and with a polished out pontil mark. 6 x 1 inches (15.0 x 2.5 cm) $40-50 (£30-35)

Flower holder, manufactured c.1900, formed with two one inch (2.5cm) diameter, clear glass tubes, each decorated with an applied green glass spiral trail. The tubes are set onto a foot formed with six stylised rustic tree root feet. 5.5 x 4.25 inches (14.0 x 11.0cm) $125-140 (£85-95)

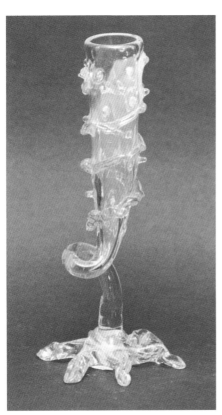

Tubular flower holder, manufactured c.1890, formed with tapering opalescent green glass tube with twisted stem, supported on an applied base with snapped off pontil, and comprising six, stylised rustic tree roots. The body is decorated with surface pull-outs and an applied spiral trail. 6.75 x 1.25 inches (17.0 x 3.0 cm) $95-110 (£65-75)

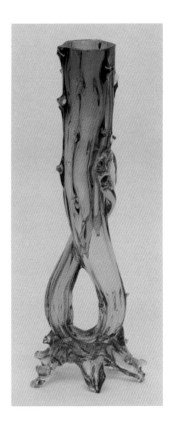

Right:
Tubular rustic pattern flower holder, manufactured c.1900. Ground off and polished rim to hexagonal section, tapering body with surface pull-outs, formed in green glass, shading to blue at the rim. The foot comprises five, tapering rustic pattern, prong shaped feet, with surface pull-outs. 8 x 2 inches (20.0 x 5.0 cm) $95-110 (£65-75)

Tubular rustic pattern flower holder, manufactured c.1900, and formed in clear glass shading into an amber-orange color at the rim. The body is supported on a clear glass foot in the shape of a squashed, spherical ball with surface pull-outs, and a polished off base. 6.25 x 1.75 inches (16.0 x 4.4 cm) $50-65 (£35-45)

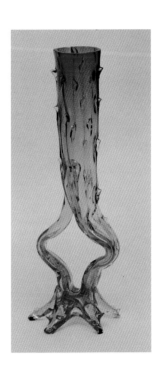

Left:
Tubular flower holder in the form of stylised tree branches, manufactured c.1900, and formed in pale green glass with surface pull-outs. The body is supported on a base, with snapped off pontil mark, and comprising six, stylised rustic tree root feet. 9.75 x 4.25 inches (24.5 x 10.5 cm) $145-175 (£100-120)

Right:
Tubular rustic pattern flower holder, manufactured c.1900. Ground off and polished rim to hexagonal section, tapering body with surface pull-outs, formed in green glass, shading to pale ruby at the rim. The foot comprises five, tapering rustic pattern, prong shaped feet, with surface pull-outs. 12 x 3.75 inches (30.5 x 9.5 cm) $125-140 (£85-95)

Double tube shaped, rustic pattern flower holder, manufactured c.1900. Ground off and polished rims to bodies, formed in iridescent finished, green glass, with surface pull-outs, and decorated with a large, applied stylised flower head formed in pincered work. A large pincered work, leaf rises from the iridescent finished foot, which comprises a free shape with seven prong shaped toes. 6 x 4.25 inches (15.0 x 10.5 cm) $125-140 (£85-95)

Miscellaneous geometric shapes

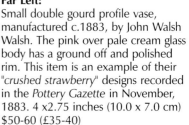

Right:
Small vase manufactured c.1880. The rim is finished with an eight-way crimp. The blue glass body has an applied, amber glass trail, and is supported on four pincered work, wishbone shaped, amber glass feet. 5.75 x 1.75 inches (14.5 x 4.5 cm) $45-50 (£30-35)

Far Left:
Small double gourd profile vase, manufactured c.1883, by John Walsh Walsh. The pink over pale cream glass body has a ground off and polished rim. This item is an example of their "crushed strawberry" designs recorded in the *Pottery Gazette* in November, 1883. 4 x2.75 inches (10.0 x 7.0 cm) $50-60 (£35-40)

Left:
Small vase, manufactured c.1880. The edge of the rim is decorated with a shallow height, rounded profile multi-crimp and finished with a second, deep profile three-way crimp. The pale, opalescent ruby glass body is formed from a mold with sixteen shallow projecting ribs. The base has a snapped off pontil mark. 5.5 x 3.25 inches (14.0 x 8.5 cm) $160-180 (£110-125)

Small tapering cylindrical vase, manufactured c.1875. The multi-crimped edge of the rim has a pale turquoise trail, and is finished with a second, four-way crimp. The opaque white glass body sits on an integral circular foot with snapped off pontil mark. 5.75 x 3.25 inches (14.5 x 80 cm) $50-60 (£35-40)

Small posy vase manufactured c.1875. The rim is ground off, and polished. The pale ruby glass body is formed from a mold with shallow projecting ribs, and is decorated with a clear glass trail of rigaree. The body is supported on five, wishbone pattern, clear glass feet. 4 x 3.25 inches (10.0 x 8.0 cm) $125-140 (£85-95)

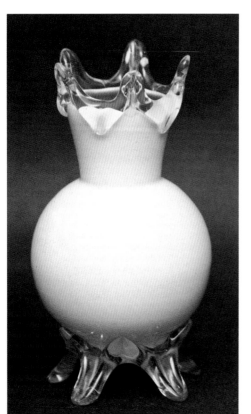

Left:
Small shaft and globe shaped vase, manufactured c.1880. The rim has a clear glass trail formed in an inverted wishbone foot pattern. The cased, white over ruby glass body has a snapped off pontil, and is supported on five, clear glass, wishbone pattern feet.6 x 3.25 inches (15.0 x 8.0 cm) $50-60(£35-40)

Right:
Small vase with perforated, stylised crown type rim, manufactured c.1890. The green glass, continuous loop trail sits on a clear glass trail applied around the rim. The body has a snapped off pontil mark, and is formed from a mold with ten shallow convex ribs, which project inside the vase. 6 x 4.5 inches (15.0 x 11.5 cm) $65-80 (£45-55)

Small specimen flower holder, manufactured c.1880. The edge of the rim has a clear glass trail, and is finished with a combination crimp comprising large and small rounded profiles, which is then completed with a second, three way deeper crimp. The opal white over pale blue glass, circular section body is set on a small circular integral foot, with a snapped off pontil mark. 5.75 x 2.75 inches (14.5 x 7.0 cm) $50-65 (£35-45)

Small conical shaped vase, manufactured c.1890. The rim is finished with a four-way crimp, pushed inwards. The blue glass body is formed from a mold with ten shallow projecting ribs. The applied circular foot has a folded under edge, and polished out pontil mark. 4.75 x 4.75 inches (12.0 x 12.0 cm) $50-65 (£35-45)

Small tapered shape vase, manufactured c.1900. The flared out rim is finished with an eight-way vertical crimp. The green glass body is formed from a mold with eight shallow projecting ribs, and has a polished out pontil mark on the base. 3.75 x 3.25 inches (9.5 x 8.5cm) $50-65 (£35-45)

Conical shaped vase, manufactured c.1900 by Stuart & Sons Lilmited. The rim is finished with a seven-way shallow crimp. The green glass body is formed from a mold with ten, shallow projecting ribs, and is set onto a small knop. The circular foot has a flat base. 6.25 x 6.75 inches (15.5 x 17.0 cm) $95-110 (£65-75)

Vases with textured finishes:

Satin finished surfaces left undecorated

Satin finished surfaces decorated with enamelling and / or gilding

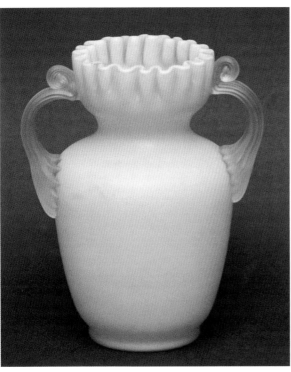

A small satin finished vase, manufactured c.1880. The circular rim is finished with a twenty-way, rounded profile, tightly set, vertical crimp. The circular section, shaded pale yellow over opal white cased glass body, has two shell ribbed handles. The integral circular foot has a snapped off pontil mark. 5.5 x 3.25 inches (14.0 x 8.5 cm) $125- 140 (£85-95)

A small satin finished vase, manufactured c. 1885. The rim is ground off and polished and decorated with gilding. The shaft and globe shaped, creamy white glass body is decorated with an enamelled floral pattern. The circular, integral foot has a flat base. 4.25 x 2.75 inches (10.5 x 7.0 cm) $50-60 (35-40)

A small satin finished vase, manufactured c. 1880. The rim has a twenty-way, rounded profile edge crimp, and is finished with a second, two-way deep crimp. The circular section body is formed in shaded pink over opal white glass. The integral foot has a snapped off pontil mark. 5 x 4 inches (12.5 x 10.0 cm) $80-95 (£55-65)

Right:
A large satin finished vase, manufactured c.1885. The rim is ground off and polished, and decorated with gilding. The circular section body is formed in shaded pale orange over creamy white, cased glass, and decorated with an enamelled floral pattern. The slightly concave base is inscribed with *1/103*. 15.25 x 6.25 inches (39.0 x 16.0 cm) $220-255 (£150-175)

Far right:
Close-up of the enamelled pattern on the vase.

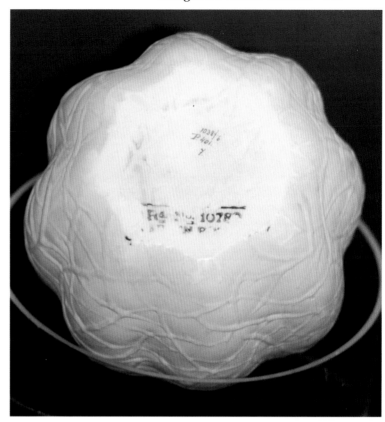

Underside of the base.

A satin finished vase, manufactured c.1890. The rim is ground off and polished. The opal white glass body is formed from a mold with eight bold projecting ribs, and is decorated all over with a pattern of interwoven, random bracken type trailing. The short neck and shoulder are decorated with an enamelled floral pattern. The base has a polished out pontil mark and is inscribed with *1038/6* above *P.401* above *7*. The edge of the base is over-stamped with a partially complete mark, which appears to read *Rd. 10780*(?). Although this number is ascribed to John Walsh Walsh, the Registered Designs book of Representations records that a certificate was not issued for this particular number. 6.75 x 4.25 inches (17.0 x 11.0 cm) $115-130 (£80-90)

Iced / Frosted / Crackled effects on translucent / opaque glass

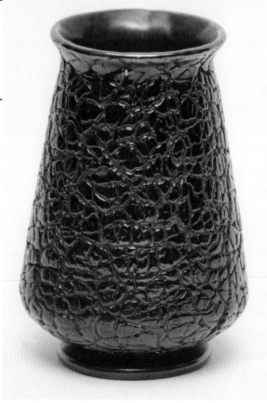

A small crackled glass vase, manufactured c.1878, by Thomas Webb & Sons Limited The tapered profile, circular shaped body is formed in a dark green glass, and given an iridescent, crackled surface finish. The applied circular foot has a polished out pontil mark. 5.0 x 3.75 inches (12.5 x 9.5 cm) $220-255 (£150-175)

Vases with applied decoration:

Transfer printed designs on translucent / opaque glass

Front view of tall vase decorated with transfer printed designs, manufactured c.1850. The rim is ground off and polished, and decorated with gilding. The white glass body is decorated with terra cotta colored Greek key pattern, and transfer printed designs of soldiers. The foot has a polished out pontil mark, and is inscribed in faint pencil with *PR/n* above another indecipherable pencil marking. 14.25 x 4.75 inches (36.0 x 12.0 cm) $260-290 (£180-200)

Transfer print design to front of vase.

Rear view of vase.

Transfer print design to rear of vase.

Enamelled designs on translucent / opaque glass

Small vase with enamelled decoration, manufactured c.1885. The rim is finished with a rounded profile, sixteen-way vertical crimp. The cream glass body is decorated with enamelled flower heads and leaf trails. The applied solid foot has a polished out pontil mark. 4.5 x 3.5 inches (11.5 x 9.0 cm) $65-80 (£45-55)

Small vase with enamelled decoration, manufactured c.1880. The rim is finished in a four-way crimp, and folded over and down to abut the body. The opal white over pale pink glass body is decorated with an enamelled fruit and leaf pattern. The integral foot with polished out pontil mark is decorated with a gilded line around the vertical edge. 4.75 x 3.75 inches (12.0 x 8.5 cm) $95-110 (£65-75)

A small vase with enamelled decoration, manufactured c. 1895. The body is formed in green glass and the lower conical shaped portion is decorated with a white enamelled floral pattern. The circular applied foot is finished with a flat base. 6.0 x 3.5 inches (15.0 x 9.0cm) 40-50 (£30-35)

A tall vase with enamelled decoration, manufactured c.1890. The rim is ground off and polished, and decorated with gilding. The cream glass body is decorated all over with a stylised, random floral pattern, formed with closely spaced enamelled dots in a stencil type format, and outlined in gilding. The circular, integral foot has a polished out pontil mark inscribed with *1153/2* above a circle containing a propeller with three blades. Beneath this circle is written *V 487*. 10.25 x 6.0 inches (26.0 x 15.0 cm) $260-290 (£180-200)

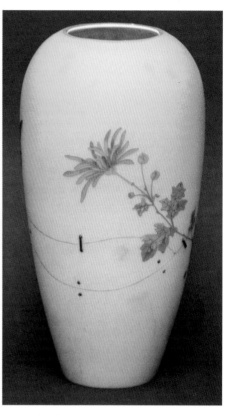

A tall vase with enamelled floral decoration, manufactured c.1887. The body is formed with opal white glass, cased over with a shaded yellow glass, and decorated all over with an enamelled floral design and a large butterfly motif. The base has a polished out pontil mark and is inscribed in pencil with *2711*. At some stage after manufacture this particular example suffered major damage and has been repaired with metal staples, and an internal application of a cement type material across the fracture lines. 10.5 x 5.5 inches (26.5 x 14.0 cm) value undamaged $400-435 (£275-300)

Side of vase showing the enamelled butterfly motif.

Rear side of vase showing the secondary enamelled floral motif.

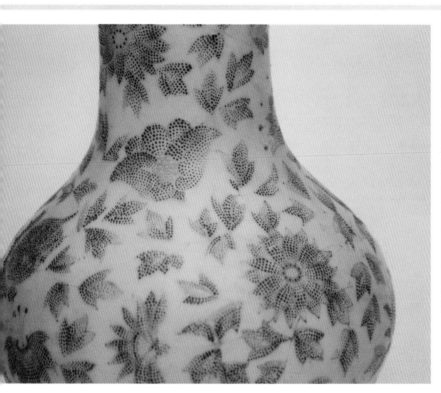

Close-up of base.

Close-up of enamelled designs.

Gilded designs on translucent / opaque glass

A small posy vase with gilded decoration, manufactured c.1885. The rim is finished with a seven-way crimp, pushed inwards. The ovular shaped body is formed in pale cream glass and is decorated with a stylised leaf trail formed with gilding. The clear glass foot has an eight-way rounded "V" shaped crimp all over, and has a snapped off pontil mark. 4 x 2.5 inches (10.0 x 6.0 cm) $110-125 (£75-85)

A small vase with gilded decoration, manufactured c.1880. The rim is ground off and polished. The circular section, mold formed, ruby glass body has a flat base and is decorated with an engraved floral pattern, highlighted with gilding. 3.5 x 2.25 inches (9.0 x 5.5 cm) $65-80 (45-55)

Gilded and enamelled designs on translucent / opaque glass

Side view no.1 of a vase with enamelled and gilded decoration, manufactured c.1885. The edge of the rim has an applied clear glass trail, and is decorated with a thirty two-way, shallow height, rounded profile crimp. The rim is also folded over and given a four-way deep crimp. The body has a polished out pontil mark and is formed in clear glass over sandy-orange glass over opal white glass. The decoration all over the body comprises an enamelled and gilded stylised floral pattern incorporating two large birds. The body is supported on a clear glass, rustic pattern trail with surface pull-outs. 8.25 x 6.0 inches (21.0 x 15.0 cm) $360-400 (£250-275)

Side view no.2 of vase.

Side view no.3 of vase.

Iridescent finish on translucent / opaque glass

An example of Registered Design No.582840, dated April 28,1911, as recorded by John Walsh Walsh. The ogee shaped, clear glass body has an iridescent finish, and is formed from a mold incorporating nine vertical stripes, each comprising five, very small, projecting, closely spaced ribs. The body sits on a clear glass knop on top of an iridescent, circular, mold formed foot with a snapped off pontil mark. The foot matches the body in design and color. 6.5 x 6.0 inches (16.5 x 15.0 cm) $95-110 (£65-75)

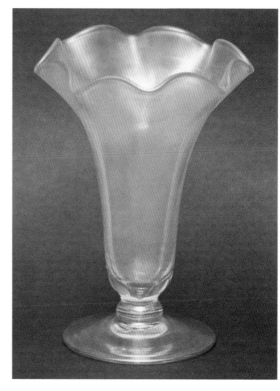

A small trumpet shaped vase, manufactured c.1910. The rim has an applied clear glass edge trail, and is finished with an eight-way crimp. The body is formed in clear glass from a mold with eight shallow projecting ribs, and is decorated all over with an iridescent finish. The matching applied circular foot has a snapped off pontil mark. 5.25 x 4 inches (13.5 x 10.0 cm) $55-70 (£40-50)

Side view no.4 of vase.

A small vase with a trefoil shaped rim, manufactured c.1911. The clear glass body has an iridescent finish, and is formed from a mold incorporating nine vertical stripes, each comprising five, very small, projecting, closely spaced ribs. The base has a polished out pontil mark. Although unmarked on the base with any form of identification, the rib pattern, together with the color and texture of the iridescent finish, strongly resembles that of items manufactured by John Walsh Walsh. 6.5 x 7.0 inches (16.5 x 18.0 cm) $75-90 (£50-60)

A small vase manufactured c.1910. The rim is finished with a fourteen-way uneven crimp. The clear glass body is decorated with diagonal machine threading over a pattern produced from a mold with sixteen, bold projecting ribs. The applied circular, clear glass foot has a polished out pontil mark. The iridescent finish applied to body and foot is very similar in texture and coloring to that used on items manufactured by John Walsh Walsh. 6.5 x 5 inches (16.5 x 12.5 cm) $110-125 (£75-85)

A small, posy vase, manufactured c.1910. The rim is finished with an eight- way crimp. The body is formed with a narrow profile, spiral rib pattern, which has been blown into a bold, projecting mold, formed with eight vertical ribs. The base is finished with a polished out pontil mark. Although unmarked on the base with any form of identification, the color and texture of the iridescent finish, strongly resembles that of items manufactured by John Walsh Walsh. 2.75 x 3.25 inches (7.0 x 8.5 cm) $50-65 (£35-45)

An example of *IRIS* glass manufactured c.1878 by Thomas Webb & Sons Limited The rim has a very narrow edge trail forming a margin to the iridescent finish, and is finished with a five-way crimp. The body has a spiral, ribbed effect, formed from a mold with twelve, shallow projecting ribs, and is decorated with an orange/gold iridescent finish. The base has a polished out pontil mark with an acid stamp mark reading: *WEBB'S IRIS GLASS*. 9 x 4.5 inches (22.5 x 11.5 cm) $110-125 (£75-85)

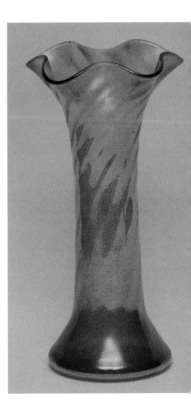

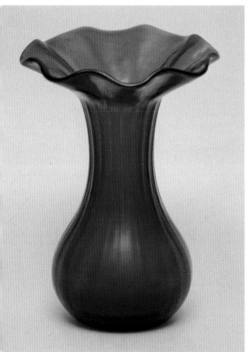

A small vase manufactured c.1900. The flared out rim is finished with an eight-way crimp. The body is formed from a mold with eighteen shallow projecting ribs, and decorated with an iridescent finish. The base has a polished out pontil mark. 4.75 x 3.25 inches (12.0 x 8.0 cm) $50-65 (£35-45)

A small vase manufactured c.1880. The square section body has been indented on each side, and decorated with an iridescent finish. The applied circular foot has a polished out pontil. 4.5 x 3.25 inches (11.5 x 8.0 cm) $90-100 (£60-70)

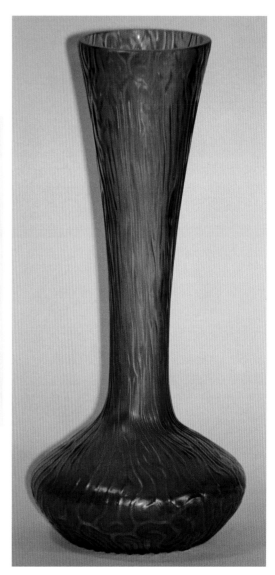

A vase manufactured c.1900. The rim is ground off and polished. The body is formed from a mold with a projecting, random abstract design pattern, and decorated with an iridescent finish. The base is patterned as from the mold. 9.75 x 4.25 inches (24.5 x 11.0cm) $125-140 (£85-95)

A small vase manufactured c.1900. The flared out rim is finished with an eight-way crimp. The body is formed from a mold with eighteen shallow projecting ribs, and decorated with an iridescent finish. The base has a polished out pontil mark. 4.75 x 3.25 inches (12.0 x 8.0 cm) $50-65 (£35-45)

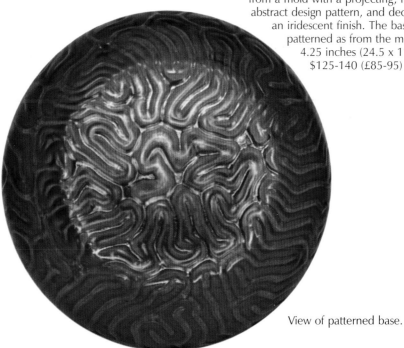

View of patterned base.

A small vase manufactured c.1880. The clear glass body is formed from a mold with fourteen shallow projecting ribs, and is decorated all over with a gold iridescent finish. The body is supported on a circular applied foot decorated with a matching finish. 5.25 x 4.25 inches (13.0 x 10.5 cm) $140-175 (£95-120)

Machine threading on translucent / opaque glass

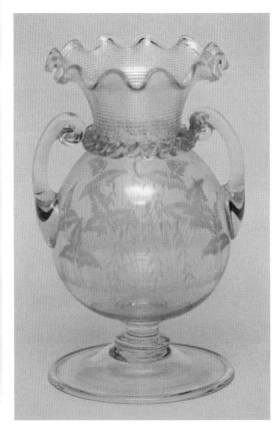

A small, threaded and engraved vase, manufactured c.1880. The edge of the rim is folded under and finished with a twelve-way rounded profile crimp. The slightly flared out neck is finished with clear glass machine threading and a trail of rigaree. The spherical, clear glass body is decorated with two applied handles and an engraved, fern type pattern, applied all around. The body sits on a small knop on top of an applied, circular glass foot with folded under edge, and snapped off pontil mark. 6.5 x 3.5 inches (16.5 x 9.0 cm) $95-110 (£65-75)

Two small vases, both manufactured c.1880. The rims are finished with amber and pale turquoise blue machine threading, and finished with an eight-way crimp. The bodies are decorated with an engraved fern type pattern all around. The applied circular feet have snapped off pontil marks. 5.25 x 1.75 inches (13.5 x 4.5 cm) $65-70 each (£45-50 each)

A small machine threaded vase, manufactured c.1880. The body is formed in clear glass with turquoise blue machine threading all over. The base has a snapped off pontil mark. 3.75 x 2.75 inches (9.5 x 7.0 cm) $50-65 (£35-45)

A small cylindrical, machine threaded vase, manufactured c.1880. The clear glass body is decorated with applied turquoise blue machine threading all over, and two trails of clear glass rigaree. The threading has been tooled to give a rope twist effect. The circular clear glass foot has a polished out pontil mark. 4.75 x 1.5 inches (12.0 x 4.0cm) $60-70 (£40-50)

A small machine threaded vase, manufactured c.1880. The flared out rim is finished with a three-way crimp. The clear glass body is decorated with applied turquoise blue machine threading all over, and a trail of clear glass rigaree beneath the rim. The base has a snapped off pontil mark. 4 x 2.75 inches (10.0 x 7.0cm) $60-70 (£40-50)

A small machine threaded vase, manufactured c.1880. The clear glass body is decorated with applied, pale turquoise blue machine threading and two applied shell ribbed handles. The applied, clear glass circular foot has a polished out pontil mark. 4.25 x 3.0 inches (10.5 x 7.5 cm) $50-65 (£35-45)

A small machine threaded vase, manufactured c.1880. The clear glass, tapered body is decorated with applied turquoise blue machine threading all over, and with two applied vertical trails of pincered work. The body sits on a short clear glass stem on top of a circular clear glass foot, with polished out pontil mark. 5 x 1.5 inches (12.5 x 4.0 cm) $60-70 (£40-50)

An example of pattern no.8075, manufactured by Hodgetts, Richardson & Son c.1880. The rim is decorated with an applied trail of clear glass rigaree. The clear glass body is decorated with applied, pale turquoise blue machine threading and two applied shell ribbed elongated trails. The applied, clear glass circular foot has a snapped off pontil mark. 4.0 x 2.5 inches (10.0 x 6.5 cm) $50-65 (£35-45)

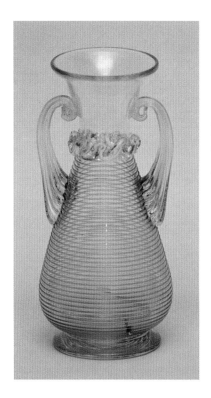

A small machine threaded vase, manufactured c.1880. The clear glass body is partially decorated with applied, pale blue machine threading, two clear glass shell ribbed handles, and a trail of clear glass rigaree around the neck. The applied clear glass foot has a polished out pontil. 4.75 x 2.25 inches (12.0 x 5.5 cm) $80-95 (£55-65)

A small machine threaded vase, manufactured c.1880. The opal white body is decorated all over with blue machine threading and a trail of white rigaree around the neck. The body sits on a similar trail, on top of the circular white foot, which has a folded under edge and polished out pontil mark. 4 x 2.25 inches (10.0 x 6.0 cm) $110-125 (£75-85)

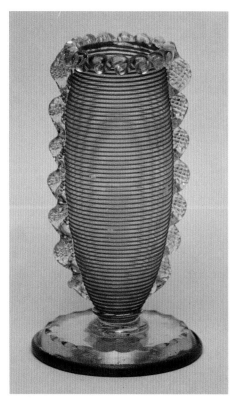

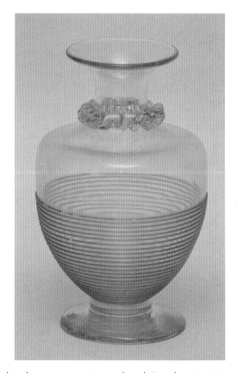

An example of pattern no.6953 as manufactured by Hodgetts, Richardson & Son c.1880. The rim is decorated with an applied trail of clear glass rigaree. The clear glass body is decorated with applied, blue machine threading and two applied vertical trails of clear glass pincered work with a cross-ribbed pattern. The body sits on a circular mirror plateau. 4.74 x 1.5 inches (12.0 x 4.0 cm) $95-110 (£65-75)

An example of pattern no.6472, dated October 12,1877, manufactured by Hodgetts, Richardson & Son. The circular clear glass body is decorated with amber glass machine threading, and a trail of clear glass rigaree. The body sits on a small circular knop, on top of the circular clear glass foot, which has a polished out pontil mark. 4.75 x 2.75 inches (12.0 x 7.0 cm) $80-95 (£55-65)

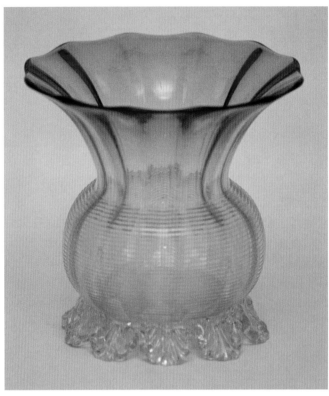

A small machine threaded vase manufactured c. 1880. The flared-out rim is finished with a three-way crimp. The clear glass body is decorated all over with pale ruby threading and a trail of clear glass rigaree beneath the rim. The base has a snapped-off pontil mark. 3.25 x 2.25 inches (8.0 x 6.0 cm) $60-70 (£40-50)

An example of pattern no. 13948 dated April 20, 1891, as manufactured by H.G.Richardson. The flared out rim is finished with a very shallow twelve-way crimp. The clear glass body is decorated with *Aurora* color shading, and applied clear glass machine threading to the lower part. The body has a snapped off pontil mark, and is supported on a continuous trail of clear glass pincered work. 4.25 x 4.25 inches (10.5 x 10.5 cm) $140-165 (£95-115)

A small machine threaded vase, manufactured c.1880. The rim is finished with an eight-way crimp. The clear glass body is formed from a mold with twelve shallow projecting ribs, and is decorated with ruby glass machine threading and a trail of clear glass rigaree. The body sits on a short stem on a circular clear glass foot which has a snapped off pontil mark. 5.25 x 2 inches (13.0 x 5.0cm) $80-95 (£55-65)

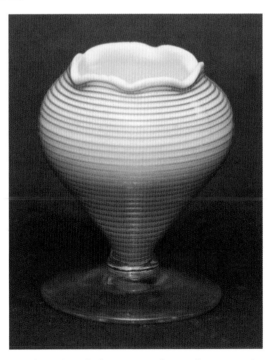

A small machine threaded vase, manufactured c.1880. The rim is finished with a six-way very shallow crimp. The pale cream body is decorated with applied ruby glass machine threading, and sits on a clear glass circular foot with a polished out pontil. 2.75 x 2.25 inches (7.0 x 5.5 cm) $50-65 (£35-45)

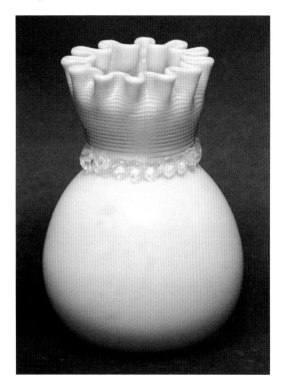

A small vase manufactured c.1880. The rim is finished with a twelve-way vertical crimp. The circular section, pale cream glass body is decorated with pale ruby machine threading from shoulder to rim, and also with an applied trail of clear glass rigaree. The base has a snapped off pontil mark. 5.25 x 3.5 inches (13.0 x 9.0 cm) $80-95 (£55-65)

Intaglio cut patterns on machine threading on translucent glass

An example of pattern no.19198, manufactured by Stevens & Williams Limited, c.1894. The clear glass body is covered with very fine section, clear glass machine threading, which is decorated with three panels of intaglio cut, stylised floral motifs and cross cut panels. 4.0 x 3.5 inches (10.0 x 9.0 cm) $255-290 (£175 –200)

Side view showing intaglio cut decoration between the three main panels.

A small machine threaded vase, manufactured c.1880. The rim is decorated with an applied trail of clear glass rigaree. The tapered, clear glass body is decorated with turquoise blue machine threading, and an alternate pattern of three long and three short, vertical clear glass, drop trails with raspberry prunts. The body has a clear glass raspberry prunt over the pontil mark, and is supported on three plain profile clear glass stub feet. 5.5 x 4.0 inches (14.0 x 10.0 cm) $110-125 (£75-85)

Machine threading with tooled surface on translucent / opaque glass

Right:
A small machine threaded vase, manufactured c.1880. The shaft and square section body is formed in clear glass, and decorated with machine threading which has been finished with an oval pattern tooled effect. The four sides have been pushed inwards, and the base has a snapped off pontil mark. 5.5 x 2.5 inches (14.0 x 6.5 cm) $80-95 (£55-65)

Below:
A small machine threaded vase, manufactured c.1880. The clear glass edge of the rim is folded over and finished with a ribbed tooled effect. The body is formed in clear glass and decorated with machine threading comprising two abutting strands of clear and pale pink threads, all finished with a tooled rope twist effect. The body is pushed in on four sides, and sits on an applied, circular clear glass foot with snapped off pontil mark. 4.75 x 2.5 inches (12.0 x 6.5 cm) $80-95 (£55-65)

Below:
A small machine threaded vase, manufactured c.1880. The edge of the rim is decorated with a rounded profile, shallow height crimp, and finished with a six-way, rectangular profile, deeper second crimp. The shaft and globe shaped body is formed in pale ruby glass, and decorated all over with amber glass machine threading, which has an oval pattern surface tooled effect. The base has a snapped off pontil mark. 6.5 x 4 inches (16.5 x 10.0 cm) $125-140 (£85-95)

Plan view of rim.

Mold blown designs finished with machine threading

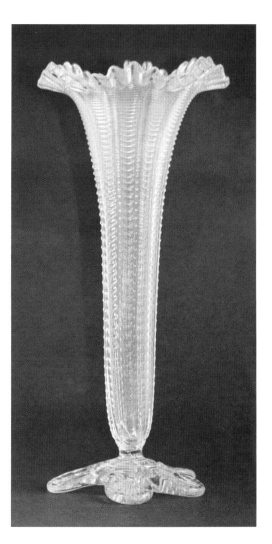

Right:
A tall machine threaded vase, manufactured c.1876. The rim has a rounded profile multi-crimped edge and is finished with a second, six-way crimp. The clear glass machine threaded body is formed from a mold with twelve projecting ribs. The base is formed with five, pincered work, prong shaped feet, and has a snapped off pontil mark. 11.75 x 5.75 inches (30.0 x 14.5 cm) $180-220 (£125-150)

A small machine threaded vase, manufactured c.1890. The rim is finished with a three-way crimp. The very pale, ruby glass body is formed from a quilted diamond patterned mold, and decorated all over with citrine color glass machine threading, and an applied trail of clear glass rigaree around the neck. The base has a polished out pontil mark. 3.5 x 3.0 inches (9.0 x 7.5 cm) $80-95 (£55-65)

A small vase decorated with the pattern recorded in Registered Design No.137288, dated November 4, 1889, by Stevens & Williams Limited, and known as *Moresque.* The rim is finished with a five-way shallow height crimp. The pale green glass body is formed from a mold, comprising stylised interlocking Moorish arches, and decorated with very fine section, closely spaced, clear glass machine threading. The base has a polished out pontil mark and is inscribed with *Rd. 137288.* 6 x 4 inches (15.0 x 10.0 cm) $255-290 (£175-200)

Encased machine threading applied to a mold blown body

An example of Stevens & Williams Limited, pattern no.14099, composite flower holder, which incorporates two, small holders decorated with their *Jewel* pattern recorded in Registered Design No. 55693, dated September 6, 1886. The large, stylised bamboo cane flower holder is formed in clear glass from a hexagonal mold with sixteen, vertical projecting ribs, and two horizontal projecting ribs. The two small ovular shaped, clear glass holders are formed from a bubble of glass covered with machine threading, which is blown into a cup of clear glass, and then blown into a mold with twelve vertical ribs. The clear glass, free shaped base is engraved on the underside with Rd, *55693*. 10.0 x 6.0 inches (25.5 x 15.0 cm) $325-360 (£225-250)

An example of Stevens & Williams Limited, Registered Design No 55693, *Jewel* pattern applied to a small vase. The body has been formed from a mold with twenty vertical projecting ribs. 4.0 x 2.5 inches (10.0 x 6.5 cm) $65-80 (£45-55)

Single spiral thread / trail

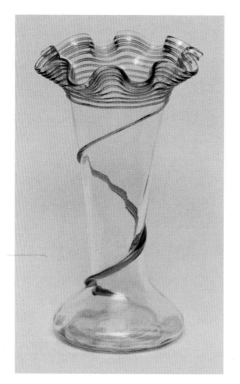

An example of a trailed vase manufactured by Stuart & Sons Limited, c.1897. The pale green glass, tapered body has an applied spiral trail from base to rim. The base has a polished out pontil mark. 5.25 x 3.0 inches (13.5 x 7.5 cm) $95-110 (£65-75)

A trailed vase manufactured c.1898. The rim is finished with an eight-way crimp. The clear glass body is formed from a mold with ten shallow projecting ribs, and is decorated with a single spiral green glass trail from base to rim. The base has a snapped off pontil mark.7.5 x 4.25 inches (19.0 x 10.5 cm) $95-110 (£65-75)

A small vase decorated with applied spiral trail, manufactured c.1890. The edge of the flared rim is finished with an eighteen-way rounded profile crimp. The pale ruby glass body is formed from a mold with eighteen shallow projecting ribs, and is decorated with an applied, green glass, pincered work trail, from base to rim. The body sits on a base formed with a trail of five, green glass, pincered work feet. 5.5 x 3.0 inches (14.0 x 7.5 cm) $140-160 (£95-110)

An example of a trailed vase manufactured by Stuart & Sons Limited, c.1897. The rim is finished with a six-way crimp. The very pale green glass, body has an applied spiral green trail from base to rim. The base has a polished out pontil mark. 5.25 x 8.0 inches (13.50 x 20.5 cm) $180-195 (£125-135)

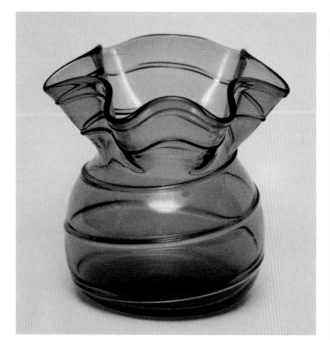

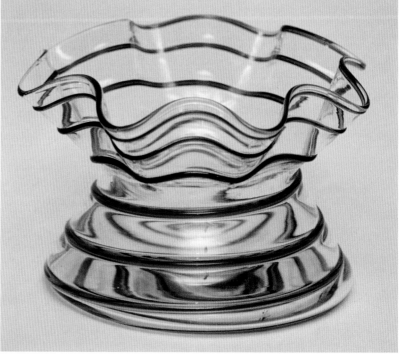

An example of a small trailed vase manufactured by Stuart & Sons Limited, c.1897. The pale green glass, body has an applied spiral trail from base to rim. The base has a polished out pontil mark. 3.5 x 3.75 inches (9.0 x 9.5 cm) $65-80 (£45-55)

Multiple vertical trails

A small vase with applied trailing, manufactured c.1900. The rim is finished with a five-way crimp. The pale green, glass body is formed from a mold with eighteen shallow projecting ribs, and is decorated with four, applied prunts and milled finish drop trails. The body sits on a small knop, on top of a matching, ribbed pattern circular foot with folded under edge and snapped off pontil mark. 6.25 x 4.25 inches (16.0 x 10.5 cm) $160-180 (£110-125)

Right:
An example of a small vase manufactured by Stuart & Son Limited, c.1900. The rim is finished with a six-way crimp. The clear glass body is formed from a mold with five shallow projecting ribs, and is decorated with five, green glass vertical trails, worked to a spiral effect around the rim. The base has a polished out pontil mark. 4.75 x 3.0 inches (12.0 x 7.5 cm) $110-125 (£75-85)

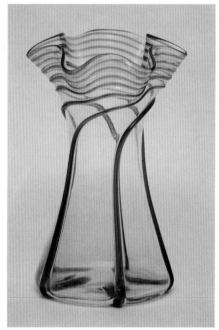

A vase with applied trailing, manufactured c.1900. The circular rim is finished with an applied green glass trail. The clear glass body is formed from a mold with ten shallow projecting ribs, and is decorated with three, green glass, vertical drop trails of rigaree. 7.0 x 3.25 inches (18.0 x 8.0cm) $125-140 (£85-95)

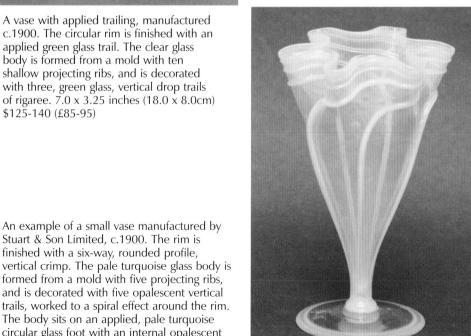

An example of a small vase manufactured by Stuart & Son Limited, c.1900. The rim is finished with a six-way, rounded profile, vertical crimp. The pale turquoise glass body is formed from a mold with five projecting ribs, and is decorated with five opalescent vertical trails, worked to a spiral effect around the rim. The body sits on an applied, pale turquoise circular glass foot with an internal opalescent edge trail and has a flat base. 4.5 x 2.75 inches (11.5 x 7.0 cm) $125-140 (£85-95)

Random pattern of threading / trails

A small vase manufactured c.1905. The rim is ground off, and polished. The green glass body is decorated all over with a random pattern of overlapping trails, and an iridescent finish. The sides of the body are pushed in on opposite sides. 3.75 x 2.75 inches (9.5 x 7.0 cm) $50-65 (£35-45)

A small vase with random trailing manufactured in Bohemia c.1900. The rim is ground off and polished. The beige over opal white, glass body has three small indentations and is decorated all over with an open, random pattern of trails. 4.25 x 3.25 inches (10.5 x 8.5 cm) $95-110 (£65-75)

A vase manufactured c.1900. The rim is finished with a very shallow eight-way crimp. The clear glass body is formed from a mold with eight shallow projecting ribs, and is decorated all over with a random pattern of tightly wound, green glass threading. The circular section body is worked to a square shape and given indented panels on each face. The flat base has a polished out pontil mark. 6.0 x 5.0 inches (15.0 x 12.5cm) $140-165 (£95-115)

Right:
A small vase with applied random trailing, manufactured c.1890. The rim is cut to a saw tooth profile and tooled with bold, vertical rib lines. The creamy white body is decorated with applied stylised coral trails formed with amber glass, and has a polished out pontil mark. The body is supported on four rustic type amber glass stub feet. 8.0 x 3.5 inches (20.0 x 8.0 cm) $255-290 (£175-200)

Stylised flower heads with leaf trails

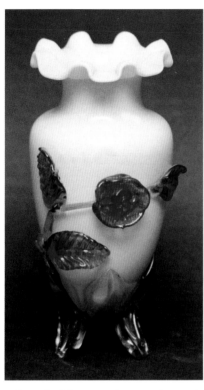

A small vase with applied flower trails, manufactured c.1890. The rim is finished with an eight-way, shallow height crimp comprising alternate rectangular and rounded profiled sections. The amphora shaped body is formed in opaque creamy white glass, and is decorated with an applied trail of stylised, colored glass pincered work leaves and a flower head. 6.0 x 2.5 inches (15.0 x 6.5 cm) $95-110 (£65-75)

A small vase with applied flower trail, manufactured c.1890. The rim is ground off and polished out. The spherical shaped body is decorated with an applied trail of stylised pincered work leaves, and a flower head. The base is flat, and has a polished out pontil mark. 4.0 x 3.5 inches (10.0 x 9.0 cm) $50-65 (£35-45)

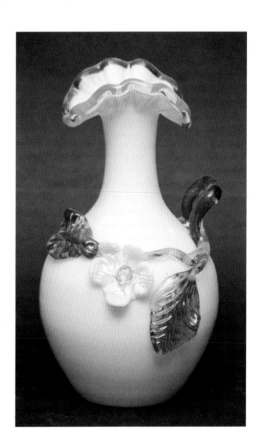

Left:
A small vase with applied flower trail, manufactured c.1890. The rim is ground off and polished out. The ovular shaped body is decorated with an applied trail of stylised pincered work leaves and a flower head. The foot comprises an amber glass looped trail. 4.25 x 2.5 inches (11.0 x 6.0 cm) $50-65 (£35-45)

Right:
A small vase with applied flower trail, manufactured c.1890. The rim is decorated with an applied green glass trail and twelve-way, shallow crimp to the edge, and is finished with a second, two-way deep crimp. The white glass body is decorated with an applied trail of stylised pincered work leaves, and a flower head. The base has a polished out pontil mark. 5.75 x 3.25 inches (14.5 x 8.0 cm) $80-95 (£55-65)

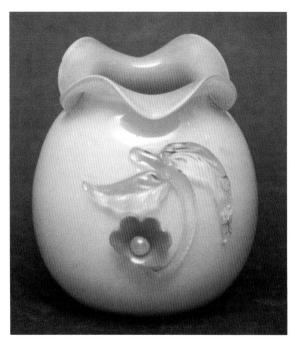

A small vase with applied flower trail, manufactured c.1890. The rim is finished with a four-way shallow crimp. The spherical shaped body is formed with clear glass, over sandy cream glass, over pink glass, and is decorated with an applied flower trail. The flower head is formed with pink over white over pale green glass, and has a green glass domed center. The base has a polished out pontil mark. 3.5 x 3.25 inches (9.0 x 8.5 cm) $110-125 (£75-85)

A small vase with applied flower trail manufactured c.1890. The rim is ground off, and polished. The mold formed body comprises shaded pink glass over opal white, and is decorated with two, white glass stylised flower heads, with amber glass leaves and stalk. The base is flat as taken from the mold. 3.5 x 3.5 inches (8.0 x 8.0 cm) $125-140 (£85-95)

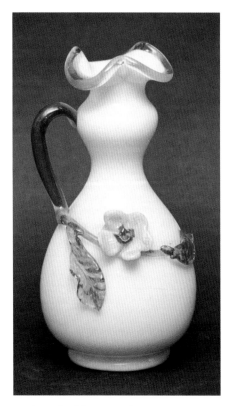

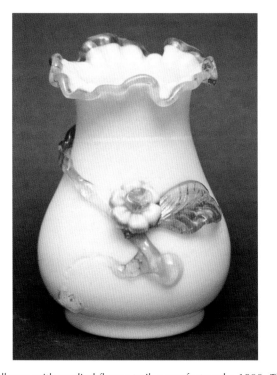

A small vase with applied flower trail, manufactured c.1890. The rim is decorated with an applied green glass trail and is finished with a three-way shallow crimp. The white glass body is decorated with an applied trail of stylised pincered work leaves, and a flower head. The integral, circular base has a polished out pontil mark. 6.0 x 3.0 inches (15.5 x 7.5 cm) $80-95 (£55-65)

A small vase with applied flower trail, manufactured c.1890. The multi-way crimped edge of the rim has an applied amber glass trail, and the rim is finished with a five-way shallow crimp. The white glass body is decorated with an applied leaf trail and flower head. The integral solid foot has a polished out pontil mark. 4.75 x 3.25 inches (12.0 x 8.0 cm) $80-95 (£55-65)

Left:
A small vase with applied flower trail, manufactured c.1895. The multi-crimped edge of the rim has an applied green glass trail and the rim is finished with a two-way deep crimp. The body is formed with shaded green glass over opal white glass, and is decorated with an applied trail of leaves and two flower heads. The base has a polished out pontil mark. 7.0 x 4.0 inches (18.0 x 10.0 cm) $180-195 (£125-135)

Right:
A tall vase with applied flower trail, manufactured c.1895. The rim has an amber glass edge trail and is finished with a rectangular stepped profile, vertical crimp. The opal white over pale ruby glass body is decorated with an applied trail of leaves and a flower head, all in amber glass. The integral foot has a ground out pontil mark. 10.5 x 5.0 inches (27.0 x 12.5 cm) $195-220 (£135-150)

Below:
A vase with applied flower trail, manufactured c.1890. The rim is decorated with a double row of opalescent, green glass pincered work trails. The ruby glass body is formed from a mold with twelve shallow projecting ribs, and is decorated with an applied trail of leaves and a large flower head. The body has a snapped off pontil mark, and is supported on a continuous trail of green glass, shell ribbed pincered work. 6.25 x 8.25 inches (16.0 x 21.0 cm) $360-400 (£250-275)

A small vase with applied flower trail, manufactured c.1895. The rim is finished in a four-way deep crimp. The amphora shaped body is formed with clear over pink, over pale green glass, and is decorated with an applied clear glass trail of leaves and a flower head. The body is supported on three, clear glass, rustic type stub feet. 6.75 x 3.5 inches (17.0 x 9.0 cm) $125-140 (£85-95)

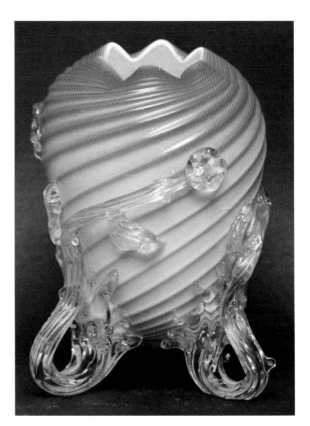

Left:
A small vase with applied flower trail, manufactured c.1885. The body comprises clear glass over very fine section green glass, pulled up machine threading, over opal white, over pale ruby glass, which has been blown into a mold with twelve projecting ribs. The body is decorated with a rustic, amber glass trail and two, stylised pink glass mold formed, flower heads. The amber glass, rustic pattern, ball shaped foot has a polished off base. 4.25 x 2.25 inches (10.5 x 5.5 cm) $255-290 (£175-200)

A vase with applied rustic flower trails, manufactured c.1885. The rim is finished with an eight-way crimp, pushed inwards. The ovular shaped body is formed in shaded pink over cream glass and decorated with a bold projecting spiral rib pattern. The pontil mark on the base of the body is covered with a clear glass, stylised flower prunt. The body is supported on three, clear glass, stylised tree branch looped trails, which rise up around the body with applied stylised flower heads and leaves. 6.5 x 4.25 inches (16.5 x 11.0 cm) $650-725 (£450-500)

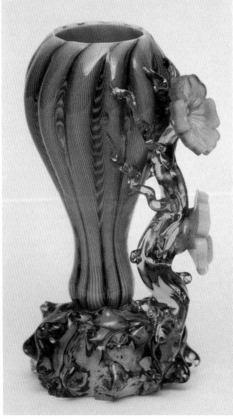

Side view.

A vase with applied rustic flower trails, manufactured c.1885. The edge of the rim is decorated with an applied clear glass, rustic pattern trail, and finished with a five-way, deep profile crimp. The amphora shaped body is formed in shaded pink over creamy white glass, and has a stylised flower head prunt over the pontil mark. The body is supported on three, clear glass, stylised tree branch looped trails, which rise up around the body with applied stylised leaves and flower heads. 9.0 x 6.0 inches (23.0 x 15.0 cm) $940-1000 (£650-700)

A vase manufactured by Stevens & Williams Limited, using their Registered Design No.15353, dated October 18, 1884, for applied floral decoration called *Mat-Su-No-Ke* (The spirit of the pine tree). The edge of the rim is finished with a twenty-way rounded profile crimp. The spherical shaped, ruby glass body is formed from a mold with ten shallow projecting ribs, and sits on a rustic pattern ball shaped knop, on top of the base. The base comprises a circular, domed hollow, ruby glass foot formed from the same mold as the body, and with a turned up edge. The pontil mark is covered by a large clear glass raspberry type prunt, and the underside of the domed base is engraved with *Rd.15353*. 6.5 x 5.5 inches (16.5 x 14.0 cm) $650-725 (£450-500)

A small flower vase manufactured c.1895. The rim is ground off and polished. The pale, translucent brown glass body is formed from a mold with eight shallow projecting vertical ribs. The body is supported on three, clear glass feet formed with double, stylised acanthus leaves. A clear glass, stylised, pincered work flower head and trail springs from each of the three feet. 4.25 x 3.5 inches (10.5 x 9.0 cm) $125-140 (£85-95)

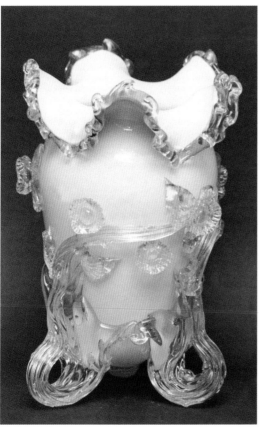

A vase with applied rustic flower trails, manufactured c.1885. The edge of the rim is decorated with an applied clear glass, rustic pattern trail, and finished with a five-way, deep profile crimp. The amphora shaped body is formed in pale shaded green glass over creamy white glass, and has a stylised flower head prunt over the pontil mark. The body is supported on three, clear glass, stylised tree branch looped trails, which rise up around the body with applied stylised leaves and flower heads. 9.0 x 6.0 inches (23.0 x 15.0 cm) $940-1000 (£650-700)

Leaves formed in two different colored halves

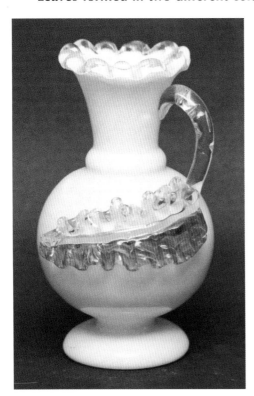

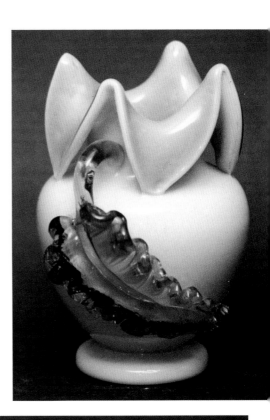

Left:
A small vase with a large leaf trail manufactured c.1885. The rim has a clear glass edge trail, which is finished with a twelve-way, shallow height crimp. The opal white opaque glass, circular section body is decorated with a pincered work, stylised acanthus leaf trail, formed in clear and very pale ruby glass. The integral circular foot has a polished out pontil mark. 5.75 x 3.25 inches (14.5 x 8.0 cm) $125-140 (£85-95)

Right:
A small vase with leaf trails manufactured c.1885. The rim is finished with a four-way deep crimp. The circular section body is formed in opal white over pale turquoise glass, and is decorated with two, pincered work, stylised acanthus leaves, each formed in pale, blending shades of green, amber and ruby. The applied circular, solid section foot has a polished out pontil mark. 5 x 3.25 inches (12.5 x 8.5 cm) $125-140 (£85-95)

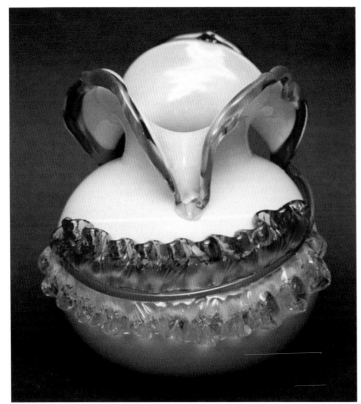

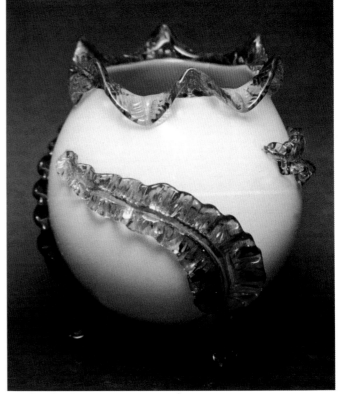

A small vase with a large leaf trail manufactured c.1885. The rim has a pale green edge trail and is finished with a three-way deep crimp. The spherical shaped body is formed in creamy white over pale ruby glass, and is decorated with a pincered work stylised acanthus leaf, formed in green and yellow glass with a pale ruby glass stem. The base has a polished out pontil mark. 5.5 x 4.75 inches (14.0 x 12.0 cm) $250-280 (£175-195)

A vase with large leaf trails, manufactured c.1885. The rim is decorated with an applied pincered work, amber glass trail finished with a six-way shallow crimp. The spherical shaped body formed in creamy white over pale ruby glass, has a pontil mark covered by an applied raspberry prunt. The body is supported on the looped stems of three, pincered work, stylised acanthus leaves, each formed in pale shades of amber and green. 6 x 5 inches (15.0 x 12.5 cm) $250-280 (£175-195)

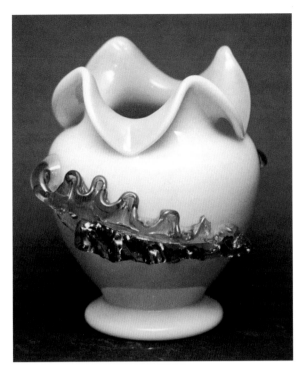

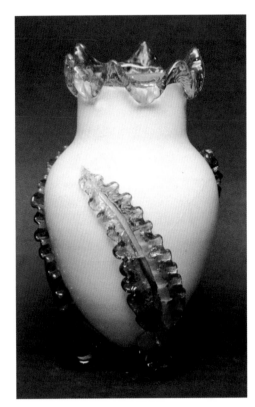

A small vase with leaf trails manufactured c.1885. The rim is finished with a four-way shallow height crimp. The circular section body is formed in opal white over pale turquoise glass, and is decorated with two, pincered work, stylised acanthus leaves, each formed in pale, blending shades of green, amber and ruby. The applied circular, solid section foot has a polished out pontil mark. 4 x 3.5 inches (10.0 x 9.0 cm) $125-140 (£85-95)

An example of a vase with applied leaf trails illustrated in an advertisement for *Autumnal Ware,* included in the *Pottery Gazette,* on May 1, 1884, by the dealers Blumberg & Company of Cannon Street London. The rim is decorated with an applied pincered work trail of amber glass, finished with a six-way crimp. The circular section body is formed in creamy white over pale ruby glass, and has an integral solid foot with a polished out pontil mark. The body is decorated with three, pincered work, stylised acanthus leaves, each formed in a blend of pale shades of amber, green and pale ruby glass. 7.5 x 4.5 inches (19.0 x 11.5 cm) $250-280 (£175-195)

An example of a vase with applied leaf trails illustrated in an advertisement for *Autumnal Ware,* included in the *Pottery Gazette,* on May 1, 1884, by the dealers Blumberg & Company of Cannon Street London. The rim is decorated with an applied pincered work trail of amber glass, finished with a six-way crimp. The amphora shaped body is formed in creamy white over pale ruby glass, and has a pontil mark covered with a clear glass raspberry prunt. The body is supported on the looped stems of three, pincered work, stylised acanthus leaves, each formed in a blend of pale shades of amber, green and pale ruby glass. 8.25 x 4.25 inches (21.0 x11.0 cm) $250-280 (£175-195)

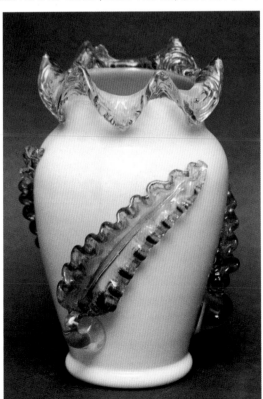

Right:
An example of a vase with applied leaf trails illustrated in an advertisement for *Autumnal Ware,* included in the *Pottery Gazette,* on May 1, 1884, by the dealers Blumberg & Company of Cannon Street London. The rim is decorated with an edge trail of amber glass, and finished with a four-way crimp. The circular section body is formed in creamy white over pale ruby glass, and has an integral solid foot with a polished out pontil mark. The body is decorated with four, pincered work, stylised acanthus leaves, each formed in a blend of pale shades of amber, green and pale ruby glass. 12 x 5 inches (30.5 x 12.5 cm) $250-280 (£175-195)

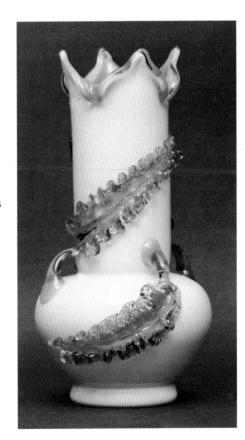

Leaves in two different colored halves with pincered daisy head pattern

Right:
A small vase with applied fruit trail, manufactured c.1885. The rim has a pale blue edge trail and is finished with a twelve-way "V" shaped vertical crimp. The circular section, opal white body has an integral solid foot with polished out pontil mark. The body is decorated with an applied trail of pale blue glass leaves and two, ruby glass cherries. 5.5 x 3.5 inches (14.0 x 9.0 cm) $175-190 (£120-130)

A small vase with applied leaf trail, manufactured c.1885. The rim has an applied blue glass edge trail finished with a twenty-four way shallow crimp. The circular section creamy white body has a ground out pontil mark, and is decorated with three, pincered work, stylised acanthus leaves, each formed in yellow and blue glass and decorated with a daisy head pincered edge pattern. The body is supported on three, rustic pattern stub feet, from which the three leaves spring. 5.25 x 3.5 inches (13.5 x 9.0 cm) $190-220 (£130-150)

Stylised fruit, nuts, or acorns with leaf trails

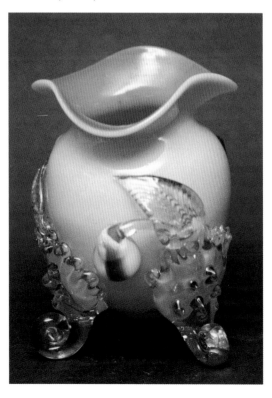

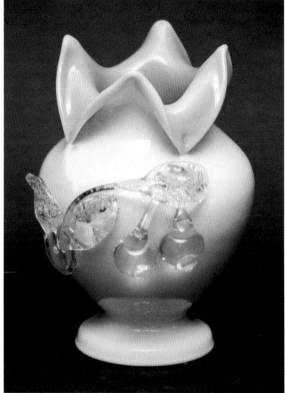

A small vase with applied fruit trail, manufactured c.1885. The rim is finished with a four-way deep crimp. The circular section body is formed in opal white over pale ruby glass, and is decorated with a clear glass trail of leaves and two stylised cherries. The applied circular, solid section foot has a polished out pontil mark. 5 x 3.5 inches (12.5 x 9.0 cm) $175-190 (£120-130)

A small vase with applied glass fruit, manufactured c.1885. The rim is finished with a three-way shallow crimp. The ovular shaped body has a polished out pontil mark, and is supported on three, clear glass, plain, snail pattern feet with rustic surface pull-outs on the haunches. The body is decorated with a stylised white and ruby striped glass cherry and clear glass leaf trail springing from each foot. 4.25 x 2.5 inches (10.5 x 6.5 cm) $175-190 (£120-130)

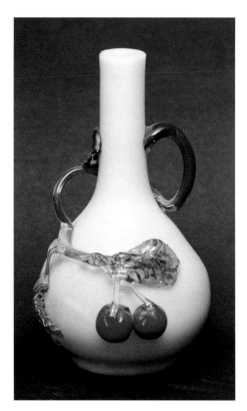

Stylised acanthus leaf motifs

A small vase with applied fruit trail, manufactured c.1885. The rim has a ground off, and polished finish. The opal white circular section, glass body has an applied circular foot with a polished out pontil mark. The body is decorated with an amber glass leaf trail and two ruby glass cherries. 5.75 x 3.0 inches (14.5 x 7.5 cm) $175-190 (£120-130)

A small vase with an applied leaf trail manufactured c.1885. The rim is finished with a very shallow, four-way crimp. The spherical body is formed with opal white over pale blue glass, and has a polished out pontil mark. The body is decorated with a large pincered work clear glass, stylised acanthus leaf. 3.75 x 3.75 inches (9.5 x 9.5 cm) $220-250 (£150-175)

Left:
A tall vase with applied leaf and nut trail manufactured c.1885. The rim has an applied clear glass edge trail decorated with a shallow height multi-crimp, and finished with a second, five-way deep crimp. The circular section body is formed in opal white glass, and has an integral foot with a polished out pontil mark. The body is decorated with an applied trail of clear glass and pale ruby glass leaves, and with a single, large stylised clear glass, horse chestnut motif. 10 x 4.5 inches (25.0 x 11.5 cm) $220-250 (£150-175)

A small vase with an applied leaf trail manufactured c.1885. The rim has a rustic pattern clear glass edge trail and is finished with a three-way deep crimp. The spherical body is formed with very pale lemon glass over very pale ruby glass, and has a polished out pontil mark. The body is decorated with a large clear glass, pincered work, stylised acanthus leaf. 5.75 x 5.0 inches (14.5 x 12.5 cm) $275-310 (£195-215)

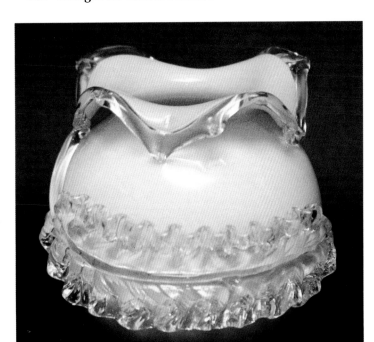

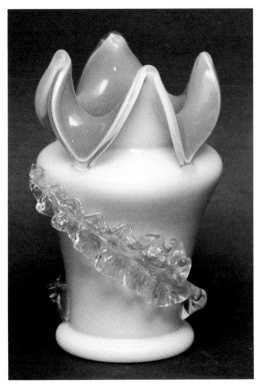

A small vase with an applied leaf trail manufactured c.1885. The rim has a rustic pattern clear glass edge trail and is finished with a four-way shallow height crimp. The spherical body is formed with opal white glass over very pale ruby glass, and has a polished out pontil mark. The body is decorated with a large clear glass pincered work, stylised acanthus leaf. 4.25 x 4.0 inches (10.5 x 10.0 cm) $250-280 (£175-195)

A small vase with applied leaf trail manufactured c.1885. The rim has a clear glass edge trail and is finished with a four-way deep crimp. The tapered, circular section body is formed in opal white over pale ruby glass and has an integral foot with a polished out pontil mark. The body is decorated with two, pincered work, clear glass, stylised acanthus leaves. 5.5 x 3.25 inches (14.0 x 8.5 cm) $220-250 (£150-175)

A small vase with applied leaf trails manufactured c.1885. The rim is finished with an eight-way crimp pushed inwards. The ovular shaped body is formed in shaded pale ruby glass over pale cream color glass, and is supported on three, clear glass, knob shaped feet. A stylised, clear glass, pincered work acanthus leaf, springs from the top of each foot. 4.25 x 3.25 inches (10.5 x 8.5 cm) $220-250 (£150-175)

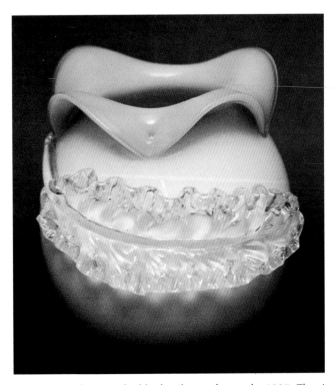

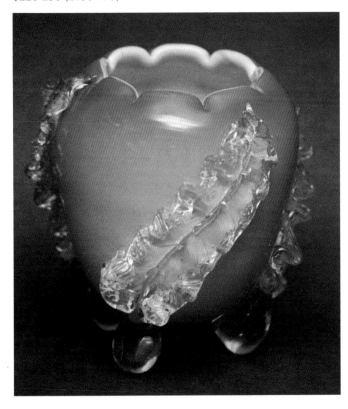

A small vase with an applied leaf trail manufactured c.1885. The rim is finished with a very shallow, four-way crimp. The spherical body is formed with opal white over pale blue glass, and has a polished out pontil mark. The body is decorated with a pincered work clear glass, stylised acanthus leaf. 3.75 x 3.5 inches (9.5 x 9.0 cm) $220-250 (£150-175)

Right:
A small vase manufactured by John Walsh Walsh, in accordance with their Registered Design No.74556, dated May 26, 1887. The stylised rustic tree trunk body with surface pullouts is formed in pale opalescent ruby glass, and has a ground out pontil mark inscribed with "Rd. 74556". The body is decorated with a large pincered work, clear glass, stylised, acanthus leaf. 3.75 x 2.5 inches (9.5 x 6.5 cm) $125-140 (£85-95)

A small vase supported on leaf shaped feet, manufactured c.1885. The rim is ground off and polished. The circular section, pale yellow glass body, is supported on three, clear glass pincered work, stylised acanthus leaf feet. 5.25 x 2.25 inches (13.0 x 5.5cm) $65-80 (£45-55)

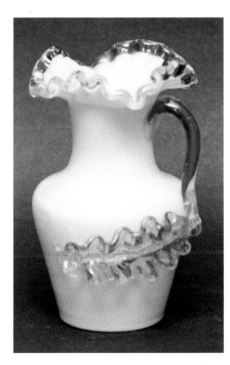

A small vase with applied leaf trail manufactured c.1885. The rim has an applied pale blue edge trail, and is finished with a four-way crimp. The circular section body is formed in opal white glass and has a polished out pontil mark. The body is decorated with a pale blue glass, pincered work, stylised, acanthus leaf. 5.25 x 3.0 inches (13.0 x 7.5 cm) $95-110 (£65-75)

A small vase with leaf trails, manufactured by Stuart & Sons Limited, c.1883. The rim is decorated with an applied trail of clear glass rigaree. The ovular shaped, ruby glass body has a clear glass, raspberry prunt over the pontil mark, and is supported on three, plain pattern, clear glass snail type feet. A large pincered work, clear glass, stylised acanthus leaf springs from the top of each foot. 5.5 x 4.0 inches (14.0 x 10.0 cm) $220-250 (£150-175)

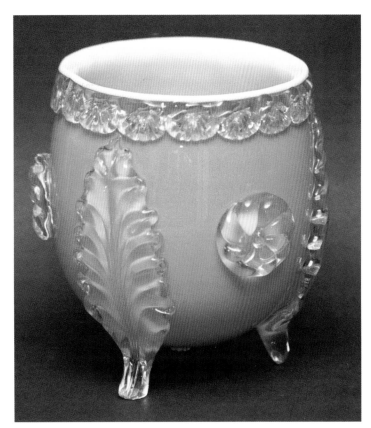

A vase manufactured by John Walsh Walsh, c.1883, and is an example from their Crushed Strawberry range as illustrated in *The Pottery Gazette*, in November 1883. The rim is decorated with an applied trail of clear glass pincered work. The circular section body is formed in a pale pink glass over a creamy white glass, and has a clear glass raspberry prunt over the pontil mark. The body is supported on three, pincered work, clear glass, stylised acanthus leaves. Three large circular clear glass stylised flower head prunts are applied to the body between the legs. 6.0 x 4.75 inches (15.0 x 12.0 cm) $220-250 (£150-175)

Short lengths of thin glass canes in random pattern (*Peloton*)

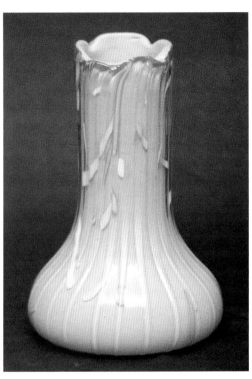

A small *Peloton* style patterned vase, manufactured c.1885. The rim is finished with a four-way shallow height crimp. The clear glass over pale pink glass, over opal white glass body is formed from a mold with twenty- two projecting ribs, and has a snapped off pontil mark. The body is decorated with a random pattern of short lengths of colored canes applied beneath the outer layer of glass. 4 x 2.75 inches (10.0 x 7.0 cm) $65-80 (£45-55)

A small vase manufactured c.1890. The rim is ground off and polished. The spherical body is formed in very pale translucent blue opalescent glass, from a mold with ten very shallow projections. The body is supported on three, pincered work, amber glass, stylised, acanthus leaf legs. 5.25 x 4.25 inches (13.5 x 10.5 cm) $110-125 (£75-85)

Horizontal and / or vertical trails of rigaree

A tall vase with applied vertical trailing, manufactured c.1885. The rim is decorated with a trail of clear glass rigaree, above two, continuous over-lapping bands of random pattern, clear glass, drop trailing. The translucent, pale brown glass body is formed from a mold with twelve, shallow projecting ribs, and has a polished out pontil mark, and is supported on three, clear glass rustic pattern stub feet. Three different patterns of long rigaree type, drop trails are applied around the body. 13.25 x 4.25 inches (33.5 x 10.5) $190-220 (£130-150)

Close-up of vertical trails.

Rigaree trails in festoon patterns with / without prunts

A small vase with applied rigaree trailing, manufactured c.1885. The rim is finished with a six-way crimp, turned inwards. The ovular shaped, clear glass over blue glass, over opal white glass body is formed from a mold with eighteen projecting ribs, and has a stylised flower head prunt over the pontil mark. The body is supported on three, shell ribbed feet. Three festoon shaped trails of clear glass rigaree and small domed prunts are applied around the body. 4.25 x 3.0 inches (11.0 x 7.5 cm) $190-220 (£130-150)

Pincered trails of shell ribbed / daisy head patterns

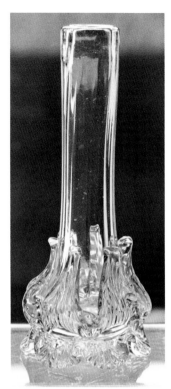

Left:
A small vase with pincered work trailing manufactured c.1880. The rim is fire polished. The body is formed in clear glass from a mold with ten, shallow projecting ribs, and is supported on a clear glass pincered trail. A trail of vertical clear glass, triangular shaped, pincered work leaves are applied around the body on top of the foot. 5.25 x 2.25 inches (13.5 x 5.5cm) $45-60 (£30-40)

Right:
A small vase with pincered work trailing, manufactured c.1880. The rim is ground off and polished. The body is shaded from clear to amber /orange color at the rim, and is formed from a mold with twelve, shallow projecting ribs. The body is supported on a clear glass pincered work trail, above which are located two further rows of clear glass pincered work trails. 8 x 2.75 inches (20.5 x 7.0 cm) $45-60 (£30-40)

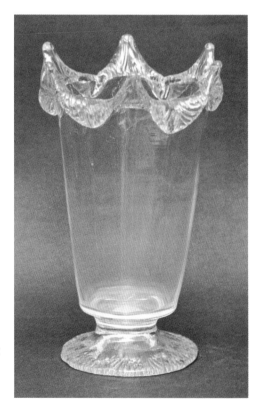

Right:
A small vase with pincered work trailing manufactured c.1880. The rim is decorated with an applied trail of clear glass triangular shaped, pincered work leaves. The clear glass body is formed from a mold with twelve shallow projecting ribs, and has a snapped off pontil mark. The lower part of the body is decorated with surface pull-outs.4.75 x 3.0 inches (12.0 x 7.5) $45-60 (£30-40)

Right:
A vase with pincered work trailing manufactured c.1880. The rim is decorated with an applied, clear glass trail of pincered work, finished with a six-way deep crimp. The tapered profile body is formed from a mold with twelve, shallow projecting ribs, and is supported on a circular foot with polished out pontil mark. The edge of the foot is decorated with a band of pincered rib patterning. 8.25 x 4.25 inches (21.0 x 10.5 cm) $80-95 (£55-65)

A small vase decorated with applied pincered work trails, manufactured c.1880 The rim is decorated with an applied trail of triangular shaped pincered work, set above a trail of clear glass, shell ribbed pincered work. The pale ruby glass body is formed from a mold with twelve, shallow projecting ribs, and has a snapped off pontil mark. The body is supported on five, clear glass, prong shaped feet. 6.5 x 3.25 inches (16.5 x 8.5 cm) $180-200 (£125-140)

A small vase with applied pincered decoration, manufactured c.1880. The rim is decorated with a trail of clear glass rigaree, beneath which is a clear glass, shell ribbed pincered work trail. The ruby glass body is formed from a mold with twelve shallow projecting ribs, and is supported on a short clear glass stem, on top of a circular, clear glass foot with snapped off pontil mark. The body is decorated with two, clear glass, shell ribbed pincered work vertical trails. 4.5 x 2.75 inches (11.5 x 7.0 cm) $145-175 (£100-120)

Stained glass designs

Right:
A vase with stained and cut decoration, manufactured c.1855. The rim is cut away to form six stylised, ogee profiled, petal shapes. The body and applied foot are formed in clear glass, coated with a ruby stain, and cut away to give six facets. 4.75 x 2.25 inches (14.5 x 5.5 cm) $110-125 (£75-85)

A small vase decorated with applied pincered work trails, manufactured by Stuart & Sons Limited, c.1883. The rim is decorated with an applied trail of triangular shaped pincered work, set above a trail of clear glass rigaree. The amber glass body is formed from a mold with sixteen, shallow projecting ribs, and has a polished out pontil mark. 3.75 x 4.75 inches (9.5 x 12.0cm) $125-140 (£85-95)

Cased glass

Underside of vase.

A cased vase manufactured c.1855. The body is formed with blue glass, over white glass over clear glass, and is decorated with a stylised floral pattern between spiral stripes, and all cut through to the clear glass. The underside of the circular base is also cut through to the clear glass. 7.75 x 4.75 inches (19.5 x 12.0 cm) $360-400 (£250-275)

Vases with internal decoration:

Amberina designs

A vase formed in heat reactive glass, manufactured c. 1885. The rim is ground off and polished. The spherical shaped *Amberina* glass body is formed from a mold with a regular pattern of indented circles, and is supported on an amber glass trail of shell ribbed pincered work. 5.25 x 4.25 inches (13.0 x 10.5 cm) $140-165 (£95-115)

Burmese designs

A vase formed in *Burmese* glass, manufactured by Thomas Webb & Sons Limited, c.1886. The rim is ground off and polished. The satin finished, cream glass body has an integral solid foot, and a polished out pontil mark inscribed with *1621* and *e/d* which are the reference number and pricing code used for this particular design. The body is decorated with an enamelled floral design. 6.75 x 4.5 inches (17.5 x 11.5 cm) $360-400 (£250-275)

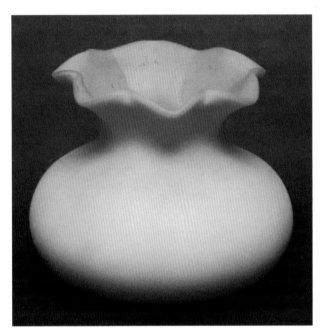

A small vase formed in *Burmese* glass, manufactured by Thomas Webb & Sons Limited, c.1886. The rim edge is finished with a seven-way petal profile. The satin finished body has a polished out pontil mark impressed with a circular stamp reading, *QUEENS BURMESE WARE PATENTED*, in a margin around the central area, which is inscribed, *Thos. WEBB & Sons*. Also inscribed around the outside of the stamp at the base is *Rd.80167*, the Registered Design reference for the petal shape rim which was recorded on September 5, 1887. 2.5 x 3.25 inches (6.5 x 8.0cm) $215-255 (£150-175)

View showing the enamelled foliage.

A small vase formed in *Burmese* glass, manufactured c.1887 by Thomas Webb & Sons Limited The satin finished body has a polished out pontil mark, and is decorated with an enamelled pattern of a bird sitting on the branch of a tree. 7.0 x 4.0 inches (18.0 x 10.0 cm) $400-435 (£275-300)

Close-up of enamelled bird.

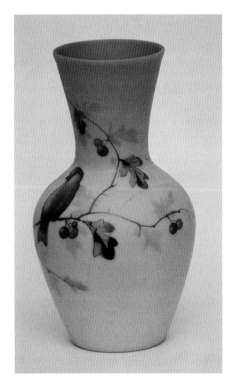

Side view of vase.

Opalescent glass designs

A small vase formed with opalescent glass, manufactured c.1890. The rim is finished with an eight-way crimp. The opalescent, yellow-green body has been formed in a mold with twelve, very shallow projecting ribs. The body sits on a small knop, on top of the matching circular glass foot which has a snapped off pontil mark. The complete item has been given an iridescent finish, the color and texture of which, is very similar to that known to have been produced by John Walsh Walsh. 5.5 x 4.0 inches (14.0 x 10.0) $140-175 (£95-120)

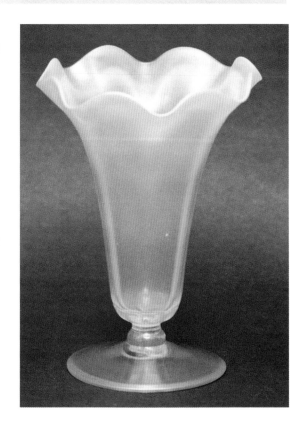

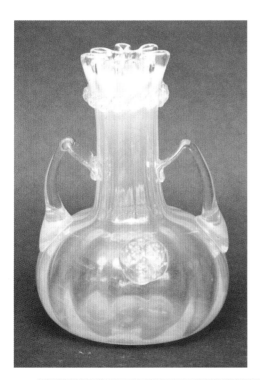

Left:
A small vase formed in opalescent glass, manufactured c.1885. The rim is finished with an eight-way, tightly set vertical crimp. The pale opalescent blue glass body is formed from a mold with twelve, shallow projecting ribs, and has a polished out pontil mark. The body is decorated with a trail of clear glass rigaree just below the rim, two, clear glass handles, and two, clear glass applied circular pads, each containing three, raspberry type prunts. 4.5 x 3.0 inches (11.5 x 7.5 cm) $95-110 (£65-75)

Right:
A small vase formed in opalescent glass, manufactured c.1890. The rim is decorated with an applied clear glass edge trail, and finished with an eighteen-way, shallow height, rounded profile crimp. The pale, opalescent blue glass body and hollow section foot is formed from a two-part mold, and the inside surface of the body is finished with an eight-way convex section vertical rib mold pattern. 6.0 x 2.5 inches (15.9 x 6.5 cm) $65-80 (£45-55)

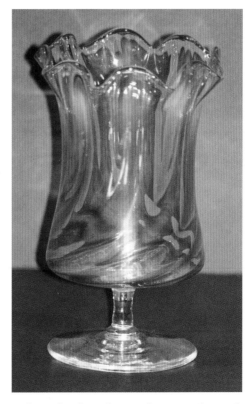

A small vase formed in opalescent glass, manufactured c.1895. The edge of the rim is decorated with a vertical, green glass trail of half-daisy pattern pincered work. The pale translucent green, opalescent glass body is formed from a mold with twelve, shallow, projecting ribs. The body is supported on a foot with a snapped off pontil mark, and comprising five, green glass, triangular shaped, stylised leaves. 4.5 x 3.0 inches (11.5 x 7.5 cm) $149-170 (£95-115)

A small vase formed with opalescent glass, manufactured c.1890. The rim is finished with an eight-way crimp. The opalescent, pale green glass body is formed from a mold with eight, shallow projecting ribs, and is supported on a clear glass circular foot with a short stem. 4.75 x 3.25 inches (12.0 x 8.0 cm) $110-125 (£75-85)

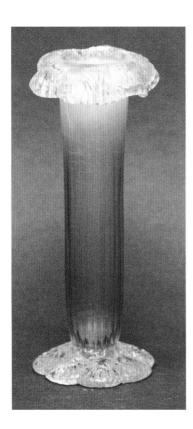

A small vase formed with opalescent glass, manufactured c.1885. The rim is decorated with an applied, clear glass pincered work trail, folded downwards in a six-way crimp. The opalescent, pale blue glass body is formed from a mold with eighteen shallow projecting ribs, and has a snapped off pontil mark. The clear glass foot is formed with a trail of daisy head pattern pincered work. 6.0 x 2.5 inches (15.0 x 6.5 cm) $80-95 (£55-65)

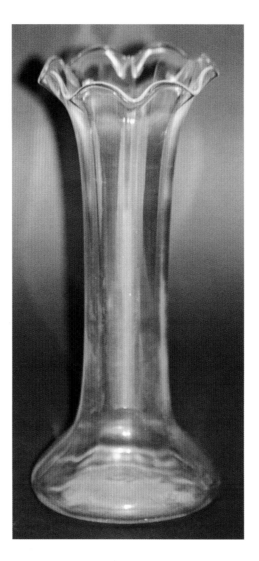

A small vase formed with opalescent glass, manufactured c.1890. The rim is finished with an eight-way shallow crimp. The yellow-green opalescent glass body is formed from a mold with eight, shallow projecting ribs. 8.25 x 3.5 inches (21.0 x 9.0 cm) $80-95 (£55-65)

A small vase formed with opalescent glass, manufactured c.1890. The rim is finished with a five-way crimp. The opalescent, yellow-green glass body is formed from a mold with four, shallow projecting ribs, and is supported on an applied circular foot. 4.5 x 2.75 inches (11.5 x 7.0 cm) $95-110 (£65-75)

A small vase formed with opalescent glass, manufactured c.1895. The rim is decorated with an applied non-opalescent edge trail and finished with an eighteen-way shallow height crimp. The opalescent, yellow-green glass body is formed from a mold with twelve, shallow, projecting ribs. The body is supported on a base with a polished out pontil mark, and formed with five, pincered work, triangular shaped green glass feet. 7 x 2.75 inches (18.0 x 7.0 cm) $140-160 (£95-110)

A trumpet shaped vase formed with opalescent glass, manufactured c.1890. The rim has a non-opalescent green glass edge trail and is finished with a composite patterned edge crimp of four, shallow height crimps set between four, large half-round crimps. The opalescent, very pale green body is formed from a mold with twelve, shallow projecting ribs, and sits on a circular foot with a snapped off pontil mark. 9.25 x 5.5 inches (23.5 x 14.0 cm) $160-190 (£110-130)

A trumpet shaped vase formed with opalescent glass, manufactured c.1885. The rim is decorated with an applied pale blue glass edge trail, and finished with an eighteen-way, shallow height edge crimp, and a second, deep profile three-way crimp. The opalescent pale blue glass body is formed from a mold with twelve, shallow projecting ribs. The applied, opalescent pale blue glass foot is decorated with an eighteen-way shallow height crimp all over, and has a snapped off pontil mark. 10.25 x 6.0 inches (26.0 x 15.0 cm) $220-250 (£150-175)

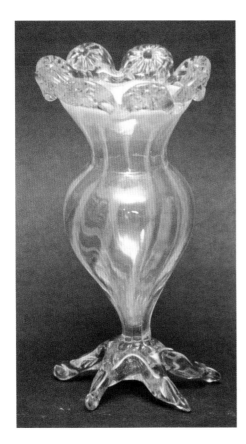

A small vase formed from opalescent glass, manufactured c.1895. The rim is decorated with a pincered work, green glass vertical trail. The clear glass body is formed from a mold with ten, shallow projecting ribs, and is decorated with ten, vertical opalescent trails. The base has a snapped off pontil, and comprises eight, green glass, stylised tree root type feet. 6.0 x 3.25 inches (15.0 x 8.0 cm) $140-160 (£95-110)

A trumpet shaped vase formed with opalescent glass, manufactured c.1885. The inside of the rim area is finished with a heat reactive glass that has been struck ruby. The edge of the rim is finished with a fourteen-way, tightly set, rounded profile, vertical crimp. The opalescent pale blue glass body is formed from a mold with sixteen, shallow projecting ribs, and is decorated with very thin vertical opalescent trails set between the rib lines, and an applied trail of clear glass rigaree. The circular foot has a snapped off pontil mark , and is decorated all over with an eighteen-way, shallow height crimp. 9.75 x 5.25 inches (25.0 x 13.5 cm) $220-250 (£150-175)

A small vase formed with opalescent glass, manufactured c.1885. The edge of the rim has a non-opalescent pale green glass trail, and is finished with an eight-way shallow crimp. The opalescent, pale green glass body is formed from a mold with twelve, projecting ribs. The clear glass base has a snapped off pontil mark, and comprises, three, tapering, prong shaped feet, with surface pullouts. 4.0 x 2.0 inches (10.0 x 5.0 cm) $80-95 (£55-65)

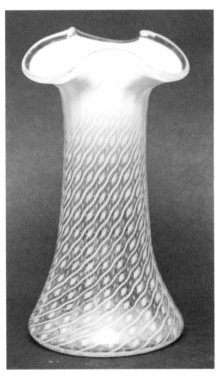

A tall vase formed from opalescent glass, manufactured c.1885. The rim is finished with an eight-way crimp. The shaded opalescent, pale blue glass body is formed from a mold with nine, shallow projecting ribs, and is supported on a circular, clear glass foot with a snapped off pontil mark. 10.5 x 3.25 inches (27.0 x 8.5 cm) $180-195 (£ 125-135)

A small vase formed with opalescent glass, manufactured c.1890. The rim has a pale green non-opalescent edge trail, and is finished with a three-way crimp. The opalescent green glass body is formed from a mold with twenty, shallow projections, and has a snapped off pontil mark. 5.5 x 3.0 inches (14.0 x 7.5 cm) $175-195 (£120-135)

A small vase formed with opalescent glass, manufactured c.1885. The rim has a non-opalescent green glass trail around the six- petal profile, and is finished with a six-way crimp. The opalescent pale green glass body is formed from a mold with twelve, shallow projecting ribs, and is decorated with an applied trail of clear glass rigaree. The base has a snapped off pontil mark, and is formed with clear glass, shell ribbed pattern pincered work. 4.75 x 2.5 inches (12.0 x 6.5 cm) $110-125 (£75-85)

A small vase formed in opalescent glass, manufactured c.1890 by Thomas Webb & Sons Limited. The edge of the rim is decorated with a six-petal profile and is finished with a six-way crimp. The opalescent, pale green glass body is formed from a mold with twelve, shallow projecting ribs, and has a snapped off pontil mark. 2.75 x 3.0 inches (7.0 x 7.5 cm) $95-110 (£65-75)

This vase by Thomas Webb & Sons Limited has been reheated at the glory hole to bring out only a small amount of opalescence.

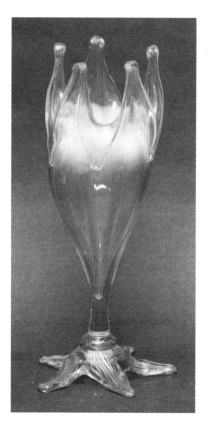

A small vase formed with opalescent glass, manufactured c.1890. The rim is finished with a five-way deep crimp. The opalescent pale green body is formed from a mold with twelve, shallow projecting ribs, and has a snapped off pontil mark. The base is formed with five, pincered work, green glass, triangular shaped, stylised leaves. 8.0 x 2.5 inches (20.0 x 6.5 cm) $125-140 (£85-95)

A rare example of a *Vesta Venetian* pattern vase as manufactured by John Walsh Walsh c.1909. The body and foot are formed from a gather of an opalescent yellow-green glass mix, covered with machine threading, and blown into a mold with sixteen vertical ribs, and brought to the final shape by hand. The item was reheated at the glory hole to bring out the opalescent effect, and then completed with an iridescent finish. The base of the foot has the pontil mark covered by a circular prunt, in the form of a large center half dome surrounded by six smaller half-domes. 7.5 x 8.0 inches (19.0 x 20.0 cm) $650-725 (£450-500)

Gold or silver foil inclusions in translucent / opaque glass

A small vase formed with silver foil inclusions, manufactured c.1895. The pinched together rim has a clear glass edge trail. The body is formed with clear glass, over silver foil fragments, over pale pink glass, over opal white glass. The base is slightly concave and has a snapped off pontil mark. 5.25 x 5.0 inches (13.0 x 12.5 cm) $140-165 (£95-115)

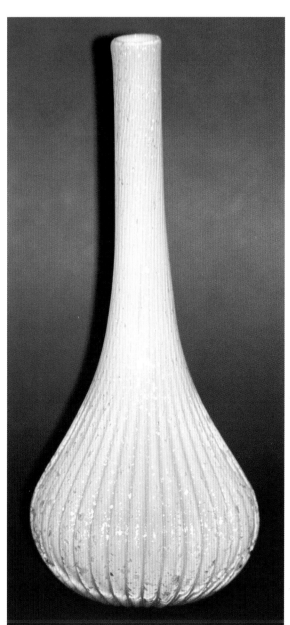

A vase formed with silver foil inclusions, manufactured c.1895. The rim is fire polished. The body is formed with clear glass over silver foil fragments, over pale pink glass, over opal white glass, and formed in a mold with thirty-six shallow projecting ribs. The base is finished as from the mold. 10.25 x 4.25 inches (26.0 x 10.5 cm) $95-110 (£65-75)

Underside of base.

A vase with silver foil inclusions manufactured c.1880. The rim is finished with a four-way deep crimp. The body is formed with pale pink glass over fragments of silver foil, over opal white glass. The integral foot has a snapped off pontil mark. 9.0 x 4.25 inches (23.0 x 10.5 cm) $125-140 (£85-95)

Vertical striped colored trails

A vase formed with silver foil inclusions, manufactured c.1890. The rim is ground off, and polished. The body comprises small fragments of silver foil trapped between two layers of green glass, and formed in a mold with twelve, shallow projecting ribs. The integral hollow foot has a snapped off pontil mark. 10.75 x 3.75 inches (27.5 x 9.5 cm) $95-110 (£65-75)

A small cased glass vase with vertical striped patterning, manufactured c.1885. The rim is decorated with a clear glass edge trail and sixteen-way crimp, and finished with a second, two-way deep crimp. The body is formed with clear glass over multi-colored glass vertical trails, over opal white glass. The circular integral foot has a snapped off pontil mark. 6.75 x 3.25 inches $95-110 (£65-75)

A vase with vertical striped patterning, manufactured c.1895. The Jack-in-the-Pulpit type rim has a multi-crimped edge. The trumpet shaped body is formed in pale green glass with six, vertical white stripes, marvered into the surface, and set on a triangular shaped, green glass foot with a multi-crimped edge. 11.5 x 3.75 inches (29.0 x 9.5cm) $190- 202 (£130-150)

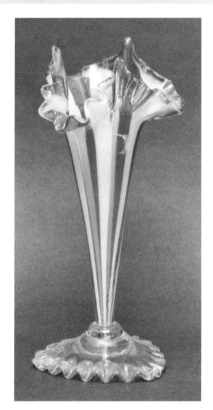

A vase with vertical striped patterning, manufactured c.1895. The rim has a multi-crimped edge, and is finished with a three-way deep crimp, with the three sides between this crimp, turned upwards. The trumpet shaped body is formed in pale ruby glass with six white glass, vertical stripes, marvered into the surface, and set on a triangular shaped, green glass foot with a multi-crimped edge. 7.75 x 3.5 inches (19.5 x 9.0cm) $190- 202 (£130-150)

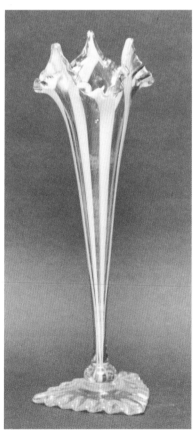

A small vase with vertical striped patterning, manufactured c.1895. The rim is finished with a rounded profile tightly set, twelve-way crimp. The very pale ruby glass is decorated with twelve, vertical opalescent glass stripes, and is supported on three amber glass feet in the form of stylised pincered work leaves. 5.75 x 3.5 inches (14.5 x 9.0 cm) $175-200 (£125-140)

A vase with vertical striped patterning, manufactured c.1895. The rim has a multi-crimped edge, and is finished with a three-way deep crimp, with the three sides between this crimp, turned upwards. The trumpet shaped body is formed in pale green glass with six white glass, vertical stripes, marvered into the surface, and set on a triangular shaped, green glass foot with a multi-crimped edge. 11.5 x 3.75 inches (29.5 x 9.5cm) $190- 202 (£130-150)

Spiral trailing

A small vase with internal spiral trailing, manufactured c.1890. The rim is fire polished. The body is formed in pale green glass, with eight, white spiral stripes marvered into the surface, and is decorated with an applied, amber glass stylised oak leaf trail. The integral circular foot has a snapped off pontil mark. 6.0 x 3.5 inches (15.0 x 3.5 cm) $140-165 (£95-115)

Pulled up threading

A small vase with internal pulled up trailing, manufactured c.1876 by Hodgetts, Richardson & Son. The rim is fire polished. The ovular shaped body is formed with clear glass, over pale ruby glass pulled up trailing, over opal white glass, and is decorated with four, vertical trails of clear glass rigaree. The circular, applied foot has a folded under edge, and a snapped off pontil mark. 5.5 x 2.75 inches (14.0 x 7.0 cm) $175-195 (£120-135)

Tartan type colored patterning

A small vase with a tartan style patterning, manufactured c.1885. The edge of the Jack-in-the-Pulpit type rim is decorated with a rounded profile multi-crimp. The satin finished body is formed with a spiral trail of pale yellow glass applied over twelve, vertical trails of opal white glass. The applied circular foot is formed in satin finished clear glass, and has a snapped off pontil mark. 5.5 x 4.75 inches (14.0 x 12.0 cm) $175-195 (£120-135)

A small trumpet vase with internal pulled up trailing, manufactured c.1880. The edge of the rim is decorated with a twenty four-way crimp, and is finished with a second, six-way deeper, rectangular profiled crimp. The satin finished body is formed with clear glass, over opal white pulled up trailing, over pale ruby glass. The circular, applied foot is formed in satin finished clear glass, and has a twenty four-way rounded profile edge crimp, and a snapped off pontil mark. 10.5 x 5.25 inches (26.5 x 13.0 cm) $195-210 (£135-145)

A small vase with internal, diagonally pulled up trailing, manufactured c.1900. The rim is fire polished. The oval section, clear glass body is decorated internally with diagonally pulled up composite trails. Each trail is formed with a central wide trail of green glass edged each side with a narrow, white trail. The base has a polished out pontil mark. 5.25 x 5.0 inches (13.5 x 12.5 cm) $175-195 (£120-135)

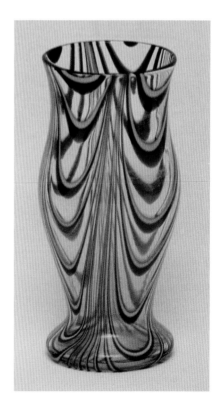

Left:
A small vase with internal, diagonally pulled up trailing, manufactured c.1900. The rim is finished with a six-way crimp. The spherical clear glass body is decorated internally with diagonally pulled up trails. Each trail is formed with a central wide trail of green glass edged each side with a narrow, white trail. The base has a polished out pontil mark. 4.25 x 3.5 inches (10.5 x 9.0 cm) $140-160 (£95-110)

Right:
A small vase with internal pulled up trailing, manufactured c.1900 by Thomas Webb & Sons Limited The rim is fire polished. The clear glass, circular section body is decorated internally with pulled up composite trails. Each trail is formed with a brown glass band on each side of a central white glass band. The base has a polished out pontil mark. 6.25 x 2.75 inches (15.5 x 7.0 cm) $125-140 (£85-95)

Air trap pattern - Diamond shape

A large air trap patterned vase, manufactured c.1885. The rim is ground off and polished. The satin finished body is formed in pale ruby glass, shading into pale pink over a diamond air trap pattern, over opal white glass. The base is slightly concave and is inscribed in pencil with *5771, 1/4, 1/1, L/u/-.* 8 x 8 inches (20.0 x 20.0cm) $360-400 (£250-275)

A large vase with internal pulled up trailing, manufactured c.1900 by Thomas Webb & Sons Limited The rim is fire polished. The clear glass, circular section body is decorated internally with pulled up composite trails. Each trail is formed with abutting bands of blue, green, yellow and black glass. The base has a polished out pontil mark. 12.0 x 4.75 inches (30.0 x 12.0 cm) $220-250 (£150-175)

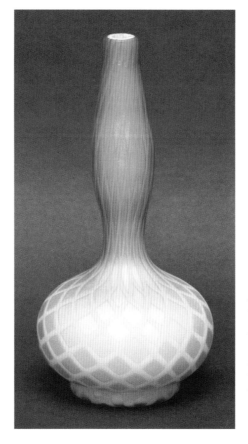

An air trap patterned vase, manufactured c.1885. The rim is ground off and polished. The satin finished body is formed in pale ruby glass, shading into pale pink, over a diamond air trap pattern, over opal white glass. The circular integral foot has a polished out pontil mark. 9.5 x 4.5 inches (24.0 x 11.5 cm) $145-175 (£100-120)

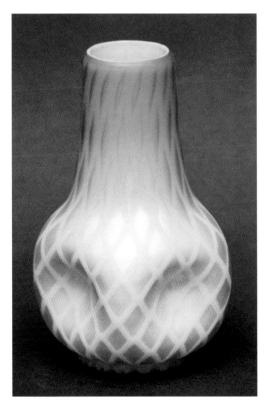

A small air trap patterned vase, manufactured c.1885. The rim is fire polished. The satin finished body is formed with pale blue glass shaded to clear glass, over a diamond air trap pattern, over opal white glass, and with the lower section of the body pushed inwards four times. The base has a polished out pontil mark. 5.5 x 2.75 inches (14.0 x 7.0 cm) $140-165 (£95-115)

Air trap pattern - Diamond shape with motif in centre of diamond

A small air trap patterned vase, manufactured c.1885. The rim is ground off and polished. The satin finished body is formed with pale ruby glass shading into pale pink glass, over a diamond air trap pattern incorporating a four-point star motif, over opal white glass. The body is further decorated with an applied surface pattern of four-point stars formed in a *Coralene* glass bead technique. 5.25 x 4.25 inches (13.5 x 11.0 cm) $180-195 (£125-135)

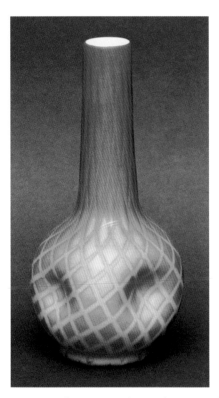

A small air trap patterned vase, manufactured c.1885. The rim is fire polished. The satin finished body is formed with ruby glass shaded to orange-pink glass, over a diamond air trap pattern, over opal white glass, and with the lower section of the body pushed inwards four times. The base has a polished out pontil mark. 7.5 x 3.25 inches (19.0 x 8.0 cm) $140-165 (£95-115)

Air trap design - Herring bone pattern

A small vase formed with an air trap pattern, manufactured c.1885. The edge of the rim is decorated with an eighteen-way rounded profile shallow crimp, and finished with a second, two-way deep crimp. The satin finished, circular section body is formed with a very pale ruby glass shading into pale pink glass, over a herring-bone, air trap pattern, over opal white glass. The base has a snapped off pontil mark. 3.0 x 3.0 inches (7.5 x 7.5 cm) $65-80 (£45-55)

A small vase formed with an air trap pattern, c.1885. The rim is ground off and polished. The body is formed with a pale blue glass shaded into clear glass, over a herringbone air trap pattern, over opal white glass. The integral solid foot has a polished out pontil mark. 6.25 x 3.25 inches (16. x 8.0 cm) $125-140 (£85-95)

A small vase formed with an air trap pattern, manufactured c.1885. The rim is ground off and polished. The satin finished, spherical shaped body is formed with a pale yellow glass, shading into clear glass, over a herringbone, air trap pattern, over opal white glass. The base has a snapped off pontil mark. 4.25 x 3.5 inches (11.0 x 9.0 cm) $95-110 (£65-75)

A small vase formed with an air trap pattern, manufactured c.1885. The rim has an applied, clear glass trail, and is finished with a two-way deep crimp pinched together in the middle. The satin finished, oval section body is formed with clear glass over a herringbone air trap pattern, over light blue glass. The base has a ground out pontil mark. 5.25 x 5.25 inches (13.5 x 13.5 cm) $160-180 (£110-125)

A small vase formed with an air trap pattern, manufactured c.1885. The rim is ground off and polished. The satin finished, circular section body is formed with pale ruby glass shading to pale pink glass over a herringbone air trap pattern, over opal white glass. The integral, circular solid section foot has a polished out pontil mark. 7.0 x 3.0 inches (17.5 x 7.5 cm) $125-140 (£85-95)

Air trap design - Circular / oval patterns

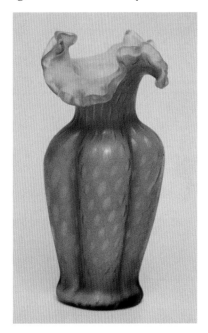

Air trap design - Stylised floral designs

A small vase formed with an air trap pattern, manufactured c.1885. The edge of the rim is decorated with an applied trail of clear glass, and finished with an eighteen-way rounded profile, shallow crimp, and a second, three-way deep crimp. The satin finished body is formed with a pale, sandy brown colored glass, over an oval air trap pattern, over opal white glass. The body has a rounded diamond section, formed from a mold with four, very bold, rounded profile vertical ribs. The integral foot has a ground out pontil mark. 7.0 x 3.75 inches (18.0 x 9.5 cm) $140-160 (£95-110)

A rare vase formed with an air trap pattern, manufactured c.1885. The trefoil shaped rim is fire polished. The satin finished, circular section body is formed with pale blue glass, over stylised floral air trap pattern, over opal white glass. The base has a polished out pontil mark. 7.0 x 5.75 inches (18.0 x14.5 cm) $325-360 £225-250

Air trap design - Miscellaneous patterns

A small vase formed with an air trap pattern, manufactured c.1885. The edge of the rim is decorated with a twenty-way shallow, rounded profile crimp, and finished with a second, two-way deep crimp. The satin finished, oval section body is formed with pale blue glass shading into clear glass, over a stylised swag trail air trap pattern, over opal white glass. The base has a ground out pontil mark. 6.0 x 3.25 inches (15.0 x 8.5 cm) $140-160 (£95-110)

Imitation stone patterns decorated with enamelling and / or gilding

Above right:
A small vase formed with *Carneol,* pattern imitation marble effect glass as manufactured by Loetz c.1896. The ground off and polished rim is decorated with gilding. The four-sided body is indented on each side, and is formed with a marbled effect ruby glass, over an opal white glass. The neck is decorated with an enamelled pattern. The applied circular glass foot is decorated with gilding 6.5 x 6.0 inches (16.5 x 15.0 cm) $175-195 (£120-135)

Left:
A small vase formed with *Carneol,* pattern, imitation marble effect glass, as manufactured by Loetz c.1896. The ground off and polished rim is decorated with gilding. The mold formed body with flat base, comprises a marbled effect ruby glass, over an opal white glass. The neck is decorated with an enamelled pattern. 4.5 x 2.75 inches (11.5 x 7.0 cm) $175-195 (£120-135)

Right:
A large vase formed in imitation marble effect glass, manufactured c.1890. The rim is ground off and polished. The multi-colored, marbled effect is formed over a pale ruby glass, oval section body. 16.0 x 8.0 inches (40.5 x 20.5 cm) $280-325 (£195 –225)

Color splashed designs in translucent / opaque glass

A small color splashed glass vase, manufactured c.1890. The turned over rim is decorated with a twenty-way crimped edge, and an applied vertical trail of five, triangular shaped, pincered work motifs. The body is formed with a random pattern of white splashes within a pale translucent yellow glass. The integral circular foot has a snapped off pontil mark. 5.25 x 2.75 inches (13.0 x 7.0 cm) $65-80 (£45-55)

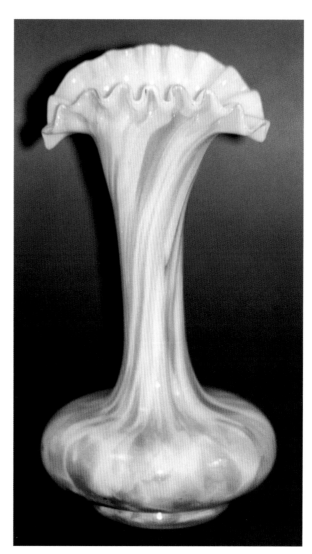

A small color splashed vase, manufactured c.1890. The rim is decorated with a twenty-way, shallow height, rounded profile, edge crimp and a second, two-way deep crimp. The body is formed with clear glass over a random vertical pattern of multi-colored splashes, over opal white glass. The integral solid foot has a snapped off pontil mark. 6.0 x 3.25 inches (15.5 x 8.5 cm) $65-80 (£45-55)

A small color splashed glass vase, manufactured c.1890. The rim is ground off and polished. The body is formed with clear glass over a random pattern of white and pale ruby glass splashes, over a pale amber glass. The body is supported on five feet formed from a wishbone pattern clear glass trail. 4.75 x 3.25 inches (12.0 x 8.0 cm) $65-80 (£45-55)

Vases decorated with surface reduction techniques:

Geometric cut patterns on translucent glass

Intaglio cut designs on translucent glass

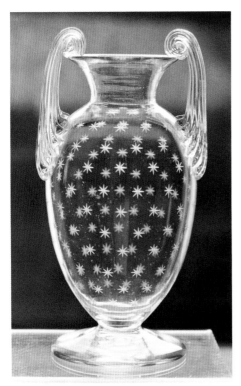

Left:
A small glass vase manufactured c. 1867, by Thomas Webb & Sons Limited The flared rim has a fire polished edge. The ovular shaped, circular section body is formed in clear glass, and decorated with a regular cut pattern of small, eight-point stars. The two applied shell ribbed handles are formed in accordance with their Registered Design No.212674, dated October 19,1867. The applied circular glass foot has a polished out pontil. 5.25 x 2.5 inches (13.0 x 6.5 cm) $95-110 (£65-75)

Cameo designs on translucent glass

A vase decorated with a cameo floral pattern, manufactured c.1895. The cameo, floral design comprises polished, pale ruby glass flower and leaf trails on a pale green glass background, which has a slightly textured surface. The applied circular, clear glass foot is decorated on the underside with a forty eight-point, cut star pattern. 8.75 x 3.75 inches (22.5 x 9.5 cm) $800-870 (£550-600)

Left:
A small intaglio cut glass vase manufactured c.1900, by Stuart & Sons Limited The slightly flared out rim is fire polished. The clear glass body is formed from a mold with six, shallow projecting ribs. The body is decorated with intaglio cut, stylised floral patterns between the ribs, and with horizontal flash cuts on each rib. The base has a polished out pontil mark. 5.25 x 3.25 inches (13.0 x 8.0 cm) $80-95 (£55-65)

Side view.

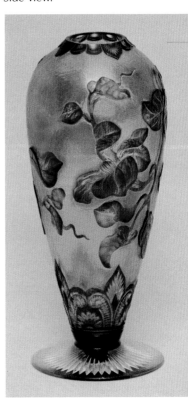

Side view.

Flower Bowls

Bowls formed with mold blown patterns:

Diamond patterns

Bold projecting rib patterns

A small flower bowl manufactured c.1885. The rim is decorated with an applied, clear glass pincered work trail finished with a six-way crimp. The pale ruby glass body is formed from a quilted diamond pattern mold. The base has a snapped off pontil mark. 4.25 x 3.5 inches (10.5 x 8.5 cm) $125-140 (£85-95)

A small mold formed flower bowl manufactured c.1880. The edge of the rim is decorated with an applied amber glass trail. The body is formed with pale, cream glass, over pale ruby glass, blown into a mold with eighteen convex projecting ribs. The body sits on an amber glass, wishbone pattern trail with six, pincered work feet. 4.0 x 4.75 inches (10.0 12.0 cm) $125-140 (£85-95)

Faint projecting rib patterns

A raised flower bowl, manufactured c.1895, by Stuart & Sons Limited The rim is finished with a shallow, ten-way crimp. The mold formed, translucent pale green glass body has ten, shallow convex ribs projecting into the bowl. The body sits on a cotton reel profile knop, set on top of a circular foot with a polished out pontil mark. 6.0 x 8.0 inches (15.0 x 20.0 cm) $140-160 (£95-110)

Festoon patterns

A small mold formed flower bowl, manufactured c.1885. The rim is decorated with an applied, pale translucent green glass pincered work trail, finished with a six-way crimp. The body is formed in a very pale ruby glass, which is shaded to amber - orange at the rim. The mold pattern comprises six, wide projecting convex profile vertical ribs, between which are set a regular pattern of horizontal, shallow projecting festoon shaped ribs. The base has a snapped off pontil mark. 4.0 x 3.75 inches (10.0 x 9.5 cm) $125-140 (£85-95)

A small mold formed flower bowl, manufactured c.1885. The rim is decorated with an applied, pale translucent green glass pincered work trail, finished with a six-way crimp. The body is formed in a very pale ruby glass, from a mold with six, wide projecting convex profile vertical ribs, between which are set a regular pattern of horizontal, shallow projecting festoon shaped ribs. The base has a snapped off pontil mark. 4.0 x 3.25 inches (10.0 x 8.5 cm) $125-140 (£85-95)

Circular / oval indented patterns

A small mold formed flower bowl, manufactured c.1880. The rim is ground off and polished. The circular section body is formed in pale translucent blue glass, from a mold with a staggered pattern of circular indents. The body is decorated with an applied trail of clear glass rigaree around the short neck. 4.25 x 4.25 inches (11.0 x 11.0 cm) $65-80 (£45-55)

Repetitive geometric patterns

A small mold formed flower bowl, manufactured c.1885. The rim is decorated with an applied, pale green glass edge trail, and finished with a thirty-way shallow crimp, and then pinched together to form three separate openings. The circular section white glass body is formed from a mold with a staggered pattern of vertical narrow diamond shapes contained within pairs of continuous projecting rib lines. The base has a polished out pontil mark. 2.5 x 4.5 inches (6.5 x11.5 cm) $95-110 (£65-75)

Plan view of rim.

Bowls formed with distinctive mold-blown / hand-formed shapes:

Miscellaneous geometric shapes

A small flower bowl manufactured c.1890. The rim is decorated with an applied pale amber glass edge trail with a shallow height multi-crimp, and is finished with a second three-way deep crimp. The body is formed in opal white glass, over pale blue glass, and is supported on an amber glass, wishbone pattern trail with five, feet. 4.0 x 5.25 inches (10.0 x 13.5 cm) $140-160 (£95-110)

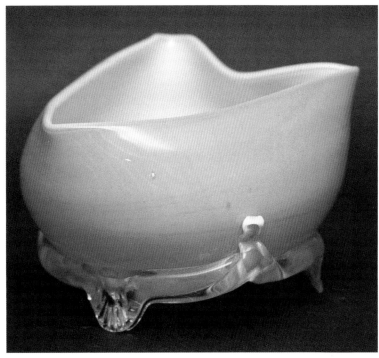

A small flower bowl manufactured c.1890. The circular rim is pushed inwards to form a heart shape, and the edge is fire polished. The body is formed with very pale ruby glass over a very pale green glass, and has a polished out pontil mark. The base comprises an opalescent, clear glass wishbone pattern trail incorporating three, pincered work vertical feet. 3.5 x 5.5 inches (9.0 x 14.0 cm) $140-160 (£95-110)

Bowls formed with textured surfaces:

Satin finished surfaces left undecorated

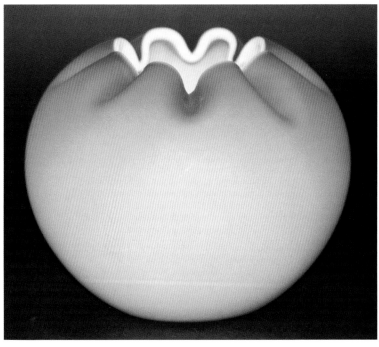

A small flower bowl manufactured c.1885. The rim is finished with an eight-way crimp, pushed inwards. The satin finished, spherical shaped body is formed with pale ruby, shading to pale pink glass, over opal white glass. The base has a polished out pontil mark. 4.5 x 5.25 inches (11.5 x 13.5 cm) $125-140 (£85-95)

A small flower trough manufactured c.1893. The rims of each container are ground off and polished. The three, spherical inter-connecting containers are formed in clear glass and decorated with two narrow bands, and one wide band of acid etching. A wheel shaped, clear glass prunt is applied to the sides of the two end containers. 2.75 x 9.25 inches (7.0 x 23.5 cm) $110-125 (£75-85)

Satin finished surfaces decorated with enamelling and / or gilding

A small flower bowl manufactured c.1890. The rim has an eight-way crimp, and is decorated with gilding to the edge. The satin finished, cream glass body is decorated with an enamelled and gilded floral trail, and is supported on a satin finished, clear glass circular foot with a polished out pontil mark. 2.5 x 3.0 inches (6.5 x 7.5 cm) $175-200 (£120-140)

A small flower bowl manufactured c.1890. The edge of the rim is decorated with an eighteen-way crimp, comprising alternate rectangular and rounded profiles, creating a folded linen effect. The satin finished body is formed with opal white glass, over pale blue glass, and is decorated internally with an enamelled floral trail. The base has a polished out pontil mark and is inscribed with *R610*. 4.0 x 6.75 inches (10.0 x 17.5cm) $220-250 (£150-175)

Bowls formed with applied decoration:

Gilded designs on translucent / opaque glass

A small flower bowl manufactured c.1890. The rim is decorated with a double trail of clear glass pincered work. The circular section body is formed in a cream glass and has a polished out pontil mark, and is decorated with two, gilded floral trails. The body sits on three, clear glass ribbed pattern, stub feet. 4.0 x 2.5 inches (10.0 x 6.5 cm) $180-215 (£125-150)

A small flower bowl manufactured c.1890. The rim is finished with an eight-way crimp, and turned inwards. The satin finished, spherical body is formed with pale green glass over opal white glass, and is decorated with an enamelled floral trail. The base has a snapped off pontil mark. 2.75 x 3.5 inches (7.0 x 9.0 cm) $95-110 (£65-75)

Iridescent finish on translucent / opaque glass

A small flower bowl manufactured c.1900. The rim is ground off and polished. The body is formed from a small, random quilted pattern mold, and is decorated with an applied yellow-green glass trail of leaves, and an iridescent finish all over. The base has a polished out pontil mark. 4.5 x 5.25 inches (11.5 x 13.0 cm) $110-125 (£75-85)

Machine threading on translucent / opaque glass

A small flower bowl manufactured c.1880. The rim is decorated with an applied trail of clear glass pincered work, finished with a four-way crimp. The spherical shaped body is formed in clear glass, and decorated with a shallow band of green glass machine threading. The base has a snapped off pontil mark. 3.75 x 3.5 inches (9.5 x 8.5 cm) $110-125 (£75-85)

A small flower bowl manufactured c.1880. The rim is decorated with an applied trail of clear glass pincered work, finished with a four-way crimp. The spherical shaped body is formed in clear glass, and decorated with a shallow band of ruby glass machine thread-ing. The base has a snapped off pontil mark. 3.75 x 3.5 inches (9.5 x 8.5 cm) $110-125 (£75-85)

A small bowl decorated with machine threading, manufactured c.1885. The rim is finished with a seven-way vertical crimp. The pale, amber glass body is decorated with a narrow band of amber glass, closely spaced, machine threading. The base has a polished out pontil mark. 2.75 x 4.25 inches (7.0 x 10.25 cm) $50-65 (£35-45)

A small bowl decorated with machine threading, manufactured c.1885. The rim is finished with an eight-way vertical crimp. The clear glass body is formed from a mold with sixteen shallow projecting ribs, and is decorated with a narrow band of closely spaced, ruby glass machine threading. The base has a snapped off pontil mark. The body is supported on a clear glass, wishbone pattern trail incorporating twelve feet. 3.25 x 5.0 inches (8.5 x 12.5 cm) $95-110 (£65-75)

A small bowl decorated with machine threading, manufactured c.1885. The rim is finished with a twelve-way crimp. The pale ruby glass body is decorated with a wide band of acid etched floral patterning, contained between two narrow bands of closely spaced, blue glass machine threading, which have a tooled surface effect. The base has a polished out pontil mark. 2.0 x 4.5 inches (5.0 x 4.25 cm) $110-125 (£75-85)

A small bowl decorated with machine threading, manufactured c.1885. The rim is finished with an eight-way vertical crimp. The pale green glass body is decorated with widely spaced, green glass machine threading, and is supported on a short green glass stem and circular foot, with a polished out pontil mark. 3.5 x 4.4 inches (9.0 x 11.5 cm) $65-80 (£45-55)

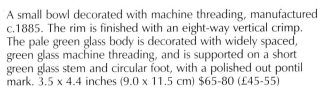

Encasing machine threading applied to a mold blown body

A small *Jewel* pattern bowl manufactured c.1886, by Stevens & Williams Limited The pale green glass body is formed from a bubble of glass covered with machine threading, encased in another layer of glass and finally blown into a mold with sixteen vertical ribs. The polished out pontil mark is inscribed with *Rd.55693,* which relates to this particular design which was registered on September 6, 1886. 2.25 x 2.5 inches (5.5 x 6.5 cm) $50-65 (£35-45)

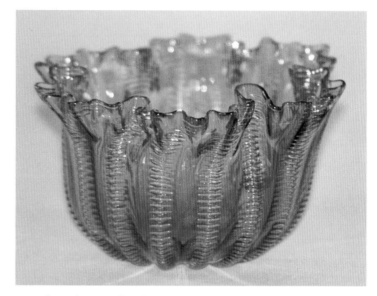

A small *Jewel* pattern bowl manufactured c.1886, by Stevens & Williams Limited The pale green glass body is formed from a bubble of glass covered with machine threading, encased in another layer of glass and finally blown into a mold with sixteen vertical ribs. The polished out pontil mark is inscribed with *Rd.55693,* which relates to this particular design which was registered on September 6, 1886. 2.0 x 4.0 inches (5.0 x 10.0 cm) $95-110 (£65-75)

A group of small *Jewel* pattern bowls set on a rustic log, manufactured c.1886, by Stevens & Williams Limited *Rd.55693* is inscribed on the rustic log. 2.75 x 9.0 inches (7.0 x 23.0 cm) $190-220 (£130-150)

Random pattern of threading / trails

A small flower bowl with random applied trailing, manufactured c.1900, in the style of items manufactured by Pallme-König. The rim is ground off and polished. The clear glass body is formed from a mold with six, bold, rounded profile projecting vertical ribs, and decorated with a random pattern of random thickness, opal white trailing, and then completed with an iridescent finish all over. 4.25 x 3.75 inches (10.5 x 9.5 cm) $95-110 (£65-75)

Underside of bowl.

Stylised flower heads with leaf trails

A small flower bowl with applied leaf trails, manufactured c.1895. The rim is finished with an eight-way, shallow height, rectangular profile crimp. The circular section body is formed with opal white glass over pale pink glass, and has a polished out pontil mark. The body is supported on three rustic pattern, amber glass stub feet, and is decorated with an applied trail of pincered work green glass leaves. 4.0 x 4.25 inches (10.0 x 10.25 cm) $125-140 (£85-95)

A small flower bowl with applied flower trails, manufactured c.1895. The rim is finished with a four-way, shallow height, wide profile rectangular crimp. The circular section body is blown to an ogee profile, and is formed with opal white glass over pale turquoise glass. Three, rustic branch type legs are attached to an amber glass trail around the body at mid-height, and then folded back to under the center of the body. Trails of pincered work leaves and flower heads are applied all around the body. 7.25 x 5.25 inches (18.5 x 13.5 cm) $220-255 (£150-175)

A small flower bowl with applied flower trail, manufactured c.1895. The rim is decorated with a rectangular profile, shallow height, nine-way crimp. The body is formed with opal white glass over pale turquoise glass, from a mold with eight, rounded profile, bold projecting ribs, and has a polished out pontil mark. The body is supported on four, applied rustic pattern stub feet. A large stylised flower head and pincered work leaf trails are applied to the body. 4.75 x 4.25 inches (12.0 x 10.5 cm) $180-195 (£125-135)

Stylised fish / reptile motifs

A small flower bowl manufactured c.1882 by Thomas Webb & Sons Limited The edge of the rim is decorated with a trail of pale green pincered work, and is finished with a six-way shallow crimp. The style of the crimp is in the form of Registered Design No.390104, dated November 11, 1882. The body is formed in an *Amberina* type glass, shading from pale translucent amber at the base, up to ruby at the rim. The pontil mark is covered with a prunt impressed with a Registered Diamond mark, incorporating the date code for November 11, 1882. The body is decorated all around with an enamelled floral trail and butterflies. Each of the three green glass feet, are in the stylised form of a seal. 3.75 x 4.25 inches (9.5 x 10.5 cm) $255-285 (£175-195)

A small flower bowl manufactured c.1882 by Thomas Webb & Sons Limited The rim is decorated with an applied, clear glass edge trail finished with a six-way shallow crimp. The style of the crimp is in the form of Registered Design No.390103, dated November 11,1882. The body is formed from a mold with fourteen, shallow projecting ribs, and comprises clear glass, over multi-colored splashes, over fragments of silver foil, over ruby glass, and decorated with two, large amber glass lizard type creatures. The pontil mark is covered with a prunt impressed with a Registered Diamond mark, incorporating the date code for November 11, 1882. The body is supported on four, rustic style stub feet. 3.75 x 8.75 inches (9.5 x 22.0) $360-400 (£250-275)

End view.

A small flower bowl manufactured c.1882. The oval shaped rim is fire polished. The body is formed from a mold with twelve, shallow projecting ribs, and comprises pale translucent blue glass, over fragments of silver foil, over ruby glass, and has a polished out pontil mark. The body is decorated with two, clear glass lizard type creatures, and is supported on four, clear glass rustic pattern stub feet. 3.25 x 5.5 inches (8.0 x 14.0 cm) $220-250 (£150-175)

A small flower bowl manufactured c.1882. The rim is decorated with a clear glass pincered work, shell ribbed trail. The crackled effect body is formed with clear glass, over gold foil, over pale ruby glass and is supported on two, plain, clear glass stub feet and two, clear glass feet in the form of stylised fishes. 3.5 x 6.5 inches (8.5 x 16.5 cm) $220-250 (£150-175)

A small flower bowl manufactured c.1883. The rim is fire polished. The circular section body is worked to a triangular shape at rim level, and is formed with pale ruby glass machine threading, over pale amber glass, and has a snapped off pontil. The body is supported on three, pale amber glass, stylised fishes. (The ends of the tails are missing from the example illustrated) 2.5 x 4.0 inches (6.5 x 10.0 cm) $220-250 (£150-175)

A small flower bowl manufactured c.1883. The edge of the rim is fire polished. The dark, red-brown glass body is formed from a mold with twelve, shallow projecting ribs, and has a square opening at the rim. The body has a polished out pontil mark, and is supported on four, gilded legs, in the form of stylised fishes. The four panels between the legs are decorated with gilded floral motifs. 4.25 x 3.75 inches (10.5 x 9.5 cm) $250-280 (£175-195)

Side view.

A small *Flora* pattern flower bowl manufactured c.1884 by John Walsh Walsh. The oval shaped rim is decorated with an applied trail of clear glass, shell ribbed pattern pincered work. The body is formed with ivory colored glass over ruby glass, and is supported on two clear glass legs in the form of stylised fish, and two clear glass legs in the stylised form of an acanthus leaf. The body has a ground out pontil mark. 2.5 x 6.5 inches (6.5 x 16.5 cm) $220-255 (£150-175)

End view of bowl.

Rigaree trails in festoon patterns with / without prunts

Left:
A small flower bowl manufactured c.1885. The rim is finished with a six-way crimp, turned inwards. The pale ruby glass body is formed from a mold with fourteen, shallow projecting ribs, and has the pontil mark covered by a clear glass, raspberry prunt. The body is decorated with three, clear glass rigaree festoons, small raspberry prunts, and drop trails, and is supported on three, clear glass ribbed shell type feet. 4.0 x 4.75 inches (10.0 x 12.0 cm) $180-220 (£125-150)

Right:
A small flower bowl manufactured c.1885, by Stuart & Sons Limited The rim is fire polished. The circular section, pale ruby glass body, is formed from a mold with twelve shallow projecting ribs, and has the pontil mark covered by a clear glass raspberry prunt. The body is decorated with three, festoons of clear glass rigaree and six, small raspberry prunts, and is supported on three clear glass ribbed shell pattern glass feet. 4.25 x 3.25 inches (10.5 x 8.0 cm) $180-220 (£125-150)

A small flower bowl manufactured c.1885. The fire polished rim is finished with a six-way crimp, turned inwards. The pale green glass, over pale cream glass body has the pontil mark covered by a clear glass, raspberry prunt. The body is decorated with three, clear glass rigaree festoons, and three, small raspberry prunts, and drop trails, and is supported on three, clear glass ribbed shell type feet.(the curled toes of the feet on this example are missing) 4.0 x 4.75 inches (10.0 x 12.0 cm) $180-220 (£125-150)

A small flower bowl manufactured c.1885 by Stuart & Son Limited The rim is fire polished. The spherical shaped, pale blue glass body is formed from a mold with twelve, shallow projecting ribs, and has a pontil mark covered with a clear glass raspberry prunt. The body is supported on three, ribbed shell pattern, clear glass feet, and is decorated with three festoons of clear glass rigaree, and six, clear glass raspberry prunts. 4.0 x 3.75 inches (10.0 x 9.5 cm) $180-220 (£125-150)

A small flower bowl manufactured c.1885 by Stuart & Son Limited The rim is fire polished. The spherical shaped, ruby glass body is formed from a mold with twelve, shallow projecting ribs, and has a pontil mark covered with a clear glass raspberry prunt. The body is supported on three, ribbed shell pattern, clear glass feet, and is decorated with three festoons of clear glass rigaree, and six, clear glass raspberry prunts. 4.5 x 4.5 inches (11.5 x 11.5 cm) $180-220 (£125-150)

A small flower bowl manufactured c.1885 by Stuart & Son Limited The rim is fire polished. The spherical shaped, amber glass body is formed from a mold with twelve, shallow projecting ribs, and has a pontil mark covered with a clear glass raspberry prunt. The body is supported on three, ribbed shell pattern, clear glass feet, and is decorated with three festoons of clear glass rigaree, and six, clear glass raspberry prunts. 4.0 x 4.0 inches (10.0 x 10.0 cm) $180-220 (£125-150)

A small flower bowl manufactured c.1885 by Stuart & Son Limited The spherical shaped, clear glass body is formed from a mold with sixteen, shallow projecting ribs, and has a pontil mark covered with a clear glass raspberry prunt. The body is supported on three, ribbed shell pattern, clear glass feet, and is decorated with three festoons of clear glass rigaree, between three, clear glass raspberry prunts. A trail of clear glass, half daisy pattern pincered work is applied to the body between these prunts at rim level. 3.5 x 4.0 inches (9.0 x 10.0 cm) $180-220 (£125-150)

Small glass beads set out in patterns using a *Coralene* type process

Small glass beads set out in a regular pattern

A large flower bowl manufactured c.1885. The rim is finished with a nine-way shallow height, rectangular profile crimp. The orange-ruby glass body is supported on three, amber glass rustic trail feet, and has a polished out pontil inscribed – *W PATENT* The body is decorated all around with a pattern of small birds on the branch of a tree, and all formed using the *Coralene* technique of small colored glass beads. 8.0 x 10.0 inches (20.0 x 25.5cm) $360-400 £250-275

A small flower bowl manufactured c.1905. The rim is fire polished and finished with a six-way shallow crimp turned inwards. The satin finished, clear glass body is formed from a mold with twenty-four shallow projecting ribs, and has a polished out pontil mark. The body is decorated with a regular pattern of small ruby ovals. 3.0 x 3.75 inches (7.5 x 9.5 cm) $125-140 (£85-95)

Side view.

A small flower bowl manufactured c.1905. The rim is finished with a six-way rounded profile crimp. The clear glass body is formed from a mold with twelve shallow projecting ribs, and is decorated with a regular pattern of turquoise blue glass beads on the ribs, in a manner similar to that patented in 1905 by H. Wilkinson of Amblecote, near Stourbridge, West Midlands.

Cased glass

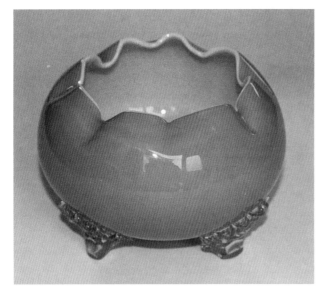

A small flower bowl from the *Crushed Strawberry* pattern range as manufactured c.1883, by John Walsh Walsh. The rim is finished with an eight-way crimp. The body is formed in pale pink glass, over a creamy white glass, and is supported on four, clear glass rustic pattern stub feet. The pontil mark is covered with a clear glass raspberry prunt. 2.5 x 4.5 inches (6.5 x 11.5 cm) $125-140 (£85-95)

Bowls formed with internal decoration:

Opalescent glass designs

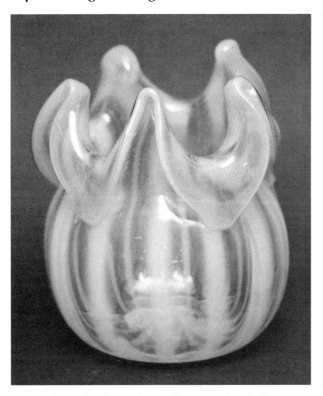

A small flower bowl manufactured c.1880. The rim is finished with a five-way deep crimp. The body is formed from a mold with twelve, shallow projecting ribs, and has a snapped off pontil mark. The clear glass body shades to light green at the rim, and is decorated with twelve, full height vertical opalescent stripes. 3.5 x 3.0 inches (9.0 x 7.5cm) $110-125 (£75-85)

A small flower vase manufactured c.1885. The rim is ground off and polished. The pale, opalescent blue glass body is formed from a mold with a staggered pattern of indented circles. 3.5 x 4.0 inches (9.0 x 10.0 cm) $80-95 (£55-65)

Translucent shaded glass designs – single color shading into clear glass

A small bowl manufactured c. 1890. The rim is finished with an eight-way rectangular staggered profile, vertical crimp. The body is formed in a yellow glass with an integral solid foot, with a polished out pontil mark. The inside of the neck is finished with a ruby color, shading down into the yellow. 3.0 x 4.25 inches (7.5 x 10.5 cm) $95-110 (£65-75)

Plan view of rim.

Pulled up threading

A small flower bowl manufactured c.1880, by Stuart & Sons Limited The rim is finished with an eight-way crimp, pushed inwards. The body is formed with closely spaced, very fine section clear glass machine threading, over pale pink pulled up festoon trailing, over a very pale yellow glass. The pontil mark is covered by a clear glass raspberry prunt. The body is supported on three, clear glass, ribbed shell pattern feet. 2.75 x 4.0 inches (7.0 x 10.0 cm) $255-280 (£175-195)

Regularly spaced "V" shaped pulled up patterning

A small flower bowl manufactured c.1885, by Stevens & Williams Limited The rim is decorated with a shallow height, rounded profile multi-crimp to the edge, and finished with a second, six-way vertical crimp. The satin finished, circular section body is formed with clear glass over a stylised interlocking scale, air trap pattern over pale brown, "V" pattern pulled up, closely spaced machine threading, over a cream-white glass. The base has a polished out pontil mark. 4.0 x 5.0 inches (10.0 x 12.5 cm) $650-700 (£450-475)

Plan view of rim.

Air trap design - Diamond shape

A small flower bowl manufactured c.1880. The rim is finished with an eight-way crimp, pushed inwards. The satin finished spherical body is formed with clear glass shading to pale blue, over a diamond air trap pattern, over opal white glass. The base has a polished out pontil mark. 2.75 x 3.0 inches (7.0 x 7.5 cm) $125-140 (£85-95)

A small flower bowl manufactured c.1880. The rim is finished with a six-way crimp, pushed inwards. The spherical body is formed with clear glass, over pale pink, pale yellow, and pale blue splashes around the rim, over a diamond air trap pattern, over opal white glass. The base has a snapped off pontil mark. 3.0 x 3.5 inches (7.5 x 9.0 cm) $125-140 (£85-95)

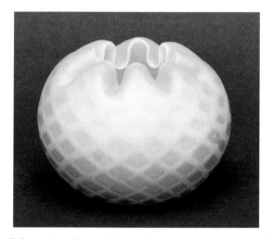

A small flower bowl manufactured c.1880. The rim is finished with a six-way crimp, pushed inwards. The satin finished spherical body is formed with clear glass shading to pale yellow, over a diamond air trap pattern, over opal white glass. The base has a snapped off pontil mark. 3.0 x 4.0 inches (7.5 x 10.0 cm) $125-140 (£85-95)

Air trap design - Herring bone pattern

A small flower bowl manufactured c.1880. The rim is finished with a six-way crimp. The satin finished, circular section body is formed with clear glass over a pattern of pale yellow glass, pale pink glass, and pale blue glass vertical stripes, over a herringbone air trap pattern, over opal white glass. The base has a polished out pontil mark. 3.25 x 3.25 inches (8.0 x 8.0 cm) $175-190 (£120-130)

Vertical / spiral hollow rib patterns

Bowls decorated with surface reduction techniques:

Cameo designs on translucent glass

A small flower bowl manufactured c.1885. The rim is finished with an eight-way crimp, turned inwards. The satin finished, circular section body is formed with pale blue glass in a spiral air trap rib pattern, over opal white glass. The base has a polished out pontil mark. 2.75 x 3.75 inches (7.0 x 9.5 cm) $175-190 (£120-130)

A small flower bowl manufactured c.1895. The rim is finished with an eight-way crimp, turned inwards. The spherical body is formed with two layers of clear glass. The outer layer is cut back in a floral cameo pattern. The base has a polished out pontil mark. 3.25 x 3.5 inches (8.0 x 9.0 cm) $250-300 (£175-200)

Baskets

Baskets with distinctive rim designs:

Pinched together rims with multiple openings

A flower basket manufactured c.1880. The rim is decorated with an applied rustic pattern clear glass trail. The circular section body is formed with clear glass with a random pattern of surface pull-outs, over pale yellow glass, over opal white glass, and is pinched together in the middle at rim level to form two separate openings. The body has a snapped off pontil mark, and is supported on a trail of six, clear glass, half-daisy pattern, pincered work. The rustic briar pattern, heart shaped handle is formed in clear glass. 6.0 x 5.5 inches (15.0 x 14.9 cm) $140-175 (£95-120)

A flower basket manufactured c.1885. The color combination and more importantly, the design of the acanthus leaf feet, suggests that it might be from the *Flora* range produced by John Walsh Walsh. (See Chapter 2B – Item 5.6K-9 for comparison) The rim is fire polished. The body is formed with ivory colored glass over pale ruby glass, and is pinched together at rim level to form three, separate openings, and has an amber glass rustic, briar pattern handle. The body has a ground out pontil mark, and is supported on three amber glass feet, in the form of stylised acanthus leaves. 8.75 x 7.25 inches (22.0 x 18.5 cm) $180-215 (£125-150)

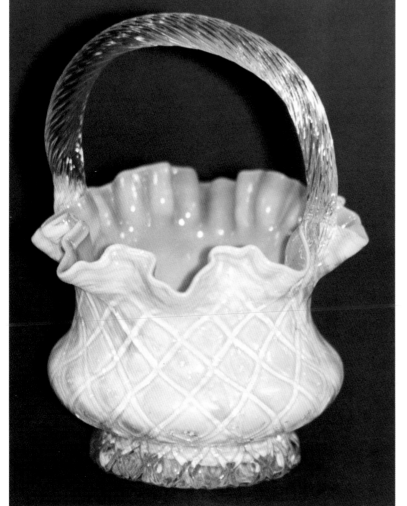

Baskets formed with mold formed patterns:

Diamond patterns

A flower basket manufactured c.1885. The rim has a shallow height, rounded profile, multi-crimped edge, and is finished with a second, eight-way deep crimp. The body is formed with pale blue glass, cased over with opal white glass with fragments of silver foil and very pale green glass splashes, cased over with clear glass, and blown into a mold with a projecting diamond rib pattern. The circular, integral foot has a snapped off pontil mark. The clear glass handle is formed in a rope twist pattern. 5.5 x 4.25 inches (14.0 x 11.0 cm) $125-140 (£85-95)

Bold projecting ribs

A flower basket manufactured c.1880. The edge of the rim is decorated with a rounded profile, shallow height multi-crimp, and is finished with a second, four-way deep crimp. The pink glass body is formed from a mold with alternate projecting vertical ribs of two different sizes. The clear glass handle is formed in a stylised rustic, briar pattern. 6.75 x 6.75 inches (17.0 x 17.0 cm) $125-140 (£85-95)

Faint projecting rib patterns

A small flower basket manufactured c.1880. The rim has a shallow height, rounded profile multi-crimped edge, and is finished with a second, four-way deep crimp. The ruby glass body is formed from a mold with fourteen rounded profile shallow projecting ribs, and has a snapped off pontil mark. The foot is formed with a trail of daisy head pattern pincered work. The handle is formed in clear glass with a plain circular section cane. 5.0 x 4.25 inches (12.5 x 11.0 cm) $180-200 (£125-140)

A flower basket manufactured c.1880. The rim is decorated with an applied trail of clear glass daisy head pattern, pincered work. The pale ruby glass body with surface pull-outs, is formed from a mold with ten, shallow projecting ribs, and has a snapped off pontil mark. The body is supported on a clear glass trail of daisy head pattern, pincered work. The clear glass handle is formed in a rustic briar pattern. 8.25 x 5.25 inches (21.0 x 13.5 cm) $220-255 (£150-175)

Repetitive geometric patterns

A flower basket manufactured c.1885. The rim has a shallow height, rounded profile, multi-crimped edge, and is finished with a second, two-way deep crimp. The opal white glass, over pale ruby glass body is formed from a patterned mold, and has a clear glass rustic briar pattern handle. 7.25 x 6.5 inches (18.5 x 16.5 cm) $180-200 (£125-140)

Miscellaneous geometric shapes

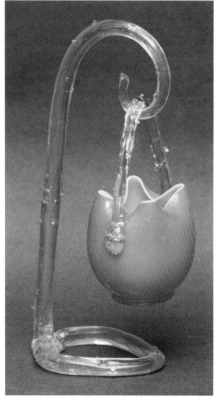

A small, hanging flower basket, which is similar in design to that shown in the pattern books of H.G.Richardson, c.1885. The rim of the basket has a four-way shallow crimp, turned inwards. The body is formed with pink glass, over opal white glass, and with an applied clear glass foot, with polished out pontil mark. The clear glass basket handle and main support frame are formed in a rustic briar pattern. 9.25 x 4.0 inches (23.5 x 10.0 cm) $145-175 (100-120)

Left:
A small, hanging flower basket, which is similar in design to that shown in the pattern books of H.G.Richardson, c.1885. The rim of the basket has a four-way shallow crimp, turned inwards. The body is formed with pale blue glass, over opal white glass, and with an applied clear glass foot, with polished out pontil mark. The clear glass basket handle and main support frame are formed in a rustic briar pattern. 8.0 x 3.75 inches (20.0 x 9.5 cm) $145-175 (£100-120)

Right:
A small hanging basket manufactured c.1885. The rim of the basket is finished with a five-point star shaped, vertical crimp. The spherical shaped body is formed with a sandy-orange colored glass over opal white glass, and has a clear glass support loop. The clear glass support frame is formed in a rustic briar pattern, and sits on a circular clear glass base, which has a snapped off pontil mark, and is decorated with a pincered work daisy head pattern all over. 6.25 x 5.0 inches (15.5 x 12.5 cm) $145-175 (£100-120)

Baskets with applied decoration:

Machine threading with tooled surface on translucent / opaque glass

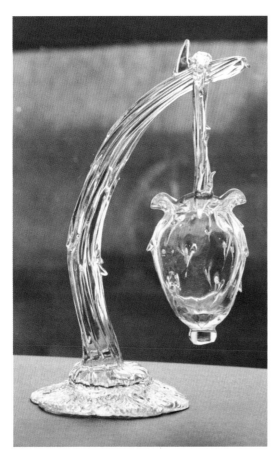

A small hanging basket, of similar in design to one shown in the pattern books of H.G.Richardson c.1888. The basket is formed in clear glass with surface pull-outs, and has a six-way crimped rim. The clear glass basket handle and the main support frame are formed in a rustic briar pattern. The base is decorated with daisy head pattern pincered work. 8.5 x 4.75 inches (22.9 x 12.0 cm) $145-175 (£100-120)

A small flower basket manufactured c.1885. The rim is finished with a four-way deep crimp. The opalescent, pale ruby glass body is formed from a mold with sixteen projecting ribs, and is decorated with amber glass machine threading which has its surface tooled with an oval pattern. The base has a snapped off pontil mark. Each end of the clear glass circular section handle terminates with a clear glass raspberry prunt. 5.25 x 3.75 inches (13.5 x 9.5 cm) $180-215 (£125-150)

View of base.

Mold blown designs finished with machine threading

A small flower basket manufactured c.1880. The edge of the rim is decorated with an applied trail of clear glass rigaree. The body is formed with very pale pink glass, blown into a quilted diamond pattern mould and then decorated with yellow-green glass, fine section, machine threading. The sides of the body are pinched inwards at the rim, to create an oval shape. The body is set on a short, clear glass stem and circular foot with a snapped off pontil mark. Each end of the rope twist pattern clear glass handle terminates with a raspberry prunt. 5.5 x 5.5 inches (14.0 x 14.0 cm) $175-195 (£120-135)

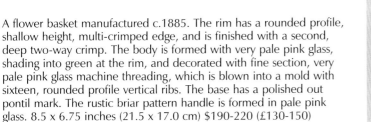

A flower basket manufactured c.1885. The rim has a rounded profile, shallow height, multi-crimped edge, and is finished with a second, deep two-way crimp. The body is formed with very pale pink glass, shading into green at the rim, and decorated with fine section, very pale pink glass machine threading, which is blown into a mold with sixteen, rounded profile vertical ribs. The base has a polished out pontil mark. The rustic briar pattern handle is formed in pale pink glass. 8.5 x 6.75 inches (21.5 x 17.0 cm) $190-220 (£130-150)

Stylised flower heads with leaf trails

A flower basket manufactured c.1885. The rim is decorated with a ruby glass edge trail, and finished with a four-way deep crimp. The circular section body is formed with amber glass machine threading, over sixteen, vertical white glass stripes, over amber glass, which shades to pale ruby at the rim. The base has a ground out pontil mark. The rustic briar pattern handle is formed in pale pink glass. 8.0 x 7.75 inches (20.5 x 19.5 cm) $190-220 (£130-150)

A flower basket manufactured c.1885. The rim is decorated with an applied edge trail of pale blue, cross-ribbed pattern, pincered work, and finished with a four-way deep crimp creating a square profile on plan. The opalescent blue glass body is formed from a mold with a quilted diamond pattern, and cased with pale blue glass machine threading. The body is supported on a clear glass circular foot, which has a folded under edge and a polished out pontil mark. The rope twist pattern handle terminates at each end with a lion head prunt. 9.5 x 7.0 inches (24.0 x 18.0 cm) $190-220 (£130-150)

A flower basket manufactured c.1895. The rim is decorated with an applied pale green glass edge trail, and is finished with a rounded profile multi-crimp. The circular section body is formed with opal white glass and is decorated with an applied flower head and pincered work leaf trail. The integral circular foot has a polished out pontil mark. 8.0 x 6.0 inches (20.5 x 15.0 cm) $180-215 (£125-150)

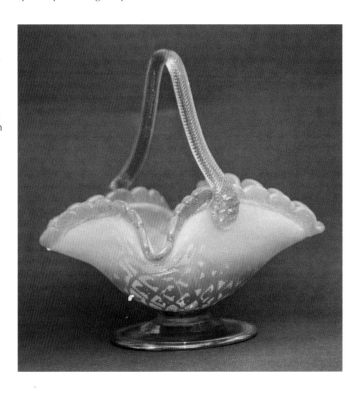

Left:
A flower basket manufactured c.1895. The rim is decorated with an applied pale green glass edge trail, and is finished with a square profile eight-way vertical crimp. The circular section body is formed with opal white glass and is decorated with an applied flower head and pincered work leaf trail. The integral circular foot has a polished out pontil mark. 8.0 x 4.25 inches (20.0 x 11.0 cm) $180-215 (£125-150)

Right:
A flower basket manufactured c.1895. The rim is decorated with an applied pale green glass edge trail, and is finished with a square profile eight-way vertical crimp. The circular section body is formed with opal white glass and is decorated with an applied flower head and pincered work leaf trail. The base has a polished out pontil mark. 8.0 x 4.25 inches (20.0 x 11.0 cm) $180-215 (£125-150)

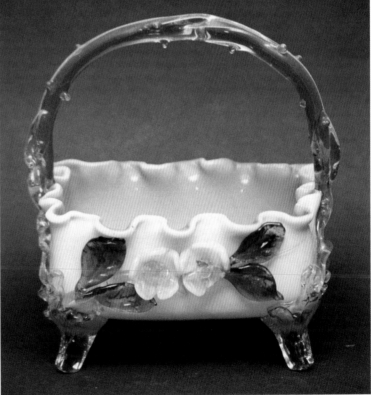

A flower basket manufactured c.1895. The rim is decorated with an applied pale green glass edge trail, and is finished with a square profile eight-way vertical crimp. The circular section body is formed with opal white glass and is decorated with an applied flower head and pincered work leaf trail. The integral circular foot has a polished out pontil mark. 8.0 x 4.5 inches (20.0 x 11.5 cm) $180-215 (£125-150)

A flower basket manufactured c.1895. The rim is finished with a fourteen-way square profile crimp. The rectangular body is formed with opal white glass, over pale pink glass, and is decorated with an applied trail of leaves and flower heads. The base has a polished out pontil mark. The body is supported on four, rustic pattern amber glass stub feet. The amber glass, rustic briar pattern handle is split into two trails just before the connection at each end of the body. 6.5 x 5.25 inches (16.5 x 13.0cm) $220-255 (£150-175)

A flower basket manufactured c.1895. The rim is decorated with an applied very pale ruby glass trail, and is finished with a four-way shallow crimp. The circular section body is formed in opal white glass, and is decorated with an applied trail of flower heads and pincered work leaves. The body has a polished out pontil mark, and is supported on four, amber glass, rustic pattern feet. The amber glass handle is formed in a rustic briar pattern. 9.0 x 6.25 inches (23.0 x 16.0 cm) $220-255 (£150-175)

A flower basket manufactured c.1895. The saw tooth profile rim is decorated with random width pincered ribbing of the vertical edge. The spherical body is formed with opal white glass, over pink glass, and has a polished out pontil mark. The body is decorated with three sprays of flower heads and leaf trails rising from each of the three rustic pattern amber glass stub feet. The handle is formed in a rustic briar pattern. 9.0 x 5.25 inches (23.0 x 13.0 cm) $220-255 (£150-175)

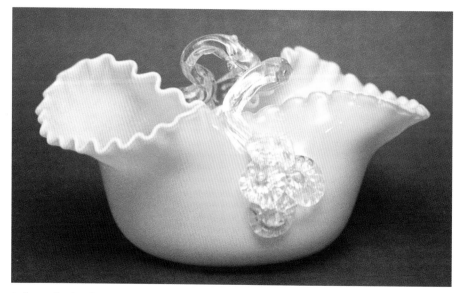

A flower basket formed with *Mat-Su-No-Ke* floral decoration manufactured c.1884 by Stevens & Williams Limited The edge of the rim is decorated with a shallow height, rounded profile, multi-crimp, and the rim is pinched together in the middle to form two, separate openings. The body is formed with clear glass over sandy-yellow glass, over creamy-white glass, and has a polished out pontil mark inscribed with *Rd. 15353*, which relates to the Registered Design dated October18, 1884, for the *Mat-Su-No-Ke* floral trail decoration. 3.25 x 6.5 inches (8.5 x 16.5 cm) $290-360 (£200-250)

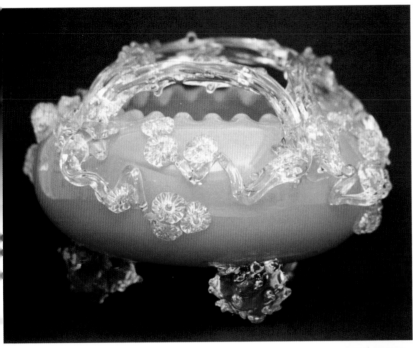

A flower basket formed with *Mat-Su-No-Ke* floral decoration manufactured c.1884 by Stevens & Williams Limited The edge of the rim is decorated with a rounded profile multi-crimp. The circular section body formed with clear glass over pink glass, has a clear glass raspberry prunt over the pontil mark, and is supported on three, clear glass rustic ball pattern feet. The underside of the body is inscribed with *Rd. 15353,* which relates to the Registered Design dated October18, 1884, for the *Mat-Su-No-Ke* clear glass floral trail decoration applied around the body. The four, clear glass, interlinked handles applied around the rim are formed in a rustic briar pattern. 4.5 x 7.0 inches (11.5 x 18.0 cm) $580-650 (£400-450)

Plan view of rim.

A flower basket manufactured c.1890. The rim is decorated with an applied amber glass trail, and is finished with an eight-way, rectangular stepped profile crimp. The body is formed with opal white glass, with an amber glass handle, and is decorated with an applied amber glass, stylised oak leaf trail. The integral foot has a ground off pontil mark. 5.25 x 6.5 inches (13.5 x 16.5 cm) $145-175 (£100-120)

Leaves formed in two different colored halves

Pincered trails of shell ribbed / daisy head patterns

A small flower basket manufactured c.1895. The edge of the rim is decorated with an applied clear glass trail and a multi-way edge crimp, and finished with a three-way vertical, crimp forming a trefoil shape. The body is formed with opal white glass, and is decorated with two stylised acanthus leaves, formed in clear and pale ruby glass, and linked to the clear glass handle. The integral foot has a polished out pontil mark. 6.0 x 6.0 inches (15.0 x 15.0 cm) $145-175 (100-120)

A flower basket manufactured c.1890, by H.G.Richardson. The rim is decorated with an applied clear glass pincered work trail, finished with an eight-way deep crimp. The body is formed in clear glass, cased with fine section machine threading, and an applied trail of half-daisy head pattern, pincered work, beneath the rim trail. The base has a polished out pontil mark. The clear glass handle is decorated with matching pincered work trails and is surmounted with a raspberry prunt. 7.5 x 5.75 inches (19.0 x 14.5 cm) $220-255 (£150-175)

Stylised fruit, nuts, or acorns with leaf trails

A glass flower basket manufactured c.1890. The pale amber glass body is formed from a mold with eight shallow projecting ribs, and is supported on four, rustic pattern, pale blue glass stub feet. The base has a polished out pontil mark. The body has a rustic briar type pale blue glass handle, and is decorated with trails of pincered work leaves and three, large plum type fruit. 7.25 x 7.25 inches (18.5 x 18.5 cm) $220-255 (£150-175)

A flower basket manufactured c.1888, by John Wash Walsh. The rim is decorated with an applied trail of clear glass pincered work. The body is made in clear glass, and decorated with applied trails of clear glass pincered work around the base and along the handle. The base of the basket has a snapped off pontil mark. The attached stylised palm tree flower holder is formed from a mold with nine projecting ribs. *Rd.100004* is impressed in the base of the tree, and relates to the palm tree design that was registered on May12, 1888. 8.5 x 5.75 inches (21.5 x 14.5 cm) $220-255 (£150-175)

A flower basket manufactured c.1890 by Stuart & Sons Limited The rim is decorated with an applied, clear glass trail of pincered work, above and below a trail of clear glass rigaree. The body is formed in clear glass from a mold with sixteen, shallow projecting ribs, and cased with fine section machine threading, and has a polished out pontil mark. The body is supported on a trail of clear glass pincered work. The clear glass, crossed-over handles are decorated with applied trails of rigaree and raspberry prunts. 11.25 x 8.75 inches (28.5 x 22.5 cm) $580-650 (£400-450)

A flower basket manufactured c.1890 by Stuart & Sons Limited The rim is decorated with an applied, clear glass trail of pincered work, above and below a trail of clear glass rigaree. The body is formed in amber glass from a mold with sixteen, shallow projecting ribs, and has a polished out pontil mark. The body is supported on a trail of clear glass pincered work. The clear glass, crossed-over handles are decorated with applied trails of rigaree and raspberry prunts. 11.0 x 9.5 inches (28.0 x 24.0 cm) $580-650 (£400-450)

A flower basket manufactured c.1890 by Stuart & Sons Limited The rim is decorated with an applied, clear glass trail of pincered work, above and below a trail of clear glass rigaree. The body is formed in ruby glass from a mold with sixteen, shallow projecting ribs, and has a polished out pontil mark. The body is supported on a trail of clear glass pincered work. The clear glass, crossed-over handles are decorated with applied trails of rigaree and raspberry prunts. 9.75 x 8.0 inches (24.5 x 20.0 cm) $435-500 (£300-350)

Cased glass designs left plain

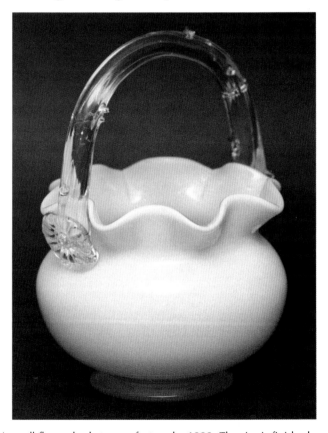

A small flower basket manufactured c.1885. The rim is decorated with an applied, double trail of clear glass pincered work. The body is formed in clear glass and is worked from a circular section to a square profile at the rim. The body has a snapped off pontil mark, and is supported on a trail of clear glass pincered work. 6.5 x 4.5 inches (16.5 x 11.5 cm) $110-125 (£75-85)

A small flower basket manufactured c.1890. The rim is finished with an eight-way crimp. The body is formed in opal white glass, over pale amber glass, and has an applied clear glass foot with polished out pontil mark. The clear glass, rustic briar pattern handle terminates each end, with a clear glass, daisy head prunt. 5 x 3.5 inches (12.5 x 9.0 cm) $95-110 (£65-75)

Vertical striped colored trails

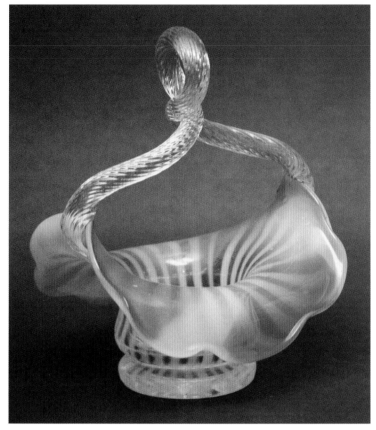

A small flower basket manufactured c.1890. The edge of the rim is decorated with a scalloped profile. The circular section clear glass body has a snapped off pontil mark, and is decorated internally with vertical opalescent white stripes, and with alternate patches of pale ruby and pale yellow around the rim. The handle is formed with a rope twist pattern, clear glass circular section. 6.5 x 5.0 inches (16.0 x 12.5 cm) $180-200 (£125-140)

Air trap design - Herring bone pattern

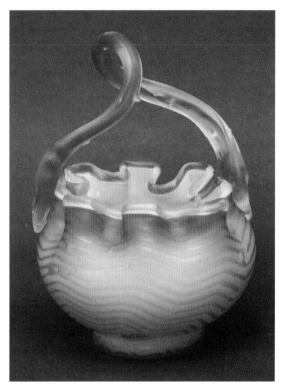

A flower basket manufactured c.1885. The rim is decorated with an applied trail of clear glass, and finished with a square profile, eight-way vertical crimp. The satin finished body is formed with pale ruby glass shading to pale pink glass, over a herring-bone air trap pattern, over opal white glass. The integral circular foot has a ground out pontil mark. The clear glass plain twisted handle is satin finished. 6.75 x 4.75 inches (17.0 x 12.0) $180-210 (£125-145)

Centre Flower Stands

Centre flower stands with applied decoration:

Machine threading on translucent glass

A center flower stand manufactured c.1880. The rim of the center trumpet vase is finished with a turned under edge and a twelve-way crimp. The trumpet shaped vase is formed in clear glass, cased all over with turquoise blue glass machine threading, and decorated with three, trails of clear glass rigaree. The circular base is formed in clear glass with a raised conical center area to which the trumpet vase is attached. The perimeter of the base is decorated with turquoise blue machine threading, and finished with an eighteen-way vertical crimp. The base has a snapped off pontil mark. 10.5 x 6.75 inches (26.5 x 17.5 cm) $290-360 (£200-250)

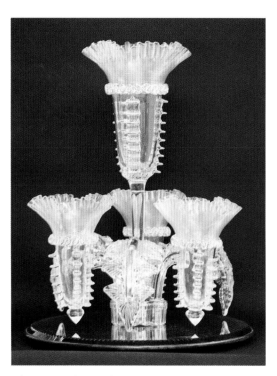

Single spiral trails

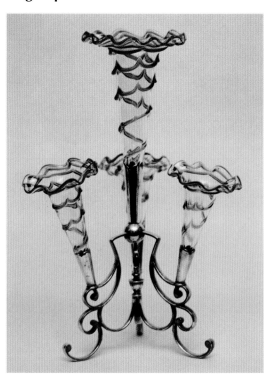

A center flower stand manufactured c.1880 by Stuart & Sons Limited. The rim of each flower holder has a multi-crimped edge and is finished with a second, eight-way crimp. Each of the four flower holders is formed in clear glass and decorated with a band of clear glass machine threading, a trail of clear glass rigaree, and four, ribbed vertical trails with projecting fins. The stems of the holders are located in a pressed glass block in the center of the circular bevelled edge mirror. 14.0 x 10.0 inches (35.5 x 25.5 cm) $945-1000 (£650-700)

A center flower stand manufactured c.1890. The rim is finished with a twelve-way shallow crimp. The clear glass body of each trumpet shaped flower holder is formed from a mold with eight, shallow projecting ribs. Each body is decorated with an applied spiral green glass trail, which is pulled up at each rib line on the body. The trumpet vases are supported in conical sockets on a silver plated decorative metal stand. 12.5 x 8.75 inches (32.0 x 22.0 cm) $360-400 (£250-275)

Close-up of center flower holder.

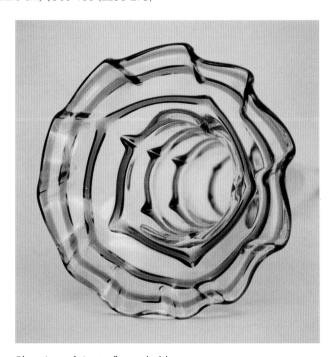

Plan view of rim to flower holder.

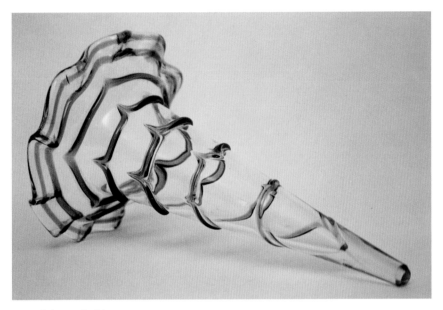

Typical flower holder.

Stylised fish / reptiles

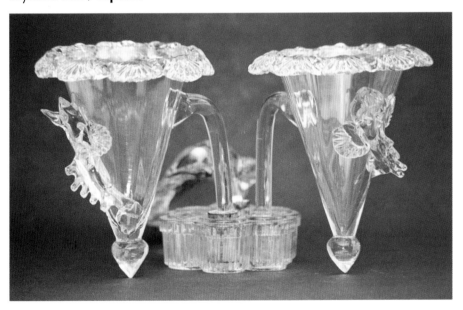

Parts of an unusual flower holder for a
center flower stand, manufactured c.1885.
Each of the conical shaped flower holders
is formed in clear glass and decorated with
an applied trail of half-daisy pincered work
around the rim, and an applied stylised fish
around the body. Each holder is 4.5 x 3.5
inches (11.5 x 9.0 cm)

An unusual bulbous leaf motif for a center
flower stand, manufactured c.1885. The
clear glass domed section body is decorated with an applied trail of half-daisy
pincered work around the rim. 4.0 x 2.75
inches (10.0 x 7.0 cm)

Centre flower stands decorated with surface reduction techniques:

Geometric cut patterns on translucent glass

An unusual clear, cut glass center flower stand manufactured c.1880. The three low level bowls and the center high level bowl are each supported on stems set into a pressed glass center block on top of a circular bevelled edge mirror. Eight, highly polished sets of cut glass pendants are attached to the center bowl at high level. The surfaces of each bowl are decorated with a cut diamond pattern. 14.25 x 9.25 inches (36.5 x 23.5 cm) $500-580 (£350-400)

Wall Mirror Flower Holders

Wall mirror flower holders with applied decoration

Machine threading on translucent glass

A small wall mirror with two, pockets for flowers, manufactured c.1880. The rim of each flower holder has a folded under edge and is finished with a twelve-way shallow crimp. The body of each holder is formed in clear glass, cased with clear glass machine threading, and decorated with a trail of rigaree, and a pointed finial. The bevelled edge mirror is decorated with a perimeter edge trail of circular cuts on the reverse side. The mirror is 13.0 x 8.5 inches (33.0 x 21.7 cm) and each flower holder is 5.5 x 3.25 inches (14.0 x 8.0 cm) $220-255 (£150-175)

A wall mirror with flower holders manufactured c.1879 by Daniel Pearce. The scalloped profile mirror has a bevelled edge and is contained in a metal tray, and supports a single flower holder. The holder is formed in clear glass, cased in machine threading, and decorated with applied pincered work trailing, a stylised flower motif and a raspberry prunt. A Registered Design, diamond shaped stamp with the coding for January 17, 1879, is applied to the back of the mirror on the metal casing, and relates to the registering of the scalloped edge design. 11.5 x 8.5 inches (29.0 x 21.5 cm) $325-360 (£225-250)

Close-up of flower holder on mirror.

Close-up of stamp on back of mirror.

Close-up of flower holder.

CHAPTER THREE
DESIGNS FOR FOOD CONTAINERS

Tazzas

Tazzas with applied decoration:

Iridescent finish

A small tazza manufactured c.1900. The rim is finished with a very shallow twelve-way crimp. The stylised leaf shaped dish is formed in clear glass from a mold with twelve equally spaced out bands of small, closely spaced, shallow projecting ribs. The dish is supported on a green glass, stylised rustic tree trunk and base formed with six, matching tree root feet. The base has a snapped off pontil mark. All surfaces of the tazza have an iridescent finish. The color and texture of the iridescent finish, and more importantly the rib pattern, suggests that the tazza was probably manufactured by John Walsh Walsh. 3.75 x 6.0 inches (9.5 x 15.0 cm) $175-195 (£120-135)

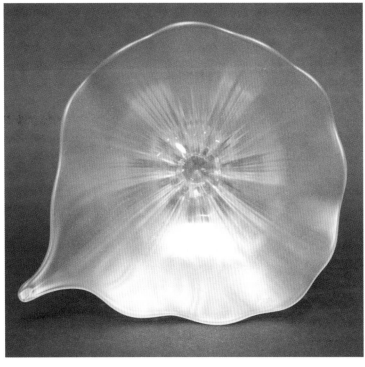

Plan view of top of tazza.

Machine threading on translucent glass

A tazza manufactured c.1878 by Hodgetts, Richardson & Son. The circular dish is formed in clear glass from a mold with twelve, very shallow projecting ribs, and is decorated with a narrow band of fine section, clear glass machine threading, around the underside of the rim. The dish sits on top of a trail of clear glass rigaree on the apex of an inverted, hollow, trumpet shaped foot. The foot is formed in clear glass, from a mold with twelve, very shallow projecting ribs, and is decorated with a narrow band of fine section, clear glass machine threading, around the top surface of the rim. 5.75 x 8.0 inches (14.5 x 20.0 cm) $125-140 (£85-95)

Machine threading over mold formed pattern

A tazza manufactured c.1880. The circular dish is formed with very pale ruby glass, blown into a quilted diamond pattern mold, and then covered with amber glass machine threading, and then finished with an eighteen-way, rounded profile crimp. The dish sits on a clear glass blade knop on top of a hollow section, inverted baluster shaped, clear glass stem, which is decorated with an applied trail of clear glass rigaree. The stem is set on a circular foot, which is formed in a similar manner to the dish, and has a snapped off pontil mark. The threaded areas on the underside of the dish, and on the top of the foot are both decorated with a gold iridescent finish. 5.5 x 7.25 inches (14.0 x 18.5 cm) $220-255 (£150-175)

A tazza manufactured c 1878. The shallow conical shaped dish is formed with very pale ruby glass, blown into a quilted diamond pattern mold, and then covered with amber glass machine threading. The dish sits on a trail of clear glass rigaree, on the apex of an inverted, hollow, trumpet shaped foot. The foot is formed in a similar manner to the dish. The threaded areas on the underside of the dish, and on the top of the foot are both decorated with a gold iridescent finish. 6.25 x 8.0 inches (15.5 x 20.0 cm) $175-200 (£120-140)

Single spiral thread trail on translucent glass

A tazza manufactured c.1880. The circular section tazza is formed in clear glass, and is decorated with a single spiral trail of clear glass, and has a polished out pontil mark. The dish inter-connects with the base. 7.75 x 8.5 inches (19.5 x 21.5 cm) $125-140 (£85-95)

Tazzas with internal decoration:

Peach Blow style designs

A small tazza manufactured c.1885, by Thomas Webb & Sons Limited The circular dish is formed with shaded ruby glass over ivory glass, and is finished with a thirty six-way rounded profile vertical edge crimp. The dish sits on an amber glass pincered work knop , on top of the domed foot which is formed in a similar manner to the dish, except that it has an eighteen way vertical edge crimp. 3.75 x 6.5 inches (9.5 x 16.0) $220-255 (£150-175)

Small Bowls And Shallow Dishes

Bowls and shallow dishes with distinctive rim designs:

Petal shaped rims

A small dish manufactured c.1880. The edge of the rim is profiled with ten, petal shapes, and is finished with a ten-way shallow crimp. The body is formed in clear glass, shaded to light green at the rim, blown into a quilted diamond pattern mold, and cased over with fine section, clear glass machine threading. The body has a polished out pontil mark, and a horizontal clear glass pincered work frill, applied to the body at mid height. 1.75 x 5.25 inches (4.5 x 13.5 cm) $110-125 (£75-85)

A small dish manufactured c.1880. The edge of the rim is profiled with ten, petal shapes, edged with a ruby glass trail, and is finished with a ten-way shallow crimp. The body is formed in clear glass, blown into a quilted diamond pattern mold, and cased over with fine section, clear glass machine threading. The body has a polished out pontil mark, and a horizontal clear glass pincered work frill, applied to the body at mid-height. 1.75 x 5.25 inches (4.5 x 13.0 cm) $110-125 (£75-85)

A small dish manufactured c.1880. The edge of the rim is profiled with ten, petal shapes, and finished with a very shallow, ten-way crimp. The body is formed in very pale green glass, shading to ruby around the rim, and is formed in a mold with twelve shallow projecting ribs. The body has a polished out pontil mark, and a horizontal pale green glass pincered work frill, applied to the body at mid-height. 1.75 x 5.5 inches (4.5 x 14.0 cm) $140-165 (£95-115)

Saw tooth profile with applied trail and pincered patterning

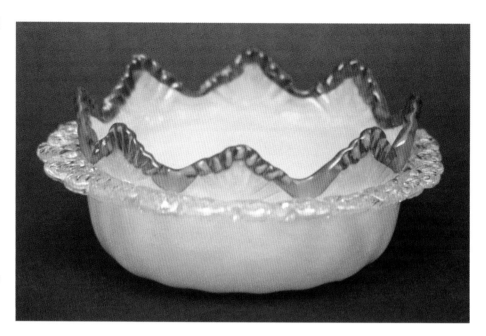

A small dish manufactured c.1880. The saw tooth profile rim is decorated with, a pincered work, pale ruby glass trail. The body is formed with pale yellow glass over opal white glass, blown into a mold with sixteen shallow projecting ribs. The body has a polished out pontil mark, and an applied clear glass pincered work frill at mid-height. 2.0 x 4.0 inches (5.0 x 10.0 cm) $175-200 (£120-140)

Rigaree trails

A shallow dish manufactured c. 1885 by Stuart& Sons Limited The rim is decorated with a trail of clear glass rigaree. The body is formed in ruby glass, from a mold with fifteen, shallow projecting ribs, and has the pontil mark covered with a clear glass raspberry prunt. The dish is supported on three, clear glass ribbed shell pattern feet. 1.75 x 5.75 inches (4.5 x 14.5 cm) $130-165 (£90-115)

Bowls and shallow dishes formed with mold blown designs:

Bold projecting rib patterns

A shallow bowl manufactured c.1880. The rim is decorated with a pale green glass, pincered work trail, set above a clear glass, horizontal pincered work frill. The body is formed in blue glass from a mold with sixteen, rounded profile, projecting ribs. The base has a polished out pontil mark. 2.0 x 4.75 inches (5.0 x 12.0 cm) $130-165 (£90-115)

A shallow bowl manufactured c.1880. The rim is decorated with a clear glass, pincered work trail, set above a clear glass, horizontal pincered work frill. The body is formed in clear glass from a mold with sixteen, rounded profile, projecting ribs. The base has a polished out pontil mark. 2.0 x 4.75 inches (5.0 x 12.0 cm) $130-165 (£90-115)

Shallow projecting rib patterns

A small raised bowl manufactured c.1885. The rim is finished with a four-way vertical crimp, creating the outline of a cross. The pale ruby glass body is formed from a mold with twelve shallow projecting ribs. The body is supported on a clear glass stem on a circular foot with a polished out pontil mark. 4.25 x 4.25 inches (10.5 x 10.5 cm) $125-140 (£85-95)

Plan view of rim.

Peacock eye patterns

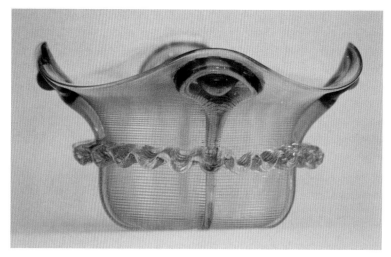

A small bowl manufactured c.1907, by H.G. Richardson. The rim is finished with a four-way crimp. The circular section body is formed with clear glass, encased with clear glass machine threading, and decorated with four, green glass mold formed stylised peacock eye trails. A clear glass pincered work frill is applied around the body at mid-height. The base has a polished out pontil mark. 2.5 x 5.25 inches (6.5 x 13.0) $140-165 (£ 95-115)

Bowls and shallow dishes formed with distinctive shapes:

Miscellaneous shapes

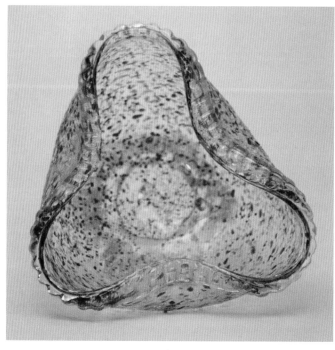

A small dish manufactured c.1880.The rim has a multi-crimped edge, folded over, and finished with a second three-way crimp, turned inwards. The body is formed in clear glass, and decorated with a random pattern of very small fragments of white and various shades of ruby glass, which project from the surface. The body has a snapped off pontil mark, and is supported on a clear glass trail of pincered work. 2.25 x 4.5 inches (6.0 x 11.5 cm) $80-95 (£55-65)

Plan view of rim.

Bowls and shallow dishes decorated with textures:

Satin finished surfaces left undecorated

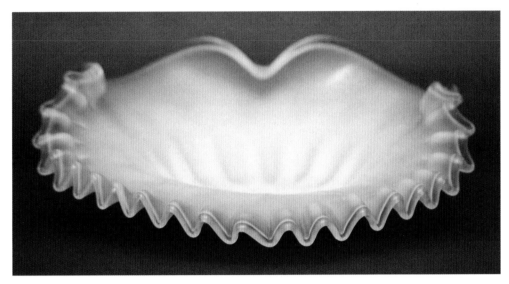

A shallow dish manufactured c.1885. The rim has an applied clear glass edge trail and is decorated with a shallow height "v" shaped edge crimp to the front part of the rim. The satin finished body is formed with opal white glass cased over with pale blue shaded glass, and formed from a mold with sixteen, rounded profile projecting ribs. The base has a ground out pontil mark. 2.5 x 8.5 inches (6.5 x 20.0 cm) $140- 165 (£95-115)

Side view.

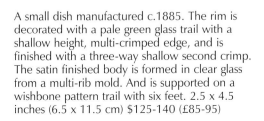

A small dish manufactured c.1885. The rim is decorated with a pale green glass trail with a shallow height, multi-crimped edge, and is finished with a three-way shallow second crimp. The satin finished body is formed in clear glass from a multi-rib mold. And is supported on a wishbone pattern trail with six feet. 2.5 x 4.5 inches (6.5 x 11.5 cm) $125-140 (£85-95)

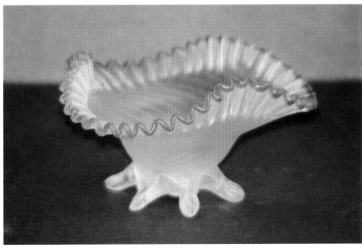

Iced / Frosted / Crackled effects on translucent / opaque glass

A small glass bowl manufactured c.1875. The recessed section rim is decorated with gilding. The body is decorated externally with a crackled glass effect. 2.75 x 5.0 inches (7.0 x 12.5 cm) $95-110 (£65-75)

Bowls and shallow dishes with applied decoration:

Gilded and enamelled designs on translucent / opaque glass

A small dish manufactured c.1895. The edge of the rim is cut and twisted into a random pattern, and gilded. The pale ruby glass body is supported on four rustic pattern stub feet. The inside surface of the dish is decorated with an enamelled floral pattern, which is illustrated in rim detail, R10A-4 in Chapter One. 2.5 x 5.0 inches (6.5 x 12.5 cm) $160-190 (£110-130)

Iridescent finish on translucent / opaque glass

A small bowl manufactured c.1895. The rim is finished with a ten-way crimp, turned inwards. The body is formed with pale ruby glass, over a very pale yellow-green glass, and is decorated with an iridescent finish. The base has a polished out pontil mark. 2.25 x 4.75 inches (5.5 x 12.0 cm) $125-140 (£85-95)

Machine threading on translucent / opaque glass

A small bowl manufactured c.1885. The rim has an applied, pale green glass pincered work trail, and is finished with an eight-way crimp. The circular section, clear glass body, which shades to light blue at the rim, is formed from a mold with twelve shallow projecting ribs, and cased with very fine section, clear glass machine threading. The body has a polished out pontil mark, and also an applied pale green glass pincered work frill at mid-height. 2.75 x 5.25 inches (7.0 x 13.0 cm) $175-200 (£120-140)

A small bowl manufactured c.1880. The rim is decorated with an applied green glass pincered work trail, and finished with a fourteen-way, rounded profile, vertical crimp. The clear glass body which shades to pale ruby at the rim, is formed from a mold with twelve shallow projecting ribs, and is cased with clear glass, fine section machine threading. The body has a polished out pontil mark, and has a green glass pincered work frill at mid-height. 2.25 x 5.5 inches (5.5 x 14.0 cm) $175-200 (£120-140)

Machine threading with tooled surface on translucent / opaque glass

A small bowl manufactured c.1885. The rim is finished with a six-way crimp. The body is formed with pale amber glass cased over with fine section machine threading with a tooled profile. The base has a polished out pontil mark. 2.5 x 5.5 inches (6.0 x 14.0cm) $110-125 (£75-85)

Mold blown designs finished with machine threading

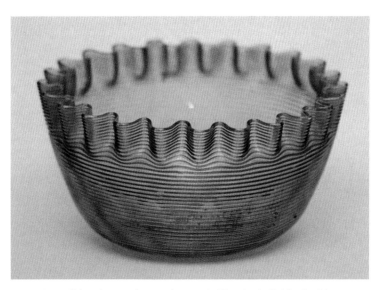

A small bowl manufactured c.1880. The rim is finished with a twenty two-way, rounded profile vertical crimp. The pale green glass body is formed from a quilted, diamond pattern mold, and cased with turquoise glass machine threading. The base has a polished out pontil mark. 2.5 x 5.0 inches (6.0 x 12.5 cm) $110-125 (£75-85)

A small bowl manufactured c.1880. The pale ruby glass body is formed from a quilted diamond mold, and cased with very fine section, pale ruby glass machine threading. The body has a polished out pontil mark, and a clear glass frill applied at mid-height. 2.25 x 3.5 inches (5.5 x 9.0 cm) $110-125 (75-85)

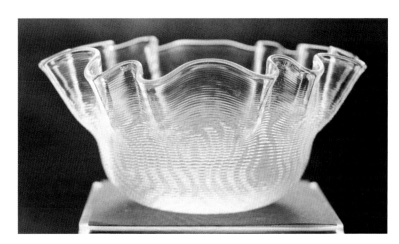

A small bowl manufactured c.1886, by Thomas Webb & Sons Limited The rim is finished with a combination crimp of six, small, rounded profile crimps alternating with six larger, rounded profile crimps. The clear glass body is formed from a mold with the stylised wave pattern recorded in Registered Design No. 58375, dated October 8, 1886. 2.25 x 5.0 inches (5.5 x 12.5 cm) $180-200 (£125-140)

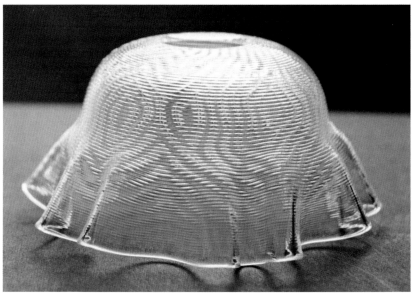

Patterning around the base.

A shallow dish manufactured c.1885. The very pale, translucent ruby glass body is formed from a quilted diamond mold, and cased with very pale, translucent ruby glass machine threading. The body is supported on three, shell ribbed pattern clear glass feet. The pontil mark is covered with a clear glass raspberry prunt. 2.5 x 6.25 inches (6.5 x 15.5 cm) $175-200 (£120-140)

Plan view.

A small raised dish manufactured c.1885. The rim is decorated with an applied trail of clear glass rigaree, and is finished with a three-way shallow crimp. The pale, translucent ruby glass body is formed from a quilted diamond mold, and cased with pale, translucent ruby glass machine threading. The body is set on a circular clear glass foot with a folded under edge. The pontil mark is covered with a clear glass raspberry prunt. The clear glass handle is formed with a shell ribbed section. 3.5 x 5.75 inches (8.5 x 14.5 cm) $190-220 (£130-150)

Stylised acanthus leaf motifs

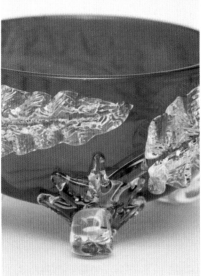

A small bowl manufactured c.1885, by Stuart & Sons Limited The ruby glass body is formed from a mold with fourteen shallow projecting ribs, and has a pontil mark covered by a large raspberry prunt. The body is decorated with large, clear glass, pincered work acanthus leaves which spring from each of the three, clear glass snail pattern feet. 4.0 x 6.25 inches (10.0 x 15.5 cm) $220-255 (£150-175)

Detail of typical foot.

Pincered trails of shell ribbed / daisy head patterns

A small bowl manufactured c.1880. The rim is decorated with a trail of clear glass, cross grid pattern pincered work, and finished with an eight-way crimp. The clear glass body is formed from a mold with twenty- two projecting ribs, and has a polished out pontil mark. A clear glass pincered work frill is applied to the body at mid-height. 2.5 x 5.0 inches (6.5 x 12.5 cm) $125-140 (£85-95)

A small bowl manufactured c.1885. The rim is decorated with a trail of clear glass pincered work, above a trail of green glass pincered work. The ruby glass body is formed from a mold with sixteen shallow projecting ribs, and has a polished out pontil mark.2.5 x 4.25 inches (6.5 x 11.0 cm) $140-165 (£95-115)

A small bowl manufactured c.1880. The rim is decorated with a trail of clear glass pincered work, and finished with an eight-way deep crimp. The amber glass body is formed from a mold with sixteen projecting ribs, and has a polished out pontil mark. 2.25 x 4.0 inches (6.5 x 10.0 cm) $110-125 (£75-85)

A small bowl manufactured c.1880. The rim is decorated with a trail of clear glass pincered work, and finished with an eight-way deep crimp. The ruby glass body is formed from a mold with sixteen projecting ribs, and has a polished out pontil mark. 2.25 x 4.75 inches (6.5 x 12.0 cm) $110-125 (£75-85)

A shallow dish with a handle manufactured c.1880. The rim is decorated with a trail of clear glass pincered work, and finished with an eight-way deep crimp. The amber glass body with clear glass handle, is formed from a mold with twelve projecting ribs, and has a polished out pontil mark. 1.5 x 5.25 inches (4.0 x 13.0 cm) $110-125 (£75-85)

A small bowl manufactured c.1880. The rim is decorated with a trail of pale green glass pincered work, and finished with an eight-way deep crimp. The ruby glass body is formed from a mold with sixteen projecting ribs, and has a polished out pontil mark. A trail of pale green glass rigaree is applied to the body beneath the rim trail. 2.25 x 4.75 inches (6.5 x 12.0 cm) $125-140 (£85-95)

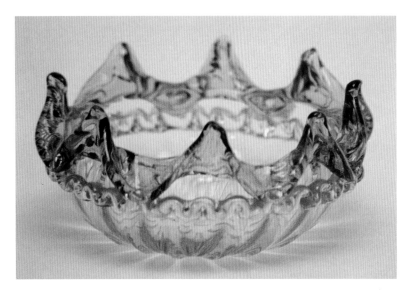

A small bowl manufactured c.1880. The rim is decorated with a trail of pale green glass pincered work, and finished with an eight-way deep crimp. The clear glass body is formed from a mold with sixteen projecting ribs, and has a polished out pontil mark. A trail of clear glass rigaree is applied to the body beneath the rim trail. 2.25 x 4.75 inches (6.5 x 12.0 cm) $125-140 (£85-95)

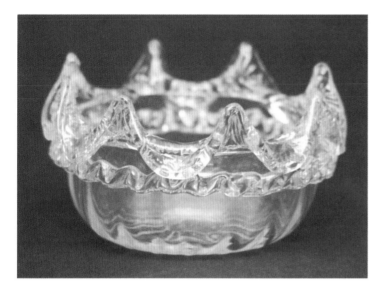

A small bowl manufactured c.1880. The rim is decorated with a trail of clear glass pincered work, and finished with an eight-way deep crimp. The clear glass body is formed from a mold with sixteen projecting ribs, and has a polished out pontil mark. A trail of clear glass rigaree is applied to the body beneath the rim trail. 2.25 x 4.0 inches (6.5 x 10.0 cm) $125-140 (£85-95)

A small bowl manufactured c.1880. The rim is decorated with a vertical trail of clear glass triangular shaped, pincered work, set above a horizontal trail of pale green glass, pincered work, triangular leaf shapes. The ruby glass body is formed from a mold with sixteen projecting ribs, and has a polished out pontil mark. A trail of pale green glass rigaree is applied to the body beneath the rim trail. 2.25 x 5.75 inches (5.5 x 14.5 cm) $140-165 (£95-115)

Projecting frills

A shallow dish manufactured c. 1880. The rim is ground off and polished. The ruby glass body is formed from a mold with sixteen, shallow projecting ribs, and has an integral circular foot. The body is decorated with an applied clear glass, crimped frill. 1.5 x 6.0 inches (4.0 x 15.0 cm). $140-165 (£95-115)

Stained glass designs

A small bowl manufactured c.1900. The rim is ground off and polished. The clear glass body has a diagonal pattern of thin ruby stained stripes and matt finished engraved clear glass stripes. The integral circular foot is decorated on the underside with a ruby stained geometric leaf pattern. 3.0 x 4.25 inches (7.5 x 12.0 cm) $125-140 (£85-95)

View showing patterned base.

Bowls and Shallow dishes with internal decoration:

Burmese designs

A shallow dish formed in *Burmese* glass manufactured c 1887, and probably used to support a fairy lamp holder. The satin finished body is formed from a circular shaped dish, with the edge folded over inwards four times to make a square shape rim. The body is decorated on all sides with an enamelled prunus type floral pattern. The circular applied foot has a polished out pontil mark. 2.0 x 6.0 inches (5.0 x 15.0 cm) $140-175 (£ 95-120)

Opalescent glass designs

A small bowl manufactured c.1885. The rim is decorated with an opalescent edge trail and is finished with a four-way deep crimp. The circular green glass body is decorated with a broad band of opalescent green glass, machine threading on the underside of the rim. The body has a snapped off pontil mark and is supported on a green glass, pincered work trail. 3.0 x 6.0 inches (7.5 x 15.0 cm) $140-165 (£95-115)

Plan view of rim.

A small bowl manufactured c.1895. The rim is finished with an eight-way crimp. The pale amber-orange glass body is formed from a mold with eight projecting ribs, which are highlighted with opalescence. The body has a polished out pontil mark, and a clear glass pincered work frill at mid-height. 2.75 x 5.25 inches (7.0 x 13.0 cm) $125-140 (£85-95)

A small bowl manufactured c.1895. The rim has a non-opalescent edge trail, and is finished with an eight-way crimp turned inwards. The amber-orange glass body is formed from a mold with eight ribs. Four of the ribs are of single, rounded profile and these alternate with four, treble rounded profile ribs. The ribs are highlighted with opalescence. 3.0 x 5.0 inches (7.5 x 12.5 cm) $160-190(£110-130)

An example of a small bowl made in accordance with Registered Design No. 583165, dated May 4,1911 as recorded by Stevens & Williams Limited The rim is finished with a rounded profile multi-crimp, and is folded inwards on one side. The body is formed in an opalescent amber glass , and blown into a mold with a stylised, vertical, herringbone rib pattern. These ribs are highlighted by the opalescence. The polished out pontil mark is inscribed with *Rd. 583165.* 2.0 x 5.0 inches (5.0 x 12.5 cm) $215-250 (£150-175)

View of base.

Translucent shaded glass designs – single color shading into clear glass

A small bowl manufactured c.1885. The rim has a shallow profile, multi-crimped edge, and is finished with a six-way rectangular profile deep crimp. The pale green, opalescent glass body is shaded to ruby at the rim, and is formed from a mold with eight, rounded profile, projecting ribs. The body has a polished out pontil mark, and is supported on a clear glass, wishbone pattern trail with three feet. 3.0 x 5.25 inches (7.5 x 13.0 cm) $175-195 (£120-135)

A small bowl manufactured c.1900, in the style of the *Grotesque* pattern manufactured by Stevens & Williams Limited The rim is finished with a four-way rounded profile, vertical crimp turned inwards. The clear glass body is shaded to amethyst at the rim, and is formed from a mold with four, projecting ribs, and has a polished out pontil mark. 3.25 x 5.25 inches (8.0 x 13.0 cm ($110-125 (£75-85)

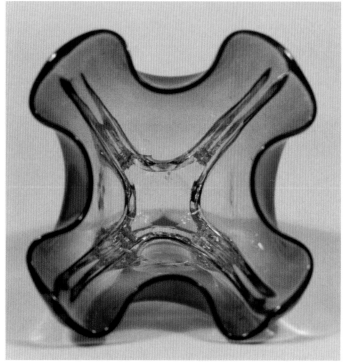

Plan view of rim.

Gold or silver foil inclusions in translucent / opaque glass

A small bowl manufactured c. 1885. The edge of the rim is finished with a twenty four-way vertical crimp. The pale ruby glass, circular section body is decorated internally with fragments of gold foil, and is finished with a crackled surface. The base has a polished out pontil mark. 2.25 x 4.25 inches (6.0 x 11.0 cm) $125-140 (£85-95)

Vertical striped colored trails

A small bowl manufactured c. 1885. The rim is decorated with a shallow height multi-way edge crimp, and is finished with a six-way rectangular profile deep crimp. The clear glass body is decorated internally with a pattern of vertical colored stripes and is formed from a mold with a vertical indented oval pattern. The body has a snapped off pontil mark, and is supported on a clear glass pincered work, trail. 3.5 x 6.0 inches (9.0 x 15.0 cm) $140-165 (£95-115)

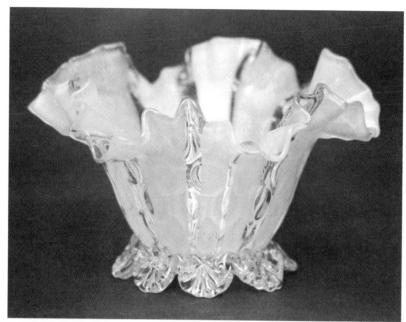

Plan view of rim.

A shallow bowl manufactured c.1885. The turned over rim is finished with a rounded profile, thirty two-way crimp. The pale green glass, circular section body is decorated internally with six pale ruby glass tapering stripes radiating from the center of the base. The body has a polished out pontil mark, and is supported on a pale green, wishbone pattern trail with six feet. 2.5 x 7 inches (6.5 x 18.0 cm) $180-200 (£125-140)

Spiral trailing

A small bowl manufactured c.1895. The rim is finished with an eight-way crimp, and turned inwards. The clear glass body is formed from a mold with eight, projecting ribs. Four of the ribs have a half-round profile, and the other four have a triple rib profile (a small rib each side of a larger center rib). The body is decorated internally with a spiral, combination trail, comprising a small section white trail on each side of a central, wider green trail. The base has a polished out pontil mark. 2.5 x 4.5 inches (6.5 x 11.5 cm) $140-160 (£95-110)

Matching Sugar Bowls And Cream Jugs

Matching sugar bowls and cream jugs formed with applied decoration:

Machine threading on translucent / opaque glass

Machine threaded jug and basin manufactured c.1890. The clear glass bodies are decorated with very fine section, clear glass machine threading, and with merging vertical bands of pale ruby, pale green, and pale blue. The jug has a circular, clear glass applied foot with a snapped off pontil mark. The basin has a clear glass, short stem on a circular foot with a snapped off pontil mark. The jug is 3.5 x 2.5 inches 9.0 x 6.5 cm) $80-95 (£55-65). The basin is 3.5 x 4.25 inches (9.0 x 10.5 cm) $95-110 (£65-75)

Machine threading over a mold blown pattern in translucent / opaque glass

Mold formed jug and basin decorated with machine threading manufactured c.1900, by Thomas Webb & Sons Limited The rims are finished with an eight-way shallow crimp. The clear glass bodies are formed from a mold with twelve projecting ribs, and have applied, circular feet with polished out pontils, which are acid stamped *Webb*. The jug is 2.5 x 2.25 inches (6.5 x 5.5 cm) $110-125 (£75-85) The basin is 2.5 x 5.0 inches (6.5 x 12.5 cm) $110-125 (£75-85)

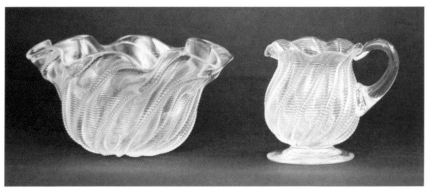

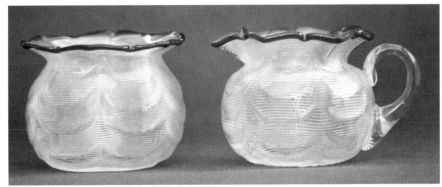

A mold formed jug and basin decorated with machine threading, manufactured c.1885. Each rim has a six-petal profiled edge, decorated with an applied ruby glass trail, and finished with a six-way shallow crimp. The clear glass bodies are formed from a mold with six, vertical panels of shallow projecting festoons. The bases have polished out pontil marks. The jug is 2.5 x 4.0 inches (6.5 x 10.0 cm) $110-125 (£75-85). The basin is 2.5 x 3.25 inches (6.5 x 8.0 cm) $110-125 (£75-85)

Pincered trails

A cream jug and sugar basin manufactured c.1885. The rims of both items are decorated with an applied, clear glass trail of pincered work, and finished with a four way crimp on the jug, and a six-way crimp on the basin. The amber glass body of each item is formed from a mold with sixteen shallow projecting ribs, and each has a polished out pontil mark. A trail of clear glass rigaree is applied beneath the rim trail. The jug is 4.0 x 2.5 inches (10.0 x 6.5 cm) $110-130 (£75-90). The basin is 3.25 x 5.0 inches (8.0 x 12.5 cm) $130-160 (£90-110)

Large Bowls

Bowls formed with applied decoration:

Enamelled and gilded designs

A large bowl manufactured c.1885. The rim is ground off and polished, and decorated with gilding. The tapered profile, circular section body is formed with blue over clear glass, and is decorated with enamelled and gilded patterns. The base has a large diameter polished out pontil mark, which exposes the inner clear glass layer. 3.5 x 8.75 inches (9.0 x 22.0 cm) $220-255 (£150-175)

Rear view.

Machine threading

A large bowl manufactured c.1885. The rim is finished with a six-way rounded profile crimp. The circular section, pale ruby glass body is formed from a mold with twelve, very shallow projecting ribs, and is decorated with a band of amber glass machine threading around the rim. The circular foot is formed in a similar manner, and has a pontil mark covered by a large clear glass raspberry prunt. 4.75 x 8.0 inches (12.0 x 20.0 cm) $250-290 (£175-200)

Pincered trails

A large bowl manufactured c.1885. The rim is decorated with an applied trail of yellow-green glass pincered work, finished with an eleven-way deep crimp. The circular section, pale yellow-green glass body is formed from a mold with twelve shallow projecting ribs, and has a snapped off pontil mark. The body is supported on a yellow-green glass, pincered work trail. 4.0 x 8.0 inches (10.0 x 20.0 cm) $220-255 (£150-175)

Bowls formed with internal decoration:

Amberina designs

A large bowl manufactured c.1885. The rim is decorated with an applied, clear glass edge trail, and finished with an eight-way crimp. The *Amberina* glass body is formed from a mold with a staggered pattern of circular indentations, and has a polished out pontil mark. The body is supported on four, clear glass rustic pattern stub feet, from which spring trails of clear glass pincered work leaves and flower heads. 5.25 x 8.0 inches (13.0 x 20.0 cm) $260-320 (£180-220)

Silver foil inclusions

A large bowl manufactured c.1885. The rim is ground off and polished, and decorated with an applied trail of clear glass rigaree. The amber glass body is decorated internally with fragments of silver foil, and is formed from a mold with thirty six, rounded profile projecting ribs, and supported on three clear glass rustic, ribbed pattern feet. 4.5 x 7.0 inches (11.5 x 17.5 cm) $140-165 (£95-115)

Bowls formed with surface reduction techniques:

Intaglio cut designs on translucent glass

A large bowl manufactured c.1893. The rim is covered with a silver band, which is stamped with the hallmarks for Sheffield, 1893. The clear glass body is decorated all over with a stylised intaglio cut floral pattern. The underside of the polished base has a thirty-two point, cut star motif. 3.75 x 8.0 inches (9.5 x 8.0 cm) $165-180 (£115-125)

Intaglio cut pattern around the base.

Biscuit Barrels

Biscuit barrels decorated with applied texture:

Gilded and enamelled designs on opaque glass

A biscuit barrel manufactured c.1888. The satin finished, cube shaped body is formed in a pale ivory glass, and has a large diameter circular indent in each face. The short, circular neck is covered by a silver plated frame, containing the lid and support for the handle. The side of the body is decorated with an enamelled and gilded pattern of stylised bamboo plants. The silver plated lid is engraved with *V.C.L.T.C* and *Open Singles 2nd Prize won by R.J.FOSBERRY July 1888.* (The silver plating on lid, frame and handle is generally worn away, exposing the brass base) 5.5 x 4.75 inches (14.0 x 12.0 cm) $255-290 (£175-200)

Rear view of biscuit barrel.

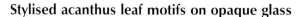

Biscuit barrels with applied decoration:

Stylised acanthus leaf motifs on opaque glass

A biscuit barrel manufactured c.1885. The circular section body is formed in very pale green glass, and has a polished out pontil mark, and is decorated with a large pincered work stylised, clear glass, acanthus leaf motif. The silver plate lid is stamped on the underside with the following marks: *A1* in one stamp, *J* and *K* in two separate stamps in old English font, *N* and *W* in one stamp in block letters, (the mark of Norton & White, Birmingham, 1883-1899), *E P* in one stamp, and *2098* in individual numbers. 8.0 x 6.0 inches (20.0 x 15.0) $325-360 (£225-250)

Biscuit barrels decorated with surface reduction techniques:

Geometric cut patterns on translucent glass

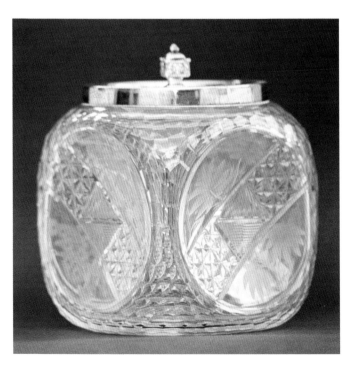

A biscuit barrel manufactured c.1886, by John Walsh Walsh. The circular rim is mounted with a silver plated frame and engraved lid. The pattern on the lid matches the design on the sides of the jar. The clear glass cube shaped body has a large circular indent on each face. The indented area on each face is decorated with engraved stylised floral patterns and diagonal bands of geometric cut patterns. The remainder of the sides around the indented areas is finished with a random pattern of polygonal cuts, which create a hammered metal effect. The polished base has a twenty-four point cut star, and is inscribed near the edge with *Rd. No. 42716*. This Registered Design was recorded on January 29, 1886. 5.25 x 4.75 inches (13.0 x 12.0 cm) $180-220 (£125-150)

Salts

Salts formed with distinctive rims:

Petal shaped rim in translucent glass

A salt manufactured c.1885. The edge of the rim is decorated with eight petal shaped profiles, with alternate petals folded up and down. The clear glass body is shaded to pale ruby at the rim, and is formed from a mold with sixteen shallow projecting ribs. The body has a snapped off pontil mark, and is supported on a pincered work, green glass trail. 2.25 x 2.75 inches (5.5 x 7.0 cm) $65-80 (£45-55)

A salt manufactured c.1885. The edge of the rim is decorated with six petal shaped profiles, and is finished with a six-way shallow crimp. The clear glass body is shaded to pale ruby at the rim, and is formed from a mold with eight shallow projecting ribs. A clear glass rigaree frill is applied at mid-height.1.75 x 2.75 inches (4.5 x 7.0 cm) $65-80 (£45-55)

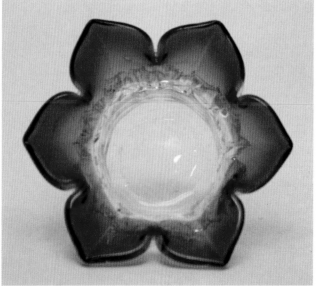

Plan view of rim.

Trellis pattern

A salt manufactured c.1880. The clear glass container has a projecting rim, which is supported on the top of a spherical shaped cage of clear glass trails formed into a diamond pattern open trellis structure. The circular flat base has a rounded profile crimped edge. 2.75 x 4.0 inches (7.0 x 10.0) $125-140 (£85-95)

Salts decorated with an applied texture:

Iced / Frosted / Crackled effects on colored translucent glass

A salt manufactured c.1885. The edge of the rim is decorated with six petal shaped profiles, and is finished with a six-way shallow crimp. The yellow-green body is cased with crackled opal white glass, and has a polished out pontil mark. 1.5 x 3.0 inches (4.0 x 7.5 cm) $65-80 (£45-55)

Plan view of rim.

Salts with applied decoration:

Multiple vertical trails

A salt manufactured c.1885. The circular section, pale blue body is formed from a mold with twelve, shallow projecting ribs, and is worked to a diamond shape at rim level. The body has a polished out pontil mark, and is decorated with four vertical trails of clear glass beads. (The feet on the base of these trails are missing) 2.0 x 4.25 inches (5.0 x 10.5 cm) $65-80 (£45-55)

Pincered trails

A salt manufactured c.1885. The circular, pale ruby glass body is decorated with a trail of clear glass, half-daisy pattern, pincered work at mid-height, and has a snapped off pontil mark. The body is supported on a trail of clear glass, half-daisy pattern, pincered work. 1.75 x 3.0 inches (4.5 x 7.5 cm) $65-80 (£45-55)

A salt manufactured c.1885. The amber-orange glass body is formed from a mold with twelve shallow projecting ribs, and has a snapped off pontil mark. The body is supported on a trail of clear glass, shell ribbed pincered work. A festoon type trail of clear glass pincered work is applied around the body at mid-height. 1.75 x 2.75 inches (4.5 x 7.0 cm) $65-80 (£45-55)

Small glass beads used to create jewel type effects on translucent glass

A salt manufactured c.1885. The circular clear glass body is decorated with three, shell ribbed prunts with central turquoise glass beads. 1.5 x 2.75 inches (4.0 x 7.0 cm) $50-65 (£35-45)

Cased glass

A salt manufactured c.1880. The rim is decorated with an applied, amber glass trail, and is finished with a ten-way shallow crimp. The circular body is formed with opal white glass, over pale ruby glass, and has a polished out pontil mark. 2.0 x 3.25 inches (5.0 x 8.0 cm) $65-80 (£45-55)

Salts with internal decoration:

Opalescent glass

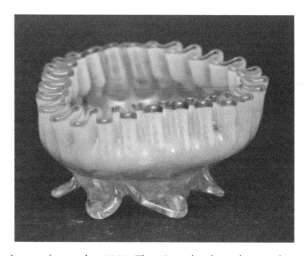

A salt manufactured c. 1885. The triangular shaped rim is decorated with a pale non-opalescent blue edge trail, and finished with a twenty six-way tightly set vertical crimp. The opalescent, very pale blue glass body is formed from a mold with eighteen shallow projecting ribs, and has a snapped off pontil mark. The body is supported on a clear glass, pincered work trail. 1.5 x 3.0 inches (4.0 x 7.5 cm) $65-80 (45-55)

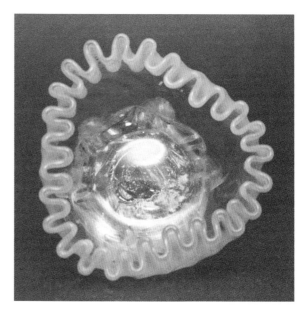

Plan view of rim.

Surface pull-outs

A salt manufactured c.1895, by Monot, Pere et Fils. The rim is finished with a four-way crimp. The body is formed with very pale ruby glass over pale amber glass, and has an integral foot with a polished out pontil mark. The body is decorated internally with ten opalescent vertical stripes. 1.5 x 1.5 inches (4.0 x 4.0 cm) $50-65 (£35-45)

A salt manufactured c.1890. The rim is finished with a ten-way shallow crimp. The pale, translucent green glass body is decorated with a random pattern of surface pull-outs, and is supported on a clear glass pincered work trail, with six pulled out feet.2.0 x 2.5 inches (5.0 x 6.5 cm) $50-65 ((£35-45)

Toothpick Holders

Toothpick holders with distinctive mold formed patterns:

Diamond patterns

A toothpick holder manufactured c.1880. The rim is ground off and polished, and decorated with an applied trail of ivory glass rigaree. The body is formed from a quilted diamond pattern mold, and is supported on three, ivory glass ribbed shell pattern feet. 3.25 x 2.75 inches (8.0 x 7.0 cm) $80-100 (£55-70)

Toothpick holders with applied decoration:

Horizontal / vertical rigaree trails

Faint projecting rib patterns

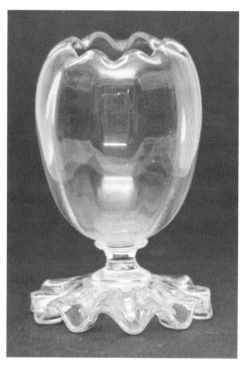

A toothpick holder manufactured c.1880. The rim is ground off and polished, and decorated with an applied trail of clear glass rigaree. The clear glass body is formed from a mold with ten shallow projecting ribs, and has a snapped off pontil mark. 2.5 x 3 inches (6.5 x 7.5 cm) $50-65 (£35-45)

Toothpick holder manufactured c.1890. The rim is finished with an eight-way shallow crimp and turned inwards. The clear glass body is formed from a mold with twelve shallow projecting ribs. The body is supported on a circular clear glass foot, finished all over with a ten-way, shallow rounded profile crimp, and has a snapped off pontil mark. 3.75 x 2.25 inches (9.5 x 6.0 cm) $65-80 (£45-55)

A toothpick holder manufactured c.1885. The circular clear glass body is decorated with a band of clear glass machine threading and a trail of clear glass rigaree. The pontil mark is covered with a raspberry prunt. The body is supported on three, clear glass, shell rib pattern feet. 2.5 x 2.5 inches (6.5 x 6.5 cm) $65-80 (£45-55)

Opalescent designs

Toothpick holders with internal decoration:

Burmese designs

A toothpick holder manufactured c.1895. The rim is decorated with an applied trail of clear glass pincered work. The spherical, opalescent, green glass body has rustic, surface pull-outs, and is formed from a mold with twelve, shallow projecting ribs. The body is supported on a trail of clear glass, daisy pattern pincered work, and the base has a snapped off pontil mark. 3.25 x 3.25 inches (8.0 x 8.0 cm) $95-110 (£65-75)

A polished *Burmese* glass toothpick holder manufactured c.1888, by Thomas Webb & Sons Limited The rim is finished with a hexagonal profile. The spherical body shades from pale yellow at the base to salmon pink at the rim. The base has a polished out pontil mark. 2.5 x 2.5 inches (6.5 x 6.5cm) $80-95 (£55-65)

Air trap design - Miscellaneous patterns

A toothpick holder manufactured c.1885. The rim is pinched together to form a trefoil shape. The satin finished body is formed with light blue glass, over a random abstract design air trap pattern, over opal white glass. The body sits on a circular satin finished base formed for mounting in a metal frame. 2.75 x 2.75 inches (7.0 x 7.0 cm) $95-110 (£65-75)

Air trap design – Vertical / spiral rib

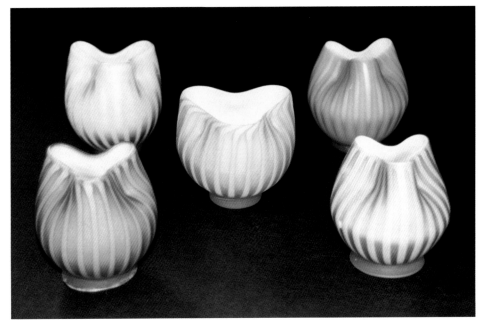

Five, *Sateen* toothpick holders manufactured c.1885 by John Walsh Walsh. The rim of each unit is pinched together to form a trefoil shape. The body of each unit is formed with a colored outer layer of glass over a vertical hollow rib, air trap pattern over opal white glass, and supported on a circular clear glass foot for mounting in a metal frame. 2.75 x 2.75 inches (7.0 x 7.0 cm). $95-110 (£65-75)

A toothpick holder and saucer manufactured c.1885. The pattern and texture of the surface is similar to the *Sateen* glass made by John Walsh Walsh. The rectangular profile rim is decorated with a multi-crimped edge. The satin finished body is formed with opal white glass, over a vertical hollow rib, air trap pattern over opal white glass, and supported on a clear glass circular foot with a ground out pontil mark. The holder sits on a matching saucer, which is circular on plan, but has three parts of the edge curled upwards, to create a tricorn shape. 2.75 x 3.5 inches (7.0 x 9.0 cm) $110-125 (£75-85)

Toothpick holders decorated with surface tooling:

Surface pull-outs

A toothpick holder manufactured c.1890. The edge of the rim is decorated with nine petal shaped profiles, and finished with a shallow, nine-way crimp. The spherical clear glass body is decorated with a random pattern of surface pull-outs, and the base has a polished out pontil mark. 2.5 x 2.5 inches (6.5 x 6.5 cm) $50-65 (£35-45)

Plates

Plates with applied decoration:

Gilded and enamelled designs

A Large plate manufactured c.1878. The blue plate is decorated all over with a pattern of gilded and enamelled, stylised floral motifs. 12.0 inches (30.5cm) diameter. $500-580 (£350-400)

Close-up of central area of plate.

Close-up of rim area of plate.

Plates with internal decoration:

Amberina designs

A circular plate manufactured c.1885. The satin finished plate is formed from a spiral trail of *Amberina* glass, applied to a gather of clear glass and blown into a mold with twelve, rounded profile, projecting ribs. The plate has a polished out pontil mark. The rim is finished with a twelve-way shallow, scalloped edge profile. 1.25 x 7.0 inches (35 x 18.0 cm) $95-125 (£65-85)

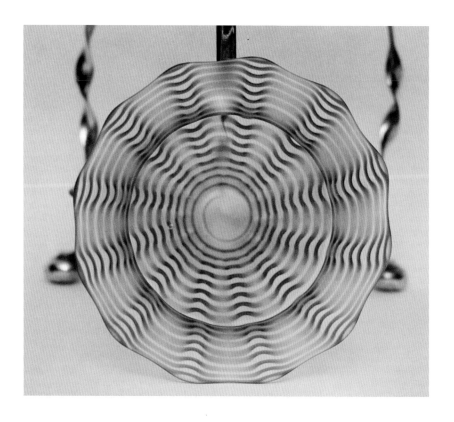

CHAPTER FOUR
DESIGNS FOR DRINKING VESSELS

Jugs

Jugs with distinctive rim designs:

Rims with petal shaped edge

A small jug manufactured c.1890. The rim has a profile formed with six petal shapes, and is finished with a shallow six-way crimp. The very pale ruby glass body is formed from a mold with twelve shallow projecting ribs, and has a polished out pontil mark. The body is decorated with a narrow band of fine section pale ruby glass machine threading, applied around the neck and beneath the rim. 4.0 x 2.75 inches (10.0 x 7.0 cm) $110-125 (£75-85)

Plan view of rim.

Jugs formed with distinctive mold blown / hand formed shapes:

Miscellaneous geometric shapes

Jugs formed with distinctive mold blown patterns:

Faint projecting rib patterns

A large jug manufactured c.1855. The rim is decorated with an applied fine section ruby glass trail. The alabaster colored body and applied strap type handle are formed in an opaline type glass. The body sits on a circular, solid section foot with a polished out pontil mark. 8.75 x 5.0 inches (22.0 x 12.5 cm) $175-220 (£120-150)

A large jug manufactured c.1880. The ruby glass body is formed from a mold with shallow projecting ribs, and with an integral circular base with a snapped off pontil mark. The clear glass handle is formed in a shell rib pattern. 7 x 6 inches (18.0 x 15.0 cm) $220-255 (£150-175)

A small jug manufactured c.1855. The rim is decorated with a trail of clear opaline glass. The pale blue glass body and applied strap handle are formed in an opaline type glass, with an integral circular solid foot with polished out pontil mark. 3.25 x 3.5 inches (8.0 x 8.5 cm) $110-125 (£75-85)

A large jug manufactured c.1867, by Thomas Webb & Sons Limited The clear glass body with integral circular solid foot, incorporates the shell rib designs for pouring lip, handle, and prunts, as recorded in Registered Designs Nos. 212674, and 212675, dated October 19,1867. 10.0 x 5.0 inches (25.0 x 12.5 cm) $125-140 (£85-95)

View of handle.

Left:
A small jug manufactured c.1875, by Thomas Webb & Sons Limited The rim has a hand formed pouring lip. The clear glass body has a polished out pontil mark, and is supported on four clear glass snail type feet. The body is decorated with four, clear glass lion head masks, each located above the feet. 5.25 x 3.5 inches (13.0 x 9.0 cm) $95-110 (£65-75)

A small jug manufactured c.1875. The clear glass body is formed from a patterned press mold, but the handle is hand formed and applied separately. 4.5 x 3.25 inches (11.5 x 8.0 cm) $45-60 (£30-40)

Jugs decorated with applied textures:

Satin finished surfaces left undecorated

A small jug manufactured c.1885. The rim has a multi-crimped edge incorporating the pouring lip. The satin finished body is formed with clear shading to pale blue over opal white glass. The integral circular foot has a snapped off pontil mark. The satin finished clear glass handle is formed in a rustic briar pattern. 6.5 x 6.5 inches (16.5 x 16.5 cm) $125-140 (£85-95)

Satin finished surfaces decorated with enamelling and / or gilding

A large jug manufactured c. 1860. The rim is profiled to form a pouring lip, and is decorated with gilding. The satin finished ivory glass spherical shaped body is supported on a hollow section foot. The body and foot are decorated with an enamelled and gilded floral pattern. The inside of the base is inscribed with *W203* above *3*. 10.0 x 6.0 inches (25.0 x 15.0 cm) $175-220 (£120-150)

Close-up of the enamelled floral decoration on item at left.

Iced / Frosted / Crackled effects on translucent / opaque glass

A large jug manufactured c.1867, by Thomas Webb & Sons Limited. The crackled glass body with integral circular solid foot, incorporates the shell rib designs for pouring lip, handle, and prunts, as recorded in Registered Designs Nos. 212674, and 212675, dated October 19,1867. 9.5 x 5.25 inches (24.0 x 13.0 cm) $125-140 (£85-95)

Jugs with applied decoration:

Gilded and enamelled designs on translucent / opaque glass

A large jug manufactured c.1848, by W.H, B.& J. Richardson. The edge of the rim, the back of the handle, and the top of the foot are decorated with gilding. The white glass body is decorated all around with an enamelled pattern of water lilies. This design is similar to that shown on the jug illustrated in Registered Design No.52328, dated June 3,1848. 8.5 x 5.0 inches (22.0 x 12.5 cm) $650-725 (£450-500)

End view of handle

Machine threading on translucent / opaque glass

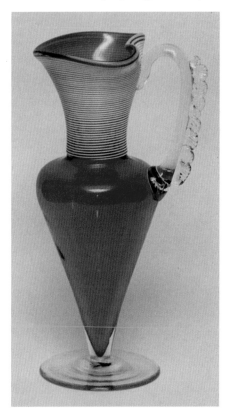

Right:
A small jug manufactured c.1885. The clear over ruby glass body is supported on a circular clear glass foot with a snapped off pontil mark. The body is decorated with white machine threading around the neck. The clear glass handle is decorated with an applied trail of half-daisy pattern, pincered work. 8.25 x 3.0 inches (21.0 x 7.5 cm) $180-220 (£125-150)

Rear view of jug, opposite page, bottom.

A jug and tumbler manufactured c.1878, by Hodgetts, Richardson & Son. The jug is formed in clear glass and decorated with two bands of turquoise blue, machine threading, and a clear glass rigaree trail. The circular clear glass foot has a polished out pontil mark. The tumbler is formed in a similar manner. Jug – 6.5 x 3.5 inches (16.5 x 9.0cm) $125-140 (£85-95). Tumbler – 3.5 x 2.5 inches (9.0 x 6.5 cm) $60-75 (£40-50)

Front view of pouring lip.

A small jug manufactured c.1877, by Hodgetts, Richardson & Son. The clear glass body is decorated with two bands of applied amber glass machine threading, two trails of clear glass rigaree and a wide central panel of engraved butterflies and floral trails, attributed to the engraver called Keller. The circular foot has a polished out pontil mark. 8.0 x 3.25 inches (20.0 x 8.0 cm) $175-200 (£120-140)

A small jug manufactured c.1880. The rim is finished with a three-way crimp. The clear glass body is decorated with applied ruby glass, machine threading around the neck, and has a ribbed shell pattern clear glass handle and three feet. 4 x 2.75 inches (10.0 x 7.0 cm) $80-95 (£55-65)

A small jug manufactured c.1880. The pale ruby glass body is decorated with amber glass machine threading and a trail of clear glass rigaree. The circular integral foot has a polished out pontil mark. 6.0 x 4.5 inches (15.0 x 11.5 cm) $125-140 (£85-95)

Mold blown designs finished with machine threading

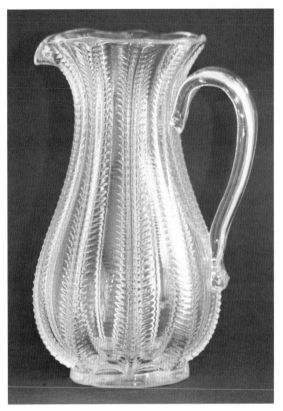

A large jug manufactured c.1876 by Hodgetts, Richardson & Son. The clear glass, machine threaded body is formed from a mold with ten, projecting ribs. The circular clear glass foot is inscribed on the underside with *1914 / 76* and *Hodgetts Patent*. 9.5 x 5.5 inches (24.0 x 14.0 cm) $180-220 (£125-150)

Side view of jug showing the ribbed handle.

A large jug manufactured c.1877 by Hodgetts, Richardson & Son. The clear glass body is decorated with two bands of applied turquoise blue machine threading, between which is a panel of engraved floral and butterfly motifs. The base has a polished out pontil mark. 9.5 x 4.75 inches (24.0 x 12.0cm) $180-220 (£125-150)

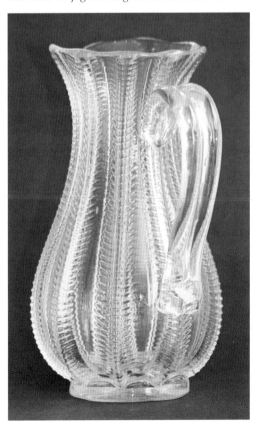

Random pattern of threading / trails

A large jug manufactured c.1885. The pale orange shading into clear glass body is formed from a mold with fourteen, rounded profile, projecting ribs, and decorated with an applied random pattern of random short lengths of clear glass canes. The base has a polished out pontil mark. 8.5 x 6.0 inches (21.5 x 15.0 cm) $180-220 (£125-150)

Stylised acanthus leaf motifs

A small jug manufactured c.1885. The clear glass body is formed from a mold with twelve shallow projecting ribs, and is supported on a circular clear glass foot with a polished out pontil mark. The body is decorated with a band of clear glass machine threading and a large applied acanthus leaf motif. 8.0 x 4.75 inches (20.5 x 12.0 cm) $180-220 (£120-150)

Side view of jug.

Horizontal and / or vertical trails of rigaree

A small jug manufactured c.1880. The pale ruby glass body is formed from a mold with twelve shallow projecting ribs, has a snapped off pontil mark. The body is supported on a clear glass trail of cross rib pattern pincered work, and is decorated with an applied trail of clear glass rigaree. 4.5 x 2.5 inches (11.5 x 6.5 cm) $110-125 (£75-85)

A large jug manufactured c.1885. The clear glass body has a polished out pontil mark and is supported on four rustic pattern stub feet. A trail of clear glass rigaree, and five pincered work clear glass leaves are applied around the rim. 5 x 4.5 inches (21.5 x 11.5 cm) $190-220 (£130-150)

Horizontal / vertical / spiral trails with short pincered projecting fins evenly spaced out along their length

A small jug manufactured c.1885. The pale ruby glass body is formed from a mold with fourteen shallow projecting ribs, and has a snapped off pontil mark, and is supported on a trail of clear glass, rib pattern pincered work. The clear glass trail around the neck is decorated with projecting, pincered work rounded profile fins. 4.25 x 2.5 inches (11.0 x 6.5 cm) $110-125 (£75-85)

Designs incorporating silver deposit patterns

Jugs with internal decoration:

Gold or silver foil inclusions in translucent / opaque glass

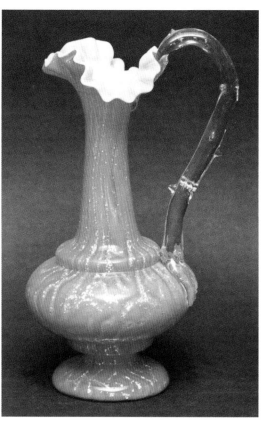

A small jug manufactured c.1850, and subsequently decorated all over with a silver deposit floral design. The body is formed in blue opaline glass, with a circular, integral foot and polished out pontil mark. 6.5 x 4.0 inches (16.5 x 10.0 cm) $220-255 (£150-175)

A small jug manufactured c.1885. The body is formed with clear glass over a pale pink glass pattern of random splashes, over silver foil fragments, over opal white glass. The integral circular foot has a snapped off pontil mark. The clear glass handle is formed in a rustic briar pattern. 8.0 x 3.75 inches (20.0 x 9.5 cm) $140-180 (£100-125)

Spiral trailing

A small jug manufactured c.1890. The amber glass body is formed from a mold with thirty-six shallow projecting rounded profile ribs. The spiral trail comprises a narrow white glass trail on each side of a wide, pale ruby glass trail, applied to the gather before being blown into the mold. 6.0 x 6.0 inches (15.0 x 15.0 cm) $190-220 (£130-150)

Air trap design - Herring bone pattern

A small jug manufactured c.1885. The rim has a multi-crimped edge and is finished with a four-way shallow crimp. The body is formed with very pale pink glass shading to pale ruby at the rim, over a herringbone air trap pattern, over opal white glass. The circular integral foot has a snapped off pontil mark. The amber glass handle is formed in a rustic briar pattern. 7.0 x 4.0 inches (18.0 x 10.0 cm) $180-220(£125-150)

Jugs decorated with surface reduction techniques:

Acid etched designs

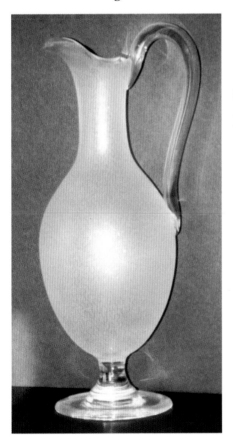

A large jug manufactured c.1855. The clear glass body is decorated all over with an acid etched vermicular pattern. 12.5 x 5.25 inches (32.0 x 13.0 cm) $180-220 (£125-150)

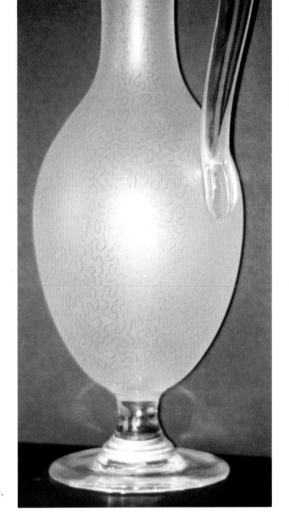

Close-up of the vermicular pattern.

A small jug manufactured c.1900, and decorated by Joseph Locke. The clear glass jug is decorated all over with an acid etched floral pattern. The base has a polished out pontil mark. The words *Locke Art* are incorporated into the floral pattern. 7.0 x 6.0 inches 18.0 x 15.0 cm) $325-360 (£225-250)

Rear view of jug.

Front view of jug.

View of etched pattern on the handle.

Geometric cut patterns on translucent glass

A small cut glass jug manufactured c.1910, and decorated with three distinctive types of cut patterns from rim to base. The base is decorated with a thirty-two point cut star pattern. 5.5 x 3.5 inches (14.0 x 9.0 cm) $95-110 (£65-75)

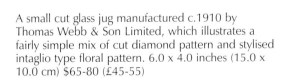

A small cut glass jug manufactured c.1910 by Thomas Webb & Son Limited, which illustrates a fairly simple mix of cut diamond pattern and stylised intaglio type floral pattern. 6.0 x 4.0 inches (15.0 x 10.0 cm) $65-80 (£45-55)

A large cut glass jug manufactured c.1910, and illustrating the technique of brilliant cutting. 11.5 x 6.0 inches (29.5 x 15.0cm) $435-500 (£300-350)

A large clear glass jug decorated with a small panel of cut diamond patterning on the neck, manufactured c.1850, and is similar to that produced   by W.H., B. & J. Richardson at that time. The circular foot is finished with a twenty-four point cut star.   8.25 x 5.0 inches (21.0 x 12.5 cm) $145-175 (£100-120)

Front view of jug.

Engraved designs

A clear glass jug manufactured c.1855, and incorporating an elongated *Greek Key* engraved pattern. The base is finished with a thirty-two point, cut star pattern. 8.25 x 4.5 inches 21.0 x 11.0 cm) $180-220 (£125-150)

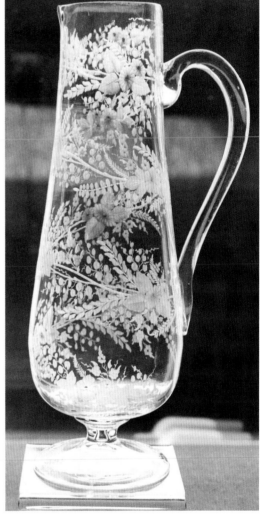

A tall clear glass jug manufactured c.1900, incorporating a vertical stylised fern engraved pattern. The circular applied foot has a polished out pontil mark. 10.75 x 4.0 inches (27.5 x 10.0cm) $180-220 (£125-140)

A tall clear glass jug manufactured c.1890, incorporating a continuous floral pattern spiral trail. The circular applied shallow domed foot is also decorated with an engraved floral trail on the top surface. 11.0 x 3.5 inches (28.0 x 9.0 cm) $180-220 (£125-140)

Right:
A tall clear glass jug manufactured c.1880, and incorporating bands of engraved stylised floral patterns and a central monogram. 13.0 x 4.25 inches (3.3 x 11.0 cm) $125-165 (£85-115)

Below, center:
Front view of jug showing engraved monogram.

Below, left:
A tall jug manufactured c.1885, and incorporating bands of *Greek Key* engraved patterns, and patterns formed with acid etching. 12.0 x 5.25 inches (30.5 x 13.0 cm) $210-255 (£145-175)

Below, right:
A tall jug manufactured c.1890, and incorporating patterns of stylised thistle trails formed with acid etching and engraving. 11.75 x 5.25 inches (30.0 x 13.0 cm) $210-255 (£145-175)

Decanters

Decanters with applied decoration:

Machine threading over a mold blown pattern in translucent glass

Right:
A decanter manufactured c.1885. The clear glass body is formed from a mold with eighteen vertical lines of staggered interlocking shallow quilted, lozenge shapes. The body is decorated with two wide bands of applied amber glass machine threading, three, horizontal trails of amber glass rigaree and eight vertical, slightly twisted amber glass trails incorporating projecting pincered work fins. The body has a snapped off pontil mark, and is supported on a circular foot formed with amber glass trellis type trailing. 11.5 x 4.75 inches (30.0 x 12.0 cm) $180-220 (£125-150)

A clear glass decanter manufactured c.1900. The body is formed from a mold with sixteen shallow projecting ribs, and finished with fine section machine threading. The base has a polished out pontil mark. The body is decorated with two trails of clear glass rigaree. 9.5 x 4.0 inches (20.4 x 10.0 cm) $175-190 (£120-130)

Decanters with internal decoration:

Pulled up festoon trails

An opaque glass decanter manufactured c.1875. The body is formed in opal white glass and decorated internally with pulled up festoon trails of pale ruby and pale blue glass. The circular integral base has a polished out pontil mark. 9.75 x 5.5 inches 25.0 x 14.0 cm) $175-220 (£120-150)

Carafes

Carafes decorated with surface reduction techniques:

Engraved designs on translucent glass

A clear glass carafe manufactured c.1890. The body is decorated all over with an engraved floral pattern. 7.5 x 3.75 inches (19.0 x 9.5 cm) $(£95-115)

Drinking glasses decorated with surface reduction techniques:

Sand blasted designs on translucent glass

A clear glass drinking glass manufactured c.1895. The bowl is decorated with three panels of a stylised floral design formed by sand blasting through a template. 5.25 x 2.75 inches (13.0 x 7.0 cm) $80-95 (£55-65)

Drinking Glasses

Drinking glasses with internal decoration:

Alexandrite designs

A small punch cup manufactured c.1900 by Thomas Webb & Sons Limited. The body is formed in *Alexandrite* glass, from a mold incorporating a quilted diamond pattern, and has an amber glass, ribbed shell pattern handle. The base has a polished out pontil mark. 2.5 x 2.75 inches (6.5 x 7.0 cm) $220-255 (£150-175)

CHAPTER FIVE
REGISTERED DESIGNS, 1850 -1914

Introduction

Between 1842 and 1883, glass manufacturers were able to register their designs at the Patents Office, in accordance with the Designs Act 1842. Glass designs came under Class Three and were protected for a period of three years.

The registration process comprised an entry in the Register, which recorded the allocated number of the design, the name and address of the owner of the design, and the quantities of items registered which was known as the bundle or parcel. It is to be noted that the owner of the design might not necessarily be the actual designer.

Illustrations of registered glass items in the form of a drawing or photograph, were recorded separately in a book called *Representations*.

The owner of the design was then issued with a registration diamond that could be applied in an appropriate manner to the body of the manufactured item(s).

The diamond shape incorporated a code confirming the day, month, and year of registration, the class code of material, and the bundle number.

If several items were registered on any one day, each item would have the same registration diamond.

Between 1842 and 1867, the class code was shown on top of the diamond, with the year letter immediately under, the month letter was on the centre left side, the day of the month on the centre right side and the bundle number at the base of the diamond.

Codes for 1842-1867

This is an example of code for 5 May (E) 1861 (R)

The year codes for this period were as follows:

A-1845
B-1858
C-1844
D-1852
E-1855
F-1847
G-1863
H-1843
I-1846
J-1854
K-1857
L-1856
M-1859
N-1864
O-1862
P-1851
Q-1866
R-1861
S-1849
T-1867
U-1848
V-1850
W-1865
X-1842
Y-1853
Z-1860

The month codes for this period were as follows:

A-December
B-October
C-January
D-September
E-May
G-February
H-April
I-July
K-November
M-June
R-August
W-March

In 1857, the mark R was used for the month code for the period September 1 to September 19.

Between 1868 and 1883, the class code was shown on top of the diamond, with the day of the month immediately beneath it, the bundle number on the centre left, the year letter on the centre right, and the month letter at the base of the diamond.

Codes for 1868-1883

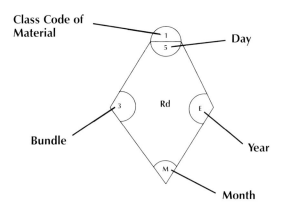

This is an example of code for 5 June (M) 1881 (E)

The year codes for this period were as follows:
A-1871
C-1870
D-1878
E-1881
F-1873
H-1869
I-1872
J-1880
K-1883
L-1882
P-1877
S-1875
U-1874
V-1876
X-1868
Y-1879

The month codes for this period were the same as for the previous period noted above. It is to be noted that for March 1 to March 6 in 1878, G was used for the month and W for the year.

The registration system was subsequently revised by The Patents, Designs and Trade Marks Act, 1883. All of the previous thirteen item classifications were replaced by a single consecutive registering system for all types of designs. In lieu of the coded diamond motif, *Rd.* and the registration number were applied to the respective item. The period of protection for designs was extended to five years.

Registered Designs recorded by British glass manufacturers

The following well-known glass manufacturers from Birmingham, Stourbridge and Manchester areas produced extensive ranges of decorative glass and recorded many Registered Designs between 1850 and 1914:

The Richardson Family Businesses
   W.H., B. & J. Richardson
   B. Richardson
   Hodgetts, Richardson & Pargeter
   Hodgetts, Richardson & Son
   Henry Gething Richardson
Stevens & Williams Limited
Stuart & Sons Limited
Thomas Webb & Sons Limited
Boulton & Mills
Burtles, Tate & Co.
John Walsh Walsh

The free-hand drawings of the Registered Designs for each of these manufacturers have been based on photo-reductions of tracings of the original illustrations in the books of Representations in the custody of the Public Records Office, Kew, London.

If required, more accurate photo-copies or photographs of the originals are available by mail order direct from the Public Records Office.

It is to be noted that descriptive text of a design is not always provided in the Register and books of Representations, which leaves the illustrations open to personal interpretation. Even without text, the illustrations still provide a useful guide to the shapes and patterns that were being produced by the respective manufacturers.

The descriptions recorded against the respective Registered Designs is the wording taken from the Registers or books of Representations. The descriptions shown within brackets are the Author's own interpretation of the illustrations where descriptive text is not provided.

The Richardson Family Businesses

Introduction

On December 25, 1829, William Haden Richardson (1785-1876) went into partnership with his brother, Benjamin Richardson (1802-1887) and Thomas Webb (1804-1869), and took over the Wordsley Flint Glassworks, creating the firm of Webb and Richardson.

In 1836 by mutual agreement, Thomas Webb left the partnership, and Jonathan Richardson joined his brothers in the business, which then became W.H.,B.,& J. Richardson. This partnership survived until 1852 when it became bankrupt. Within a year the creditors were paid off, and they had commenced trading again, this time under the name of *B.Richardson*.

In 1863 a new deed was drawn up for a partnership between William J. Hodgetts, Benjamin Richardson and Philip Pargeter, creating a business called *Hodgetts, Richardson & Pargeter*. This partnership continued until 1870, when Philip Pargeter left to take over the Red House Glassworks.

Henry Gething Richardson, (1832-1916) Benjamin's son, then entered the partnership, and the business became *Hodgetts, Richardson & Son*. In 1881, W.J. Hodgetts retired from the partnership because of ill health, and by 1882 the business was trading as *Henry Gething Richardson*.

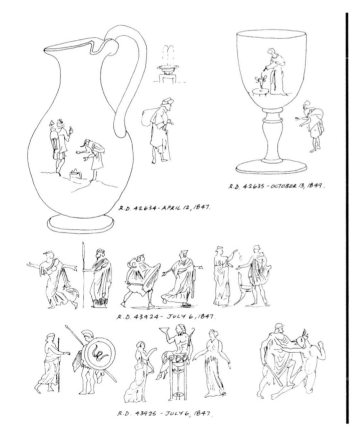

W.H., B. & J. Richardson. Registered Designs, 1836 – 1852

42634 – April 12, 1847. (Design for a water jug decorated with a transfer printed picture of two figures carrying large water containers).

42635 – April 12, 1847. (Design for a goblet decorated with a transfer printed picture of a woman pouring liquid into a large two-handled cup).

43924, 43925, 43926, 43927 – July 6, 1847. (Transfer print designs of people in various poses)

R.D. 52160 - MAY 31, 1848.

R.D. 52159 - MAY 5, 1848.

R.D. 52158 - MAY 30, 1848.

52158 – May 30, 1848. (Design for a water jug and matching goblet, decorated with an enamelled pattern of water lilies)
52159 – May 30, 1848. (Design for a large cut glass tazza)
52160 – May 30, 1848. (Design for a candle holder)

W.H., B. & J. Richardson. Registered Designs, 1836 – 1852

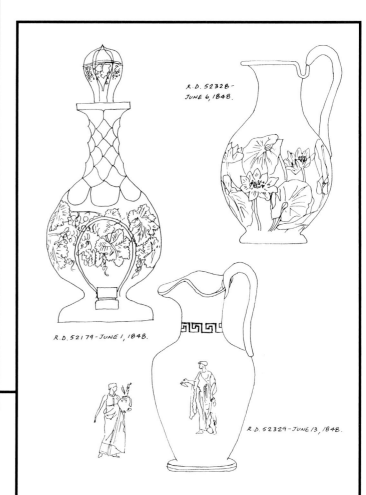

R.D. 52328 - JUNE 6, 1848.

R.D. 52179 - JUNE 1, 1848.

R.D. 52329 - JUNE 13, 1848.

52179 – June 1, 1848. (Design for a decanter incorporating a) Hollow chamber or Globe for ice
52328 – June 13, 1848. (Design for a water jug decorated with an enamelled pattern of flowering water lilies and leaves)
52329 – June 13, 1848. (Design for a jug decorated with a horizontal band of Greek key pattern, and a transfer printed figure of a woman)

R.D. 59686 - APRIL 24, 1849.

R.D. 62923 - OCTOBER 13, 1849.

PLAN OF FOOT

R.D. 75674 – JANUARY 11, 1851.

R.D. 72397 - OCTOBER 9, 1850.

R.D. 75674 - JANUARY 11, 1851.

59686 – April 24, 1849. (Design for a cut glass comport)
62923 – October 13, 1849. (Design for a cut glass tumbler)
72397 – October 9, 1850. (Design for a cut pattern on a circular dish)
75674 – January 11, 1851. (Design for a carafe with its neck decorated with a cut diamond pattern)

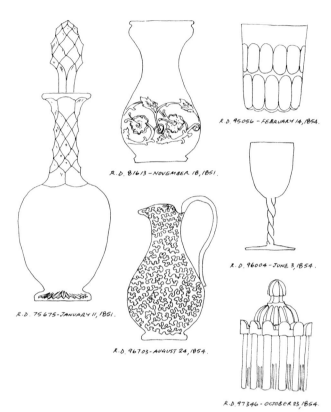

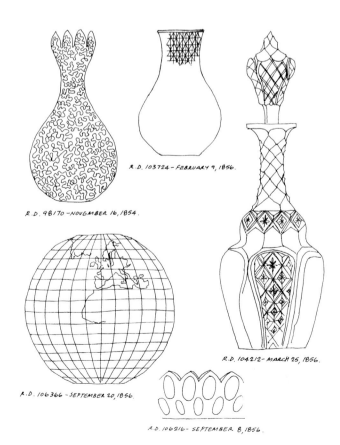

W.H., B. & J. Richardson. Registered Designs, 1836 – 1852

75675 – January 11, 1851. (Design for a decanter and stopper matching pattern to 75674 above)

81613 – November 18, 1851. (Design for a baluster shaped vasedecorated with an applied pattern of stylised flower heads and leaf trails)

Benjamin Richardson Registered Designs, 1853 – 1863

95056 - February14, 1854. (Design for a) pressed tumbler

96004 – June 3, 1854. Stems of wines

96703 – August 24, 1854. Pattern upon all kinds of table glass. (Vermicular pattern shown on a jug)

97346 – October 23, 1854. Mould blown glass for all types of table glass

Top right:

Benjamin Richardson Registered Designs, 1853 – 1863

110109 – June 9, 1857. (A small bowl formed in thick glass and decorated internally all over with a regularly spaced out bubble pattern)

111878 – November 6, 1857. (A spout of a jug and an applied twisted pattern jug handle)

114082 – June 29, 1858. For all kinds of table glass (Vertical textured pattern like a tree bark, shown applied to a tapered profile tumbler)

Hodgetts, Richardson&Pargeter Registered Designs, 1863–1870

186478 – May 3, 1865. Flower stand in flint glass

205210 – December 27, 1866. Flower stand. (Incorporates hanging baskets on rope twist pattern rods)

238052 – January 12, 1870. Ornamental design for parts of a jug and goblet

Right:

Benjamin Richardson Registered Designs, 1853 – 1863

98170 – November 16, 1854. Pattern for all kinds of glass globes, or shades or pedestals etc. (Vermicular pattern shown on a vase)

103724 – February 9, 1856. (A pattern of pyramid diamonds shown on a baluster shaped vase)

104212 – March 25, 1856. (A decanter decorated with an elaborate diamond cut pattern)

106216 – September 8, 1856. (A pattern of ovals)

106366 – September 20, 1856. (A globe with a map of the world drawn on the surface)

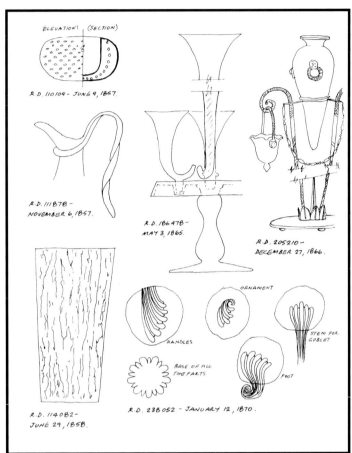

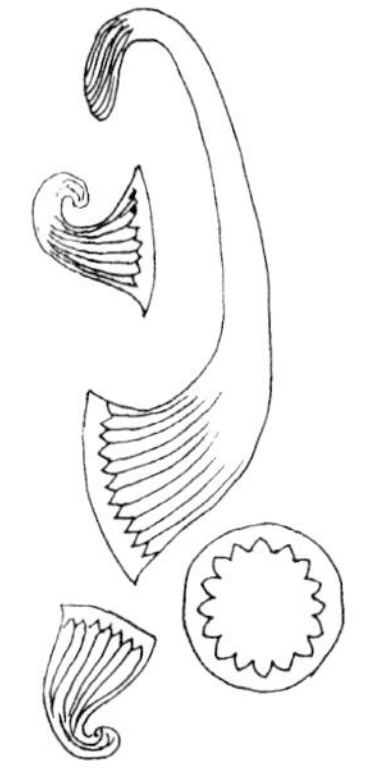

R.D. 239241- FEBRUARY 28, 1870.

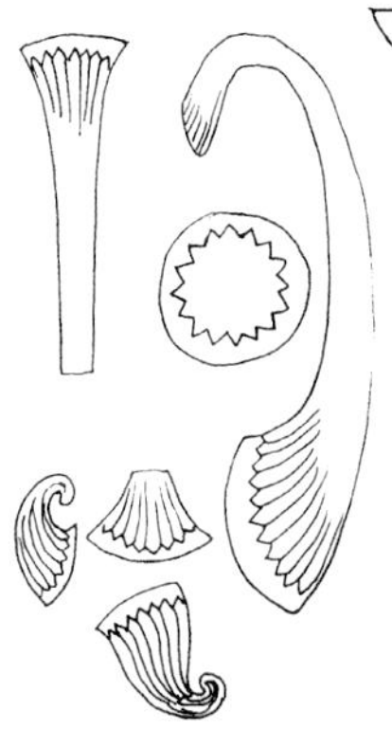

R.D. 239242- FEBRUARY 28, 1870.

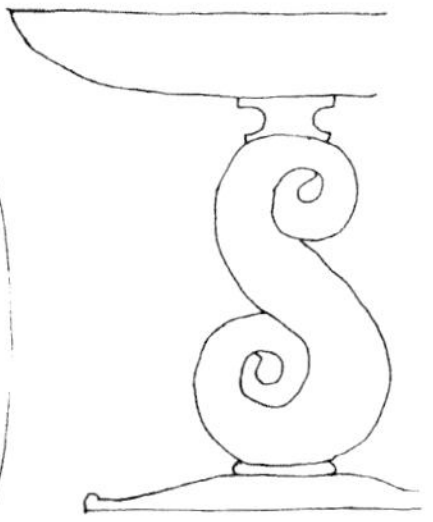

R.D. 246153- OCTOBER 22, 1870.

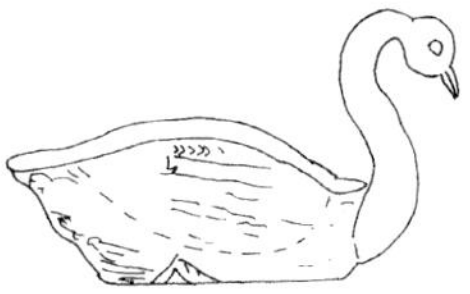

R.D. 260649 - FEBRUARY 22, 1872.

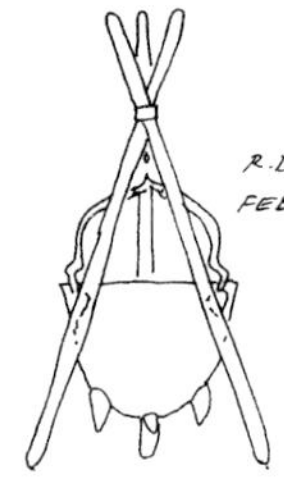

R.D. 260648- FEBRUARY 22, 1872.

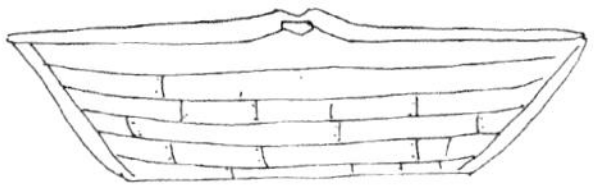

R.D. 260650 - FEBRUARY 22, 1872.

Hodgetts, Richardson&Pargeter Registered Designs, 1863–1870

239241 – February 28, 1870. Handle and ornament for parts of a ewer and bowl. All the parts hollow and indented on the inner side

239242 – February 28, 1870. Handle and ornaments for ewer and bowl

246153 – October 22, 1870. (Design for a comport comprising a shallow dish supported on a stem in the shape of a large S scroll on a circular foot)

Hodgetts, Richardson & Son. Registered Designs, 1870 – 1881

260648 – February 22, 1872. (Design for a flower holder in the form of a cauldron suspended from the top central connection of a tripod frame)

260649 – February 22, 1872. (Design for a pressed glass flower holder in the shape of a swan).

260650 – February 22, 1872. (Design for a pressed glass flower holder in the shape of a small boat)

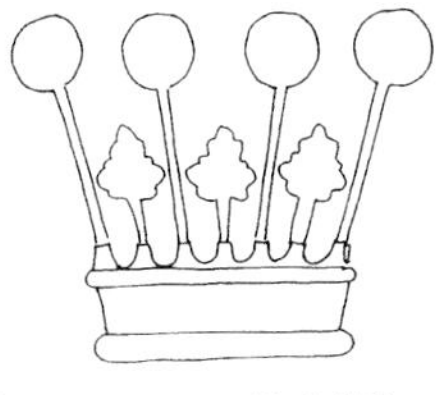

R.D. 261125 - MARCH 14, 1872.

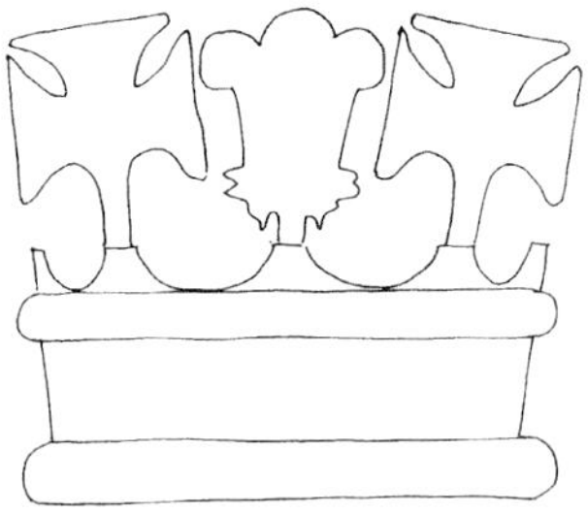

R.D. 261127 - MARCH 14, 1872.

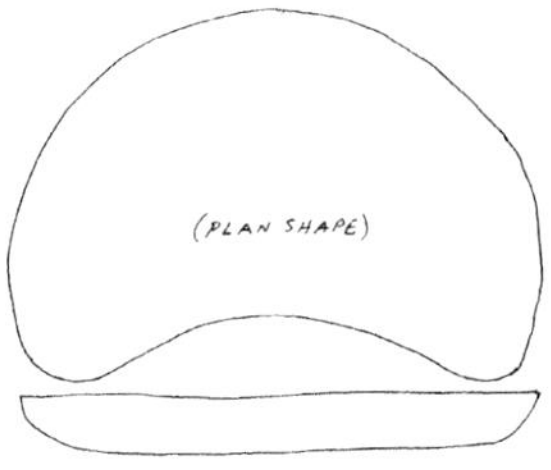

R.D. 261126 - MARCH 14, 1872.

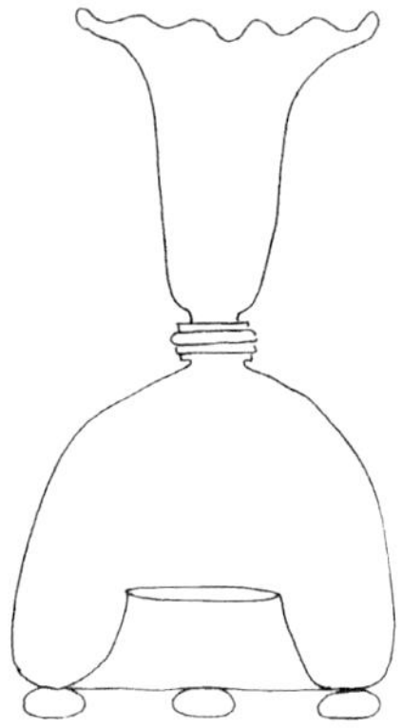

R.D. 290890 - APRIL 23, 1875.

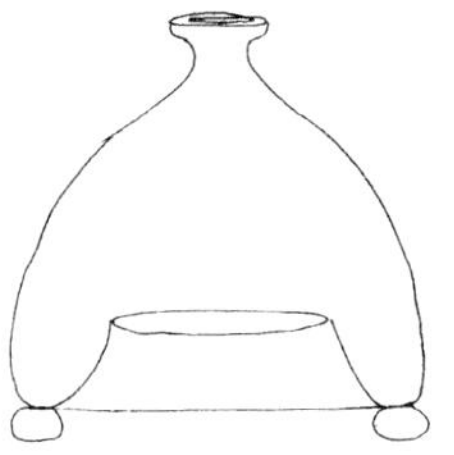

R.D. 275856 - SEPTEMBER 6, 1873.

Hodgetts, Richardson & Son. Registered Designs, 1870 – 1881

261125 – March 14, 1872. (Coronet made in glass)

261126 – March 14, 1872. (Kidney shaped shallow dish)

261127 – March 14, 1872. (Crown made in glass)

275856 – September 6, 1873. (Design for a flying insect trap)

290890 – April 23, 1875. (Design for an insect trap similar to 275856 above, but supporting a trumpet shaped flower holder, set into the narrow neck opening)

Next page:

Hodgetts, Richardson & Son. Registered Designs, 1870 – 1881

286525 – October 26, 1874. (A pair of glass hoop shaped supports with each of their ends set into a metal ferrule type section. On the crown of each hoop is set a double raspberry type prunt)

292040 – June 12, 1875. (Glass flower holder in the form of an external water pump)

292041 – June 12, 1875. Glass flower holder and fish holder

294575 – September 18, 1875. (A circular, hollow section plateau supported on three bun feet).

299158 – March 11, 1876. (Jug with slightly tapering sides, and an applied shell ribbed handle, and threading around the neck)

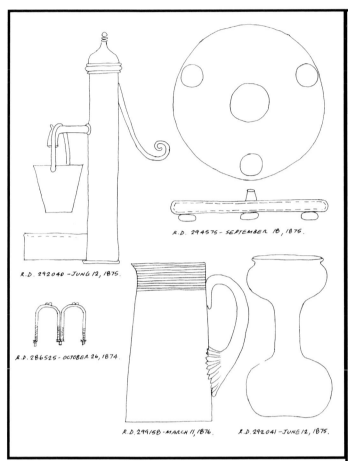

R.D. 292040 -JUNG 12, 1875.

R.D. 286525 - OCTOBER 26, 1874.

R.D. 294575 - SEPTEMBER 18, 1875.

R.D. 299158 -MARCH 11, 1876.

R.D. 292041 -JUNE 12, 1875.

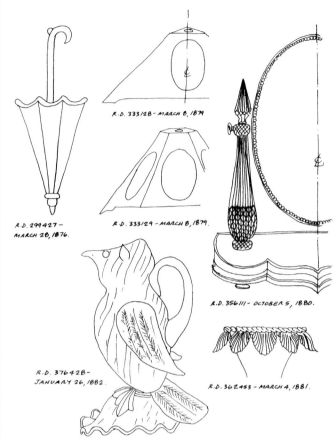

R.D. 299427 -
MARCH 28, 1876.

R.D. 333128 - MARCH 8, 1879.

R.D. 333129 - MARCH 8, 1879.

R.D. 356111 - OCTOBER 5, 1880.

R.D. 376428 -
JANUARY 26, 1882.

R.D. 362453 - MARCH 4, 1881.

Hodgetts, Richardson & Son. Registered Designs, 1870 – 1881

299427 – March 28, 1876. (A decorative flower holder in the form of an umbrella)

333128 – March 8, 1879. (Design for a three sided lamp shade)

333129 – March 8, 1879. (Design for a six sided lamp shade)

356111 – October 5, 1880. (Design for an oval, metal framed pivoting dressing table mirror)

362453 – March 4, 1881. Part of a flower vase. (Rim decorated with a trail of rigaree above a trail of ribbed, shell pattern pincered work)

376428 – January 26, 1882. A jug (In the stylised form of a bird sitting on top of an ogee profiled domed foot)

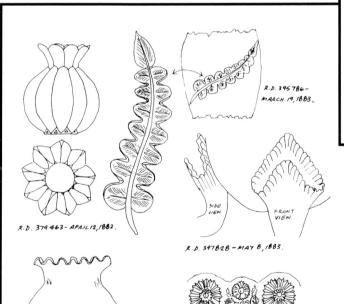

R.D. 395786 -
MARCH 19, 1883.

R.D. 379463 - APRIL 12, 1882.

R.D. 39782B - MAY 8, 1883.

SIDE VIEW

FRONT VIEW

R.D. 2959 - FEBRUARY 29, 1884.

R.D. 15256 - OCTOBER 16, 1884.

Henry Gething Richardson. Registered Designs, 1881-1916

379463 – April 12, 1882. Ornamental flower vase

395786 – March 19, 1883. (Design for a long, stylised fern leaf type trail to be applied around a vase)

397828 – May 8, 1883. Design for glass ornamentation

2959 – February 29, 1884. New design for glass globe to be used with comet fitting

15256 – October 16, 1884. Ornamental design for glass decoration

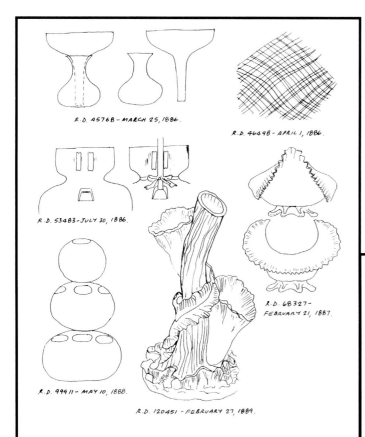

Henry Gething Richardson. Registered Designs, 1881-1916

45768 – March 25, 1886. Shape of improved "Ice drainer"

46498 – April 1, 1886. Combination of threads of glass of different shades of colour, arranged as to form a plaid, to be used in glass decoration

53483 – July 30, 1886. Design for a Hyacinth glass made with two projections on the upper or cup part, and having an indentation on the upper part of the body to carry and keep in position, a stick or other support to the plant

68327 – February 21, 1887. Shape of a flower or lamp bowl with sides turned down or lapped over, showing from side view a crescent shape.

99911 – May 10, 1888. Design for a shape of a glass flower holder formed by a configuration of separate globes with holes cut in each to hold flowers but in which there is no communication from the upper to the lower globe

120451 – February 27, 1889. Design for shape of glass flower holder.

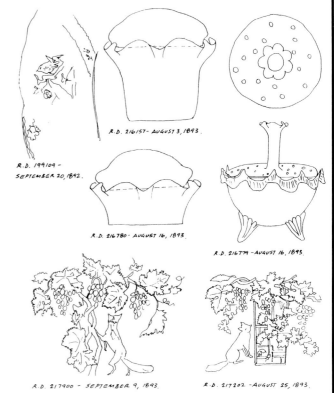

Henry Gething Richardson. Registered Designs, 1881-1916

199109 – September 20, 1892. (Ornate decorative pattern incorporating floral and bird motifs)

216157 – August 3, 1893. The red outline showing the shape of smoke consumer to be registered. (Descriptive note on the drawing)

216779 – August 16, 1893. The red outline showing the shape of the perforated flower with tube in centre to be registered. The black outline flower bowl is only to show the use of the registered perforated flower holder with tube. (Notes on the drawing)

216780 – August 16, 1893. The red outline showing the shape of smoke consumer to be registered. (Descriptive note on the drawing)

217202 – August 25, 1893. (Design for decoration) (Design for a pattern incorporating grapes and vines on a trellis frame, and with a fox shown looking up at them)

217900 – September 9, 1893. Design for the decoration of glassware (Pattern of a fox leaning up against a large vine stem attempting to get at the bunches of grapes)

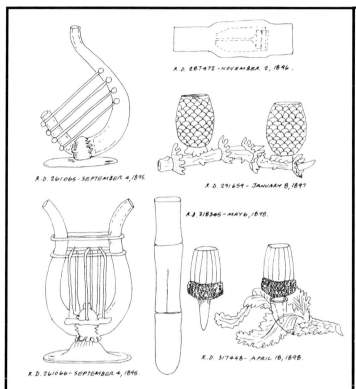

R.D. 287472 - NOVEMBER 2, 1896.

R.D. 261065 - SEPTEMBER 4, 1895.

R.D. 291659 - JANUARY 8, 1897.

R.D. 318345 - MAY 6, 1898.

R.D. 261066 - SEPTEMBER 4, 1895.

R.D. 317448 - APRIL 18, 1898.

Henry Gething Richardson. Registered Designs, 1881-1916

261065 – September 4, 1895. (Design for a tubular flower holder in the shape of a stylised harp)

261066 – September 4, 1895. (Design for a flower holder in the stylised form of a lyre)

287472 – November 2, 1896. (The illustration shows an unspecified device set into the middle of a cylindrical oil lamp funnel)

291659 – January 8, 1897. (Design for a series of flower holders in the form of fir cones)

317448 – April 18, 1898. Registered flower holder with stand, as used in combination

318345 – May 6, 1898. Bamboo Cane flower holder as registered

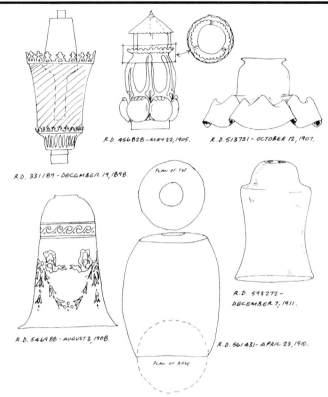

R.D. 45682B - MAY 22, 1905.

R.D. 513721 - OCTOBER 12, 1907.

R.D. 331189 - DECEMBER 19, 1898.

PLAN OF TOP

R.D. 593272 - DECEMBER 7, 1911.

R.D. 54698B - AUGUST 3, 1908.

PLAN OF BASE

R.D. 561431 - APRIL 23, 1910.

Henry Gething Richardson. Registered Designs, 1881-1916

331189 – December 19, 1898. (A decorative perforated vertical frill, drawn in a red line, around the top of a lamp shade)

456828 – May 22, 1905. (Design for a crimped rim around the top of a lamp shade)

513721 - October 12, 1907. (Design for a lamp shade with a deep projecting frill crimped rim)

546988 – August 3, 1908. (Design for a bell shaped lamp shade decorated with a pattern of ribbon bows and swag trails of small flower heads)

561431 – April 23, 1910. Glass shade gas or electric

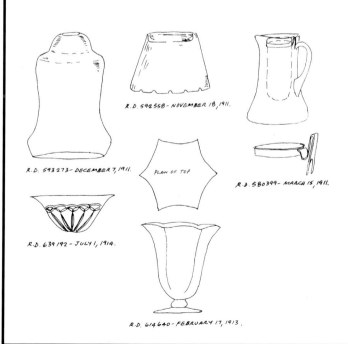

R.D. 592558 - NOVEMBER 18, 1911.

R.D. 593273 - DECEMBER 7, 1911.

PLAN OF TOP

R.D. 580399 - MARCH 15, 1911.

R.D. 639192 - JULY 1, 1914.

R.D. 614640 - FEBRUARY 17, 1913.

Henry Gething Richardson. Registered Designs, 1881-1916

580399 – March 15, 1911. An ice container to be suspended inside a jug.

592558 – November 18, 1911. Elevation view with upper part shown in vertical section, candle shade - to fit a brass carrier

593272 – December 7, 1911. The novelty claimed is for shades shape as shown made of glass for use with electric light

593273 – December 7, 1911. (All as for 593272)

614640 – February 17, 1913. Shape of top.(Rim of a vase in the form of six, shallow equal length convex sides).

639192 – July 1, 1914. The article is circular in plan. The novelty is the configuration and pattern as shown.

Stevens & Williams Limited

Introduction.

The Moor Lane Glass House was founded at Briar Lea Hill in about 1776, by Robert Honeybourne, a landowner who also owned two glass houses. Members of his family ran the works until 1821, when a lease was granted for fourteen years, to Joseph Silvers and Joseph Stevens of Silvers, Mills and Stevens. This lease was extended until 1847, when William Stevens and Samuel Cox Williams took over. In 1870 they moved to a new works built on an adjacent site.

In 1881, Frederick C. Carder (1863-1963) joined Stevens & Williams Limited as designer in charge of shapes and applied decoration.

In 1882, John Northwood (1836-1902) joined Stevens & Williams Limited as their Art Director. When he died in 1902, his son, John Northwood II (1870 - 1960), took over as Art Director. Frederick Carder who expected to succeed John Northwood, subsequently went to America and founded Steuben Glass Works with Thomas G. Hawkes.

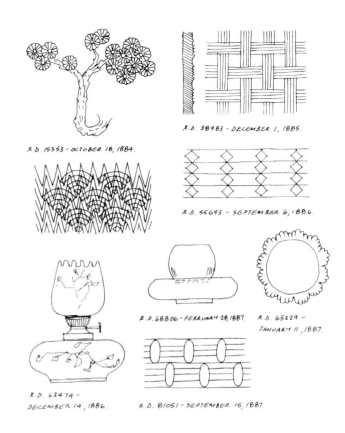

R.D. 15353 - OCTOBER 18, 1884.

R.D. 38983 - DECEMBER 1, 1885.

R.D. 55693 - SEPTEMBER 6, 1886.

R.D. 68806 - FEBRUARY 28, 1887.

R.D. 65229 - JANUARY 11, 1887.

R.D. 63474 - DECEMBER 14, 1886.

R.D. 81051 - SEPTEMBER 15, 1887.

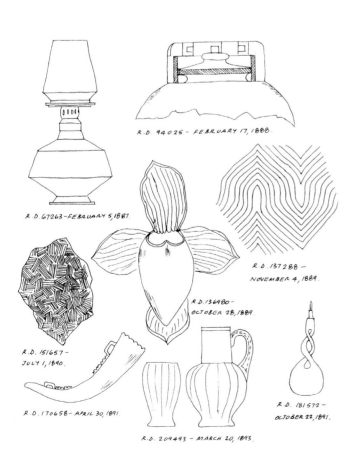

R.D. 94025 - FEBRUARY 17, 1888.

R.D. 67263 - FEBRUARY 5, 1887.

R.D. 137288 - NOVEMBER 4, 1889.

R.D. 136980 - OCTOBER 28, 1889.

R.D. 151657 - JULY 1, 1890.

R.D. 170658 - APRIL 30, 1891.

R.D. 181572 - OCTOBER 22, 1891.

R.D. 209493 - MARCH 20, 1893.

Stevens & Williams Limited Registered Designs, 1870 – 1914

15353 – October 18, 1884. Design for glass ornament to be used for decorating bowls, vases, etc. (This pattern was given the name of *Mat-Su-No-Ke*)

38983 – December 1, 1885. Pattern for the ornamentation of flint glass table ware. (A square basket weave pattern cut with a multi-mitre intaglio wheel)

55693 – September 6, 1886. Pattern for the ornamentation of glassware. (This pattern was given the name *Jewel*)

61357 – November 15, 1886. Pattern for the ornamentation of glass

63474 – December 14, 1886. Design for cameo glass lamp

65229 – January 11, 1887. Decoration of ornamental glass in colours and relief. (A large circular frame motif)

Stevens & Williams Limited Registered Designs, 1870 – 1914

67263 – February 5, 1887. Design in glass lamp

68806 – February 28, 1887. Shape in glass for table ornament

81051 – September 15, 1887. Pattern of ornamental glass

94025 – February 17, 1888. (The illustration shows a section / elevation through a lid on a jar)

136980 – October 28, 1889. (Design for a flower pocket for wall mounting, in the stylised shape of a flower, possibly an orchid)

137288 – November 4, 1889. (Decorative pattern of interlocking ogee shaped arching. (This is one of the patterns used for *Moresque* designs)

151657 – July 1, 1890. (Random straw weave decorative pattern)

170658 – April 30, 1891. (Flower holder in the shape of a hunting horn with two applied loops on the top surface, for attaching a ribbon)

181572 – October 22, 1891. (Decanter)

209493 – March 20, 1893. (Design for a jug and tumbler)

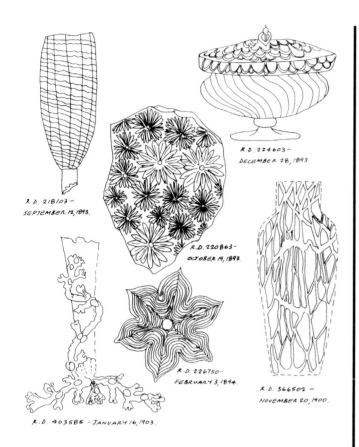

R.D. 218103 –
SEPTEMBER 12, 1893.

R.D. 220863 –
OCTOBER 19, 1893.

R.D. 224603 –
DECEMBER 28, 1893.

R.D. 226750 –
FEBRUARY 3, 1894.

R.D. 366502 –
NOVEMBER 20, 1900.

R.D. 403585 – JANUARY 16, 1903.

Stevens & Williams Limited Registered Designs, 1870 – 1914

218103 – September 12, 1893. (Flower holder)
220863 – October 19, 1893. (Pattern of closely spaced, stylised daisy type flower heads of three different sizes)
224603 – December 28, 1893. (Bowl with a grille type cover)
226750 – February 3, 1894. (Pattern, possibly for rim of vase)
366502 – November 20, 1900. (Applied pattern for decorating flower holders. This design was called *Fibrilose*)
403585 – January 16, 1903. (Design for trailing applied to a flower holder)

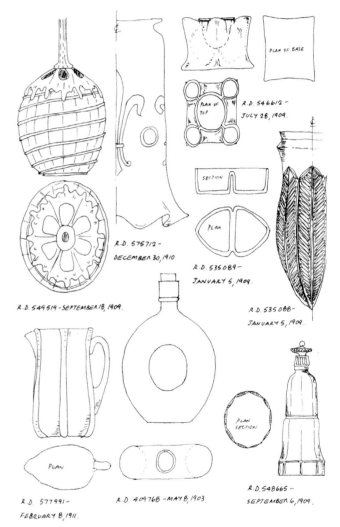

R.D. 549519 - SEPTEMBER 18, 1909.

R.D. 546612 –
JULY 28, 1909.

R.D. 575712 –
DECEMBER 30, 1910

R.D. 535089 –
JANUARY 5, 1909.

R.D. 535088 –
JANUARY 5, 1909.

R.D. 577991 –
FEBRUARY 8, 1911.

R.D. 409768 – MAY 8, 1903.

R.D. 548665 –
SEPTEMBER 6, 1909.

Stevens & Williams Limited Registered Designs, 1870 – 1914

409768 – May 08, 1903. (Decanter in the stylised shape of a lifebuoy)
535088 – January 5, 1909. (Lamp shade)
535089 – January 5, 1909. (Design for a two compartment dish)
546612 – July 28, 1909. (Shallow height combined flower holder /candle holder)
548665 – September 6, 1909. (Decorative bottle)
549519 – September 18, 1909. The novelty is a glass, earthenware or porcelain bowl of spherical form having six separated apertures at the top and a continuous coil over a surface of vertical lines, the whole surmounted by a vertical rod.
575712 – December 30, 1910. The novelty claimed is this design in a raised moulded effect on the surface of glass electric and incandescent gas shade.
577991 – February 8, 1911. The novelty claimed is a glass water jug of oval shape having 6 raised ribs or pillars as indicated.

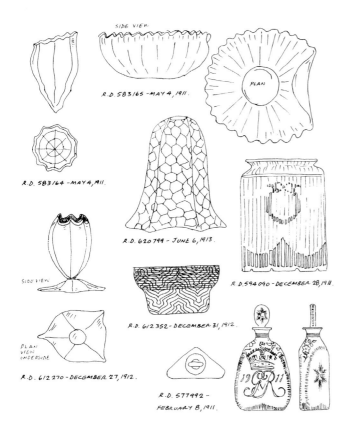

Stevens & Williams Limited Registered Designs, 1870 – 1914

577992 – February 8, 1911. The novelty claimed is a glass triangular formed bottle having a stopper, with incised decoration as indicated. No claim is made to the exclusive use of the crown device or of the letters and numerals appearing in the design.

583164 – May 4, 1911. The novelty is the shell form applied to a preserve dish or flower vase, having an irregular top edge and indentations round the body.

583165 – May 4, 1911. The novelty is the shell form applied to a dish or bowl, having a corrugated edge, and turn over back.

594090 – December 28, 1911. The novelty claimed in this design is a corrugated moulded effect on the surface with enamelled ornament applied for electric and incandescent gas shades.

612270 – December 27, 1912. The novelty claimed in the glass vase is the shaped or configuration of the leaf shaped foot or base, having ribs imitating the veins of the leaf, as shown on the representation.

612352 – December 31, 1912. The novelty claimed is the pattern as shown on representation. (This is one of the *Moresque* patterns used)

620799 – June 6, 1913. The novelty is the moulded pattern of hammered effect panels with ribs between as shown.

Stuart & Sons Limited

Introduction

In 1856, Frederick Stuart (1816 - 1900) entered into a partnership under the name of Messrs. Mills, Webb, and Stuart, at the Albert Glassworks, Wordsley. The business developed and it eventually became known as Stuart and Mills.

In 1881, Frederick Stuart acquired the lease of the Red House Glassworks from Philip Pargeter, and commenced trading on his own. This lease was then taken over by the formation of Stuart and Sons in 1885. The original partners were Frederick Stuart (Chairman), and his sons, William Henry, Frederick, and Robert.

There were four other sons: Samuel, who was later to join the Board, and Arthur, George, and Walter, who carried on the established wholesale and retail glass and china business of Stoniers, in Liverpool, which had been acquired from John Stonier in 1876.

In 1899 a cutting shop was acquired in George Street, Wordsley, and this was followed by the acquisition of a Glassworks in Brewery Street. In 1911, the business became a Limited Company and later in 1915 expanded further with the acquisition of the adjacent White House Glassworks.

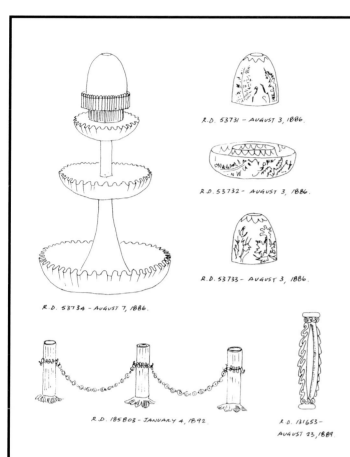

R.D. 53731 – AUGUST 3, 1886.

R.D. 53732 – AUGUST 3, 1886.

R.D. 53733 – AUGUST 3, 1886.

R.D. 53734 – AUGUST 7, 1886.

R.D. 185803 – JANUARY 4, 1892.

R.D. 131653 –
AUGUST 23, 1889.

Stuart & Sons Limited Registered Designs: 1881-1914

53731 – August 3, 1886. Pattern of a fairy lamp shade
53732 – August 3, 1886. Pattern of a flower bowl for use with fairy lamps
53733 – August 7, 1886. Pattern of a fairy lamp shade
53734 – August 7, 1886. Pattern of flower stand with fairy light on top
131653 – August 23, 1889. For the shape of configuration only, design of neck for flower stand manufactured entirely of glass by Messrs Stuart & Sons glass manufacturers, Stourbridge
185803 – January 4, 1892. (Tubular flower holders linked together with chains)

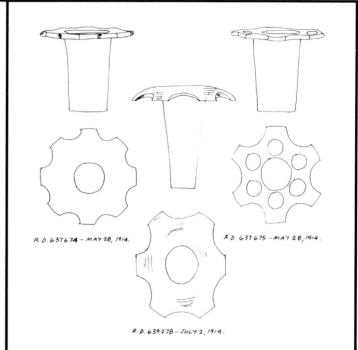

R.D. 637674 – MAY 28, 1914.

R.D. 637675 – MAY 28, 1914.

R.D. 639278 – JULY 2, 1914.

Stuart & Sons Limited Registered Designs: 1881-1914

637674 – May 28, 1914. (Design for a flower support device)
637675 – May 28, 1914. (Design for a flower support device)
639278 – July 2, 1914. (Design for a flower support device)

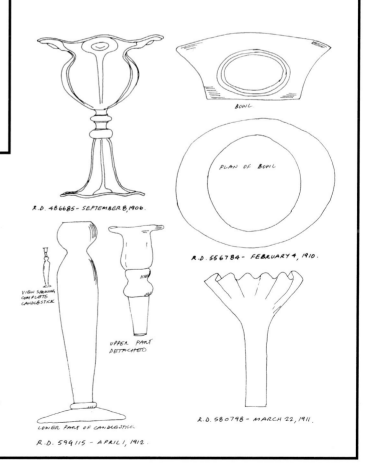

R.D. 486685 – SEPTEMBER 8, 1906.

BOWL

PLAN OF BOWL

R.D. 556784 – FEBRUARY 4, 1910.

VIEW SHOWING COMPLETE CANDLESTICK

UPPER PART DETACHED

LOWER PART OF CANDLESTICK

R.D. 599115 – APRIL 1, 1912.

R.D. 580798 – MARCH 22, 1911.

Stuart & Sons Limited Registered Designs: 1881-1914

486685 – September 8, 1906. Glass bowl to hold flowers
556784 – February 4, 1910. The novelty consists in the shape and cut oval – the body and top of the bowl being oval and the base round,- with an oval cut on each side.
580798 – March 22, 1911. The article is a glass support for use inside glass bowls or other flower holders. The novelty consists of the straight tube open at the end in conjunction with the flanged and crimped top. The crimped edge when placed inside the flower holder, leaves a distinct space at each bend of the crimp into which the stalks of flowers can be inserted.
599115 – April 1, 1912. (Combined flower holder and candlestick)

Thomas Webb & Sons Limited

Introduction

Thomas Webb (1804 - 1869), the son of John Webb, a Stourbridge farmer and butcher, went into partnership on December 25, 1829 with William Haden Richardson and Benjamin Richardson at Wordsley Flint Glass Works, where they traded as Webb & Richardson.

In 1833, John Webb went into partnership with John Shepherd at the White House Glass Works, where they traded as Shepherd & Webb. However, in 1835 John Webb died, and his share was passed to his son Thomas Webb.

In 1836, John Shepherd retired and Thomas Webb bought out his share of the business. By mutual agreement with the Richardson Brothers, Thomas Webb withdrew from their partnership in that year. Soon after this time Thomas Webb decided to build a new works adjoining Platts House, in Amblecote.

Shortly after 1851, Thomas Webb decided to move from The Platts, and by 1855 he had moved into a new works built at the rear of Dennis Hall in Dennis Park, Amblecote.

Thomas Webb had five surviving sons: Charles Webb (1835-1908), Thomas Wilkes Webb (1836 –1891), Walter Wilkes Webb (1843-1919), Henry Arthur Webb (1842-1935), and Joseph William Webb (1848-1922).

By 1860, Charles Webb and Thomas Wilkes Webb had become partners in the business, and took charge when Thomas Webb retired in 1863. In 1869, Walter Wilkes Webb joined the business. In 1886 the business became a public company, Thomas Wilkes and Charles became Managing Directors, with Clement F. Wedgwood also on the Board. Walter Wilkes however retired from the business.

Thomas Wilkes Webb died in 1891, and Charles Webb continued until his retirement in 1900. Congreve William Jackson then became the new Managing Director, a post he held for the next twenty years.

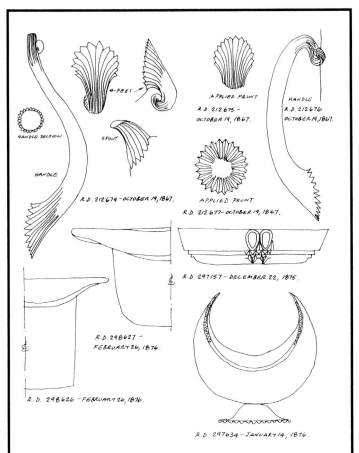

Thomas Webb & Sons Limited Registered Designs, 1860 – 1914

212674 – October 19, 1867. (Designs for a handle, pouring spout, and feet)

212675 – October 19, 1867. (Design for an applied shell shaped prunt matching the designs in 212674 above)

212676 – October 19, 1867. (The illustration shows a variation of the connection of a handle to the top of a jug that is shown in 221674 above)

212677 – October 19, 1867. (Design for an applied circular prunt, matching the designs in 212674 above)

296641 – December 6, 1875. There is no illustration for this registration in the book of Representations, and no description recorded in the Register.

297157 – December 22, 1875. Glass dish

297634 – January 14, 1876. (Design for a crescent shaped flower holder)

298626 – February 26, 1876. (Design for a flower holder in the shape of a top hat)

298627 – February 26, 1876. (Design for a flower holder in the shape of a bowler hat)

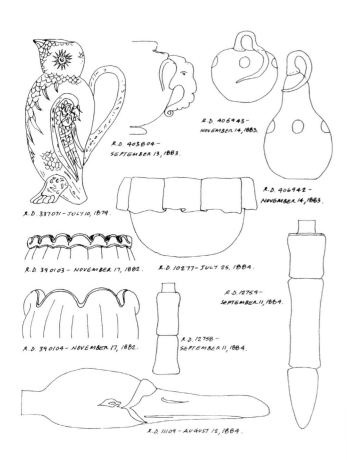

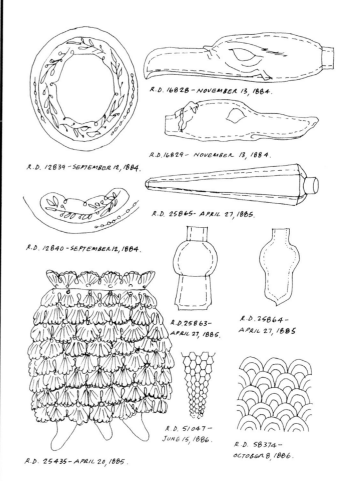

ThomThomas Webb & Sons Limited Registered Designs, 1860 – 1914

337071 – July 10, 1879. "Cock" jug

390103 – November 17, 1882. (Multi-crimped design for a rim of a vase)

390104 – November 17, 1882. (Multi-crimped design for a rim of a vase)

403804 – September 13, 1883. (Design for a vase handle in the form of a stylised head of an elephant)

406942 – November 14, 1883. (Design for a paperweight in the shape of an apple with a stalk trail)

406943 – November 14, 1883. (Design for a paperweight in the shape of a pear with a stalk trail)

10277 – July 25, 1884. Shape of valance edge glass

11109 – August 12, 1884. Scent bottle

12758 – September 11, 1884. Shape of bottle

12759 – September 11, 1884. Shape of bottle

Thomas Webb & Sons Limited Registered Designs, 1860 – 1914

12839 – September 12, 1884. Shape and decoration

12840 – September 12, 1884. Shape and decoration

16828 – November 13, 1884. Shape of scent bottle

16829 – November 13, 1884. Shape of bottle

25435 – April 20, 1885. Pattern of decoration

25863 – April 27, 1885. Shape of bottle

25864 – April 27, 1885. Shape of bottle

25865 – April 27, 1885. Shape of bottle

51047 – June 15, 1886. Pattern – hexagonal configuration with raised and sunk surfaces

58374 – October 8, 1886. Diaper of semi-circular lines forming a decorative pattern

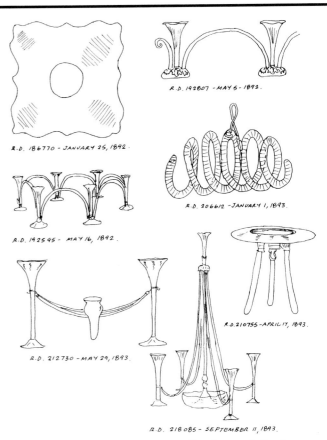

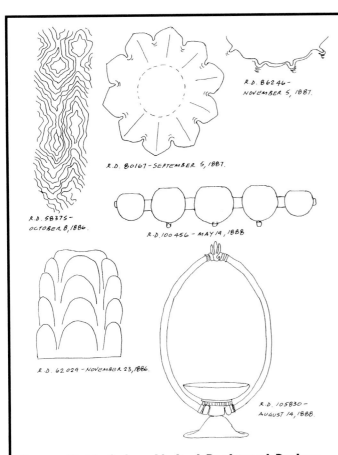

Thomas Webb & Sons Limited Registered Designs, 1860 – 1914

58375 –October 10, 1886. Diaper of irregular lines forming a watery or wavy pattern on the surface of the glass.
62029 – November 23, 1886. For the form cylindrical, tapering having six rows of arched corrugations
80167 – September 5, 1887. Shape for particular form of edge.
86246 – November 5, 1887. Shape – a particular form of edging.
100456 – May 19, 1888. (Design for a flower holder)
105830 – August 14, 1888. (Design for a tazza with an oval shaped handle)

Thomas Webb & Sons Limited Registered Designs, 1860 – 1914

186770 – January 25, 1892. (Design for a rim profile to be applied to a dish or bowl)
192807 – May 20, 1892. (Design for a set of flower holders)
206612 – January 27, 1893. (Design for a toast rack)
210755 – April 17, 1893. (Design for a raised shallow dish in the stylised form of a stool with three legs)
212730 – May 29, 1893. (Design for a centre flower stand)
218085 – September 11, 1893. Design for a centre flower stand)

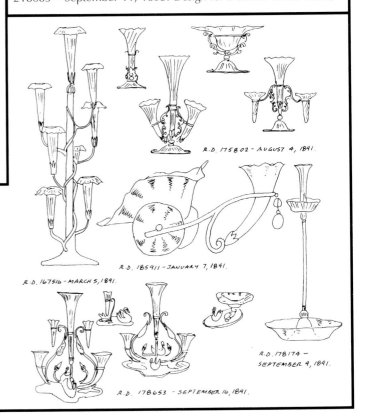

Thomas Webb & Sons Limited Registered Designs, 1860 – 1914

167516 – March 5, 1891. (Design for a centre flower holder)
175802 – August 4, 1891. (Designs for flower holders)
178174 – September 9, 1891. (Design for a centre flower stand)
178653 – September 16, 1891. (Designs for centre flower stands)
185911 – January 7, 1892. (Design for a flower holder)

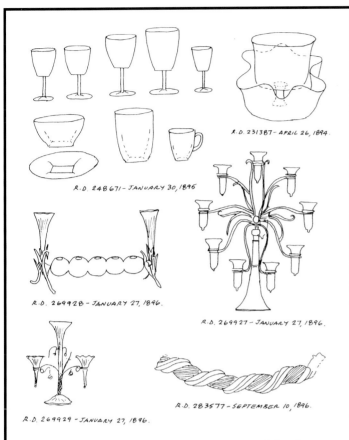

R.D. 231387 – APRIL 26, 1894.

R.D. 248671 – JANUARY 30, 1895.

R.D. 269928 – JANUARY 27, 1896.

R.D. 269927 – JANUARY 27, 1896.

R.D. 269929 – JANUARY 27, 1896.

R.D. 283577 – SEPTEMBER 10, 1896.

Thomas Webb & Sons Limited Registered Designs, 1860 – 1914

231387 – April 26, 1894. (Design for a flower holder)
248671 – January 30, 1895. (Suite of mold formed drinking glasses, cups and finger bowls and plates)
269927 – January 27, 1896. (Design for a centre flower stand)
269928 – January 27, 1896. (Design for a centre flower stand)
269929 – January 27, 1896. (Design for a variety of centre flower holders)
283577 – September 10, 1896. (Design for a rope twist type pattern for handles)

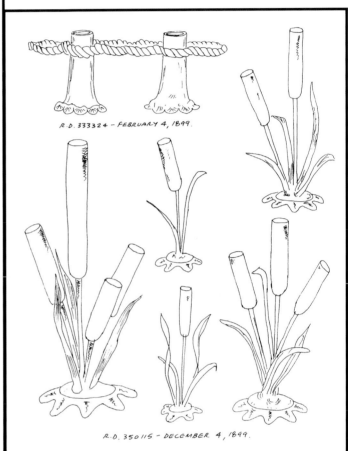

R.D. 333324 – FEBRUARY 4, 1899.

R.D. 350115 – DECEMBER 4, 1899.

Thomas Webb & Sons Limited Registered Designs, 1860 – 1914

333324 – February 4, 1899. (Design for a flower holder)
350115 – December 4, 1899. (Designs for flower holders)

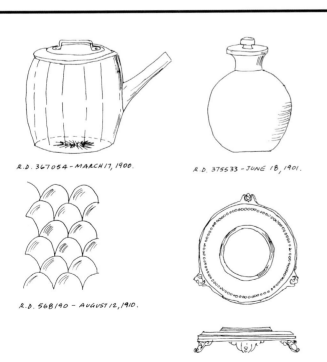

R.D. 367054 – MARCH 17, 1900.

R.D. 375533 – JUNE 18, 1901.

R.D. 568190 – AUGUST 12, 1910.

R.D. 574013 – NOVEMBER 11, 1910.

Thomas Webb & Sons Limited Registered Designs, 1860 – 1914

367054 – December 3, 1900. (Design for a covered pot)
375533 – June 18, 1901. (Design for a scent bottle)
403028 – January 5, 1903. Pattern on plate glass
568190 – August 12, 1910. (Pattern)
574013 – November 11, 1910. (Design for a mirror plateau to be set into a metal base)

Boulton & Mills

Introduction

The Audnam Glass Works at Stourbridge, changed hands many times before eventually becoming Boulton & Mills, when it was rebuilt and reorganised.

It is very difficult to attribute decorative designs to this company as only one pattern book and one trade catalogue, illustrating engraved and etched jugs, goblets, dishes, flower stands and vases are currently known to have survived. However, the Registered Designs that they recorded up to 1914 do give some indication of the range of decorative glass that they produced.

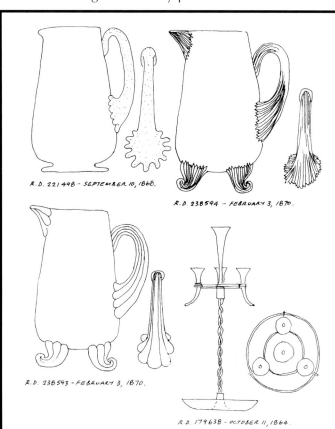

R.D. 221498 – SEPTEMBER 10, 1868.

R.D. 238594 – FEBRUARY 3, 1870.

R.D. 238593 – FEBRUARY 3, 1870.

R.D. 179638 – OCTOBER 11, 1864.

Boulton & Mills Registered Designs, 1868 – 1914

179638 – October 11, 1864. (Design for a centre flower stand)
221498 – September 10, 1868. (Design for a jug handle)
238593 – February 2, 1870. (Design for a jug handle, pouring spout, and feet)
238594 – February 2, 1870. (Design for a jug handle, pouring spout, and feet)

Boulton & Mills Registered Designs, 1868 – 1914

249882 – January 25, 1871. Glass flower stand on a silvered glass plateau.
249969 – January 28, 1871. Plateau of silvered glass with etched ornamentation with plated or gilt frame
250678 – March 4, 1871. Plateau of silvered plate glass with cut or engraved ornamentation, plated or gilt rims
250835 – March 8, 1871. Straight and curved plateau of silvered glass and plated or gilt rims

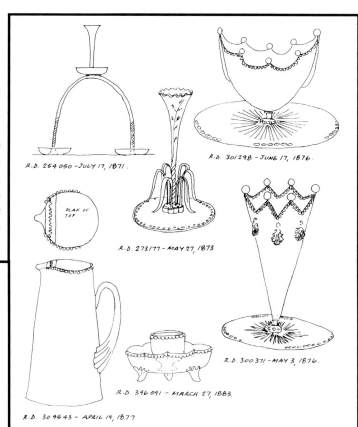

R.D. 254050 – JULY 17, 1871.

R.D. 30129B – JUNE 17, 1876.

PLAN OF TOP

R.D. 273177 – MAY 27, 1873

R.D. 300371 – MAY 3, 1876.

R.D. 396091 – MARCH 27, 1883.

R.D. 309543 – APRIL 19, 1877

Boulton & Mills Registered Designs, 1868 – 1914

254050 – July 17, 1871. Design for a centre flower stand
273177 – May 27, 1873. (Design for a centre flower stand)
300371 – May 3, 1876. Ornamental edge for articles comprised in Class 3.
301298 – June 17, 1876. Design for edge for articles comprised in Class 3.
309543 – April 19, 1877. A jug. (With a device across the rim to prevent pieces of ice from escaping when being poured)
396091 – March 27, 1883. Bowl for flowers with an inner cup for ferns attached to bowl.

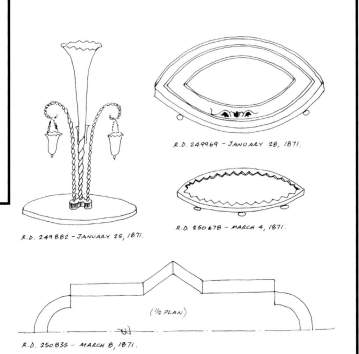

R.D. 249969 – JANUARY 28, 1871.

R.D. 250678 – MARCH 4, 1871.

R.D. 249882 – JANUARY 25, 1871.

(½ PLAN)

R.D. 250835 – MARCH 8, 1871.

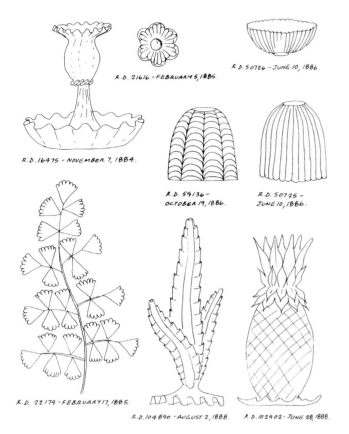

R.D. 21616 - FEBRUARY 5, 1885.

R.D. 50726 - JUNE 10, 1886.

R.D. 16475 - NOVEMBER 7, 1884.

R.D. 59136 - OCTOBER 19, 1886.

R.D. 50725 - JUNE 10, 1886.

R.D. 22179 - FEBRUARY 17, 1885.

R.D. 104890 - AUGUST 2, 1888.

R.D. 102902 - JUNE 28, 1888.

Boulton & Mills Registered Designs, 1868 – 1914

16475 – November 7, 1884. Design for a glass candlestick and flower holder combined

21616 – February 5, 1885. Design for decoration of glass

22179 – February 2, 1885. Registered Design for decoration of glass.

50725 – June 10, 1886. Glass candle shade

50726 – June 10, 1886. Candle pan in glass

59136 – October 19, 1886. Candle shade

102902 – June 28, 1888. Ornamental vase

104890 – August 2, 1888. Ornamental vase

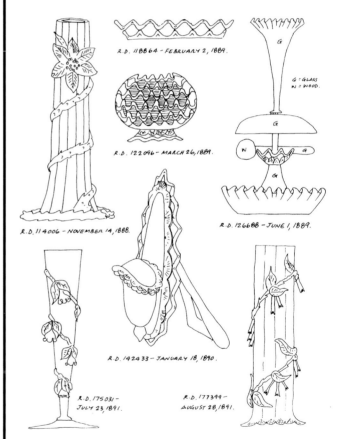

R.D. 118864 - FEBRUARY 2, 1889.

R.D. 122096 - MARCH 26, 1889.

G = GLASS
W = WOOD.

R.D. 126688 - JUNE 1, 1889.

R.D. 114006 - NOVEMBER 14, 1888.

R.D. 142433 - JANUARY 18, 1890.

R.D. 175031 - JULY 23, 1891.

R.D. 177399 - AUGUST 28, 1891.

Boulton & Mills Registered Designs, 1868 – 1914

114006 – November 14, 1888. (Vase)

118864 – February 2, 1889. (Design for a decorative trellis style rim)

122096 – March 26, 1889. (Design for a small bowl, toothpick holder or candle holder)

126688 – June 1, 1889. Design for a combined bell and flower stand)

142433 – January 18, 1890. Ornamental design for vase in glass.

175031 – July 23, 1891. Design for an ornamental flower holder in glass with raised decoration

177399 – August 28, 1891. (Design for a flower holder)

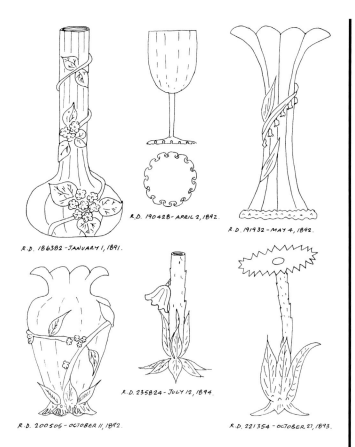

R.D. 186382 - JANUARY 1, 1891.

R.D. 190428 - APRIL 2, 1892.

R.D. 191932 - MAY 4, 1892.

R.D. 235824 - JULY 12, 1894.

R.D. 200505 - OCTOBER 11, 1892.

R.D. 221354 - OCTOBER 27, 1893.

Boulton & Mills Registered Designs, 1868 – 1914
186382 – January 15, 1892. (Design for a flower holder)
190428 – April 2, 1892. (Design of foot for a goblet)
191932 – May 4, 1892. (Design for a flower holder)
200505 – October 11, 1892. (Design for a flower holder)

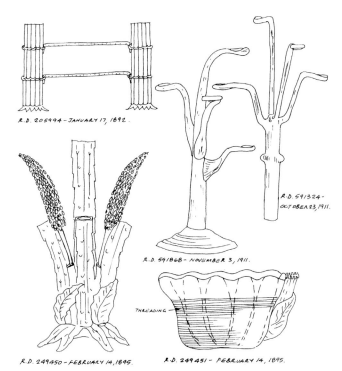

R.D. 205994 - JANUARY 17, 1892.

R.D. 591324 - OCTOBER 23, 1911.

R.D. 591868 - NOVEMBER 3, 1911.

THREADING

R.D. 249450 - FEBRUARY 14, 1895.

R.D. 249451 - FEBRUARY 14, 1895.

Boulton & Mills Registered Designs, 1868 – 1914
205994 – January 17, 1893. (Design for flower holders linked together with horizontal bars)
221354 – October 27, 1893. (Design for a flower holder)
235824 – July 12, 1894. (Design for a flower holder)
249450 – February 14, 1895. (Design for a flower holder)
249451 – February 14, 1895. Ornamental flower bowl and flower holder in glass
591324 – October 23, 1911. Design for glass flower holder
591868 – November 11, 1911. Design for flower holder to place in flower bowl

Burtles, Tate & Co.

Introduction

This glass-making factory was established in the 1850s at Poland Street, Oldham Road, Manchester. They also had another factory in Bolton called Victoria Glass Works, which was subsequently closed down in 1887 when their second Manchester factory was opened in German Street. The business was closed down in 1924.

They produced a wide range of domestic glass wares, both hand blown and press moulded, and were particularly noted for their flower holders.

Burtles, Tate & Co. Registered Designs, 1850 – 1914

The following Registered Designs are those that appear from the books of *Representations* to be for hand formed decorative glass items only. For a complete list of items registered, see *The Identification of English Pressed Glass 1842-1908* by Jenny Thompson.

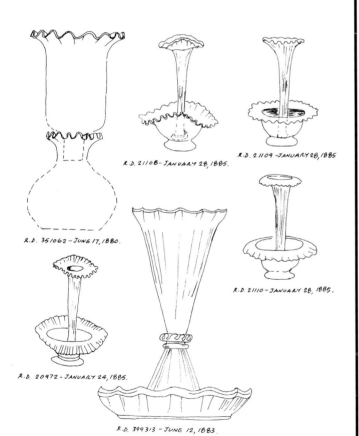

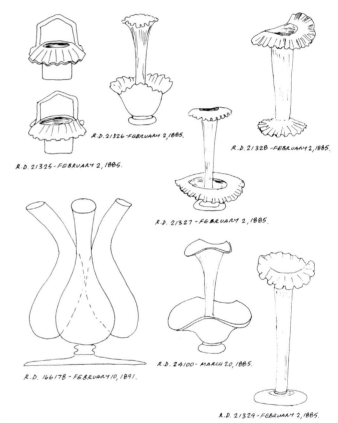

Burtles, Tate & Co. Registered Designs, 1850 – 1914

21325 – February 2, 1885. (Design for a glass basket)
21326 – February 2, 1885. Shape and pattern of flower stand
21327 – February 2, 1885. Shape and pattern of flower stand
21328 – February 2, 1885. Shape and pattern of flower stand
21329 – February 2, 1885. Shape and pattern of flower stand
24100 – March 20, 1885. Shape and pattern of flower stand
166178 – February 10, 1891. (Design for a flower holder)

Burtles, Tate & Co. Registered Designs, 1850 – 1914

351062 – June 17, 1880. (Design for a flower holder with an extension piece)
399313 – June 12, 1883. (Design for a flower holder)
20972 – January 24, 1885. Shape and pattern of flower stand
21108 – January 28, 1885. Shape and pattern of flower stand
21109 – January 28, 1885. Shape and pattern of flower stand
21110 – January 28, 1885. Shape and pattern of flower stand

John Walsh Walsh

Introduction

John Walsh Walsh, a Birmingham businessman, purchased the Soho & Vesta Glassworks in Lodge Road, Winson Green, Birmingham in 1850.

When he died in 1864, his son from his second marriage, John Walsh and the executors of his will, decided to sell the business. However, Ellen Eliza his daughter from his first marriage, persuaded her husband, Thomas Ferdinand Walker to purchase the business.

T.F.Walker then appointed Lewis John Murray to manage the business. After the death of L.J.Murray in 1912, Philip Jeffery Walker, the grandson of J.W.Walsh took over the company and ran it until his death in 1923.

John Walsh Walsh Registered Designs, 1851 – 1914

84598 – April 6, 1852. Claret decanter
90767 – April 12, 1853. Ink stand
91634 – July 9, 1853. Soda water bottle
99882 – April 18, 1855. Ink stand
356807– October 18, 1880. Jelly dish
357608 – November 3, 1880. Socket block for flower stand

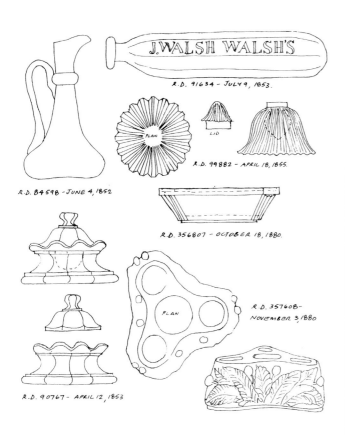

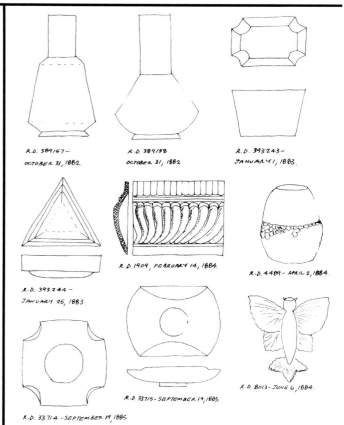

John Walsh Walsh Registered Designs, 1851 – 1914

389157 – October 31, 1882. Glass clareteen
389158 – October 31, 1882. Glass clareteen
393243 – January 25, 1883. Sugar basin
393244 – January 25, 1883. Jelly dish
1909 – February 14, 1884. Arch-topped, rolled over pillar known as the "Queen Anne" and applied to glass
4489 – April 2, 1884. Shape of the acorn
8013 – June 7, 1884. Shape
33714 – September 19, 1885. Shape
33715 – September 19, 1885. Shape

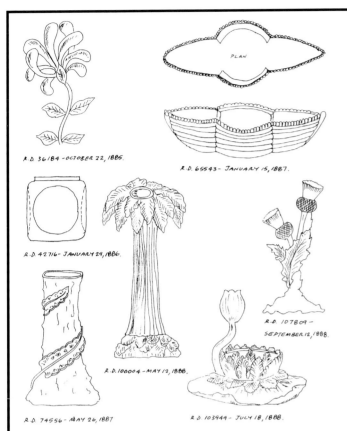

R.D. 36184 - OCTOBER 22, 1885.

PLAN

R.D. 65543 - JANUARY 15, 1887.

R.D. 42716 - JANUARY 29, 1886.

R.D. 107809 - SEPTEMBER 12, 1888.

R.D. 100004 - MAY 12, 1888.

R.D. 74556 - MAY 26, 1887

R.D. 103949 - JULY 18, 1888.

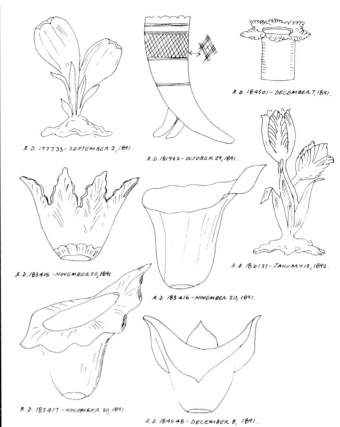

R.D. 177733 - SEPTEMBER 2, 1891.

R.D. 184501 - DECEMBER 7, 1891.

R.D. 181922 - OCTOBER 29, 1891.

R.D. 183415 - NOVEMBER 20, 1891.

R.D. 186137 - JANUARY 12, 1892.

R.D. 183416 - NOVEMBER 20, 1891.

R.D. 183417 - NOVEMBER 20, 1891.

R.D. 184548 - DECEMBER 8, 1891.

John Walsh Walsh Registered Designs, 1851 – 1914

36184 – October 22, 1885. Honeysuckle made in glass and used as a decoration on glass

42716 – January 29, 1886. Shape of biscuit jar pushed in at four sides

65543 – January 15, 1887. Shape. (Flower and candle holder)

74556 – May 26, 1887. Flower holder in the form of a tree trunk

100004 – May 12, 1888. (Design for a flower holder in the shape of a palm tree)

103949 – July 18, 1888. (Design for a combined candle and flower holder)

107808 – September 12, 1888. The Book of Design Representations records that a certificate was not issued for this registration number.

107809 – September 12, 1888. (Design for a flower holder in the form of two thistles)

John Walsh Walsh Registered Designs, 1851 – 1914

177733 – September 2, 1891. (Design for a flower holder)

181922 – October 29, 1891. Cut glass vase for holding flowers

183415 – November 20, 1891. (Design for a lamp shade)

183416 – November 20, 1891. (Design for a lamp shade)

183417 – November 20, 1891. (Design for a lamp shade)

184501 – December 7, 1891. Candle holder

184548 – December 8, 1891. (Design for a lamp shade)

186137 – January 12, 1892. Design for a Glass vase for holding cut flowers

John Walsh Walsh Registered Designs, 1851 – 1914

117086 – January 9, 1889. (Design for a flower holder in the shape of a fern leaf)

149468 – May 14, 1890. (Design for a flower holder in the shape of an owl)

155744 – September 2, 1890. Glass Rose Lamp for burning Clarks Fairy Light candle

164670 – January 14, 1891. Glass flower holder in the shape of a Wyvern.

165012 – January 20, 1891. New shaped leg for wine glasses bent round so as to look like the stem of a flower

172125 – May 29, 1891. Improvement on our Registration No.155744 dated September 2nd, 1890, consisting of a cylindrical glass vessel to be interchangeable with the candle holder, which vessel by holding water converts a "Fairy" or other candle lamp into a flower holder or lamp at will.

172810 – June 11, 1891. New shaped top for wine glasses

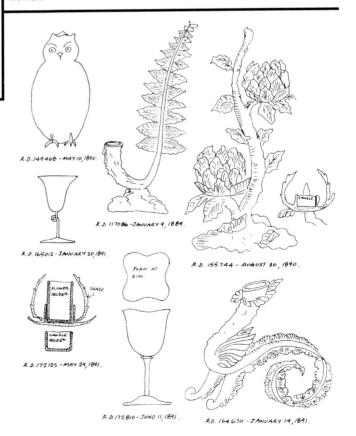

R.D. 149468 - MAY 10, 1890.

R.D. 117086 - JANUARY 9, 1889.

R.D. 165012 - JANUARY 20, 1891.

PLAN AT RIM.

R.D. 155744 - AUGUST 30, 1890.

FLOWER HOLDER   SHADE

CANDLE HOLDER

R.D. 172125 - MAY 29, 1891.

R.D. 172810 - JUNE 11, 1891.

R.D. 164670 - JANUARY 14, 1891.

R.D. 186546 - JANUARY 21, 1892.

PLAN

CONTAINER FOR ICE.

R.D. 203135 - NOVEMBER 25, 1892.

CONTAINER FOR WATER

R.D. 186567 - JANUARY 21, 1892.

R.D. 245141 - NOVEMBER 28, 1894.

R.D. 253935 - APRIL 24, 1895.

R.D. 211778 - MAY 6, 1893.

R.D. 251816 - MARCH 23, 1895.

R.D. 253934 - APRIL 29, 1895.

John Walsh Walsh Registered Designs, 1851 – 1914

186546 – January 21, 1892. (Design for a flower holder)
186567 – January 21, 1892. (Design for a fairy lamp holder)
203135 – November 25, 1892. Design for Flint glass ice pail, the object being for the hollow tubes to allow the water to be drained away from the solid ice
211778 – May 6, 1893. Design for top of glass flower vase representing pansy. Form of vase produced by Glass maker to the detail of pansy top done by a decorator.
245141 – November 28, 1894. Specimen vase flower holder.
251816 – March 23, 1895. The glass receptacle for silver mounting in the shape of horse's hoof
253934 – April 29, 1895. (Design for a flower holding device to be inserted in fan shaped vases)
253935 – April 29, 1895. Ink stand

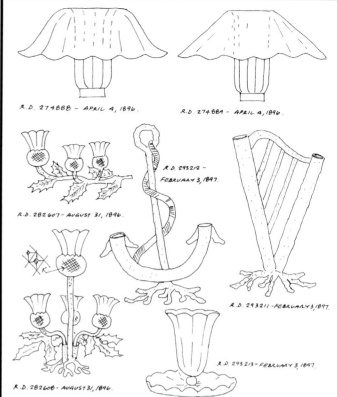

R.D. 274888 - APRIL 4, 1896.

R.D. 274889 - APRIL 4, 1896.

R.D. 282607 - AUGUST 31, 1896.

R.D. 293212 - FEBRUARY 3, 1897.

R.D. 293211 - FEBRUARY 3, 1897.

R.D. 293213 - FEBRUARY 3, 1897.

R.D. 282608 - AUGUST 31, 1896.

John Walsh Walsh Registered Designs, 1851 – 1914

274888 – April 4, 1896. (Design for a lamp shade)
274889 – April 4, 1896. (Design for a lamp shade)
282607 – August 31, 1896. (Design for a flower holder)
282608 – August 31, 1896. (Design for flower holders)
293210 – February 3, 1897. No illustration is provided for this registration, and it is recorded in the book of Representations that a certificate was not issued.
293211 – February 3, 1897. (Design for a flower holder)
293212 – February 3, 1897. (Design for a flower holder)
293213 – February 3, 1897. (Design for a flower holder)

John Walsh Walsh Registered Designs, 1851 – 1914

258147 – July 15, 1895. (Pattern)
264751 – October 29, 1895. To hold flowers
264997 – November 1, 1895. Flower holder is the shape of an easle with a vase supported on it.
271422 – February 21, 1896. (Design for a flower holder)
273414 – March 25, 1896. (Design for two ink wells and pen rest) The whole of the slab is solid glass with the exception of the two ink wells.
274887 – April 4, 1896. (Design for a lamp shade)

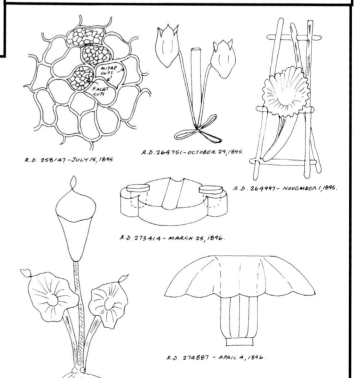

R.D. 258147 - JULY 15, 1895

MITRE CUTS

FACET CUTS

R.D. 264751 - OCTOBER 29, 1895.

R.D. 264997 - NOVEMBER 1, 1895.

R.D. 273414 - MARCH 25, 1896.

R.D. 271422 - FEBRUARY 21, 1896.

R.D. 274887 - APRIL 4, 1896.

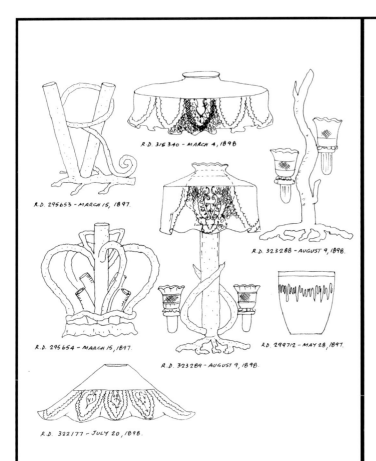

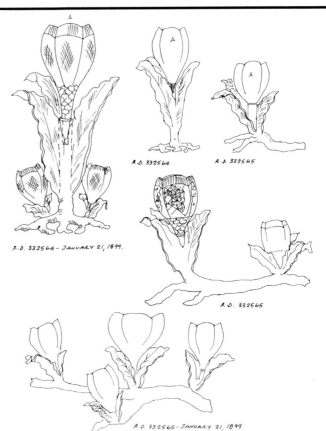

John Walsh Walsh Registered Designs, 1851 – 1914

295653 – March 15, 1897. (Design for a flower holder)
295654 – March 15, 1897. (Design for a flower holder)
299712 – May 28, 1897. Design for glass ice pail
315340 – March 4, 1898. Design for flint and opal glass shade shades, gas electric oil. It is the shape I particularly wish protected, the idea being for the sides which hang down to look like folds which when decorated give to these glass folds the appearance of lace, and the flat part of the shade at top being in opal glass throws down the light and acts as a reflector.
322177 – July 20, 1898. (Design for a lamp shade)
323288 – August 9, 1898. Cut glass vases cut and fancy glass flower holder the whole of which is made in glass. The vases are loose and drop into glass ring.
323289 – August 9, 1898. Design for a candlestick and flower holder combined for table decoration, the whole of which is made in glass, with the exception of the candle holder which is made in metal. The dotted line is a metal tube for holding the candle. The tube being placed inside the upright glass tube shown.

John Walsh Walsh Registered Designs, 1851 – 1914

332564 – January 24, 1899. Design for a set of flower holders for table decoration to be made in cut or fancy glass. The vases "A" fit into the glass tubes as shown in red ink and can be taken out when required for cleaning purposes.
332565 – January 24, 1899. Design for a set of flower holders to be made in cut or fancy glass

John Walsh Walsh Registered Designs, 1851 – 1914

333851 – February 16, 1899. Design for glass bottle for holding spirits, scents etc.
333852 – February 16, 1899. Design for a jar to be made in glass to be used for celery, biscuits etc.
333944 – February 18, 1899. Design for ink bottle to be made in glass specially for silver mounting in silver or electroplate or any other metal. The container which drops in may if necessary be utilised as a match holder, cigarette holder, toothpick holder etc. Ink well or container to drop in. Rough fitting for silver mount.
336752 – April 18, 1899. (Design for a bowl)
353374 – February 16, 1900. Design of bowl to be made in glass or chinaware representing an Imperial Yeomanry hat, for holding flowers, sweets or any other article.
375896 – June 25, 1901. Design for glass shade for incandescent gas light, electric or any other lighting purposes.

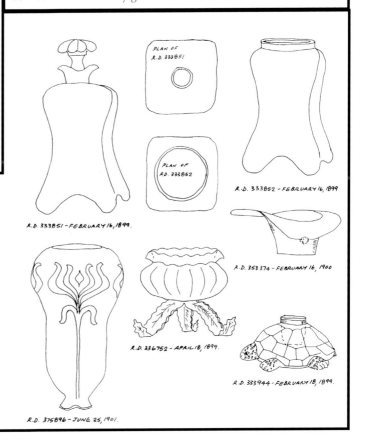

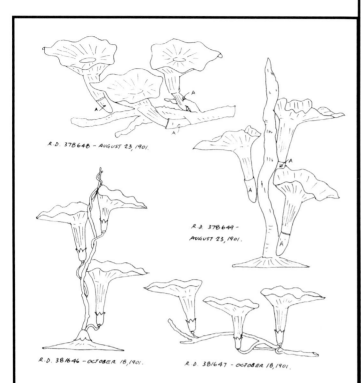

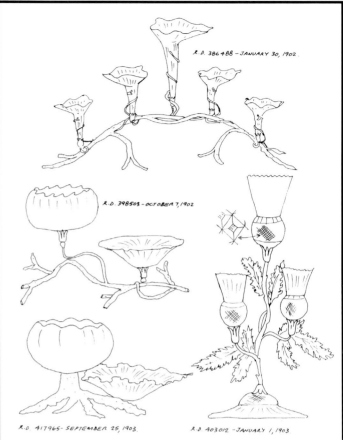

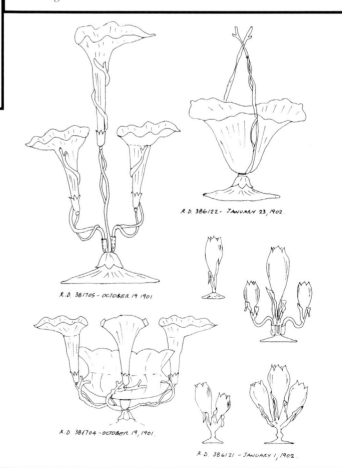

John Walsh Walsh Registered Designs, 1851 – 1914

378648 – August 23, 1901. Design for flower holder to be made in glass or china, consisting of one or more small vases in the shape of leaves, which fit into tubes marked "A" so they can be readily taken out for the purpose of cleaning.

378649 – August 23, 1901. Design for flower holders to be made in glass or china, consisting of one or more small vases in the shape of leaves, which fit into tubes marked "A" so they can be readily taken out for the purpose of cleaning.

381646 – October 18, 1901. Design for flower holder to be made in metal and glass

381647 – October 18, 1901. (Design for a flower holder)

John Walsh Walsh Registered Designs, 1851 – 1914

386488 – January 30, 1902. (Design for a centre flower stand)

398503 – October 7, 1902. Design for flower holder to be made in glass and metal combined.

403012 – January 3, 1903. Design for flower holder to be made in glass and metal combined. The thistle shape vases as foot to be made in glass and the stems and leaves in metal.

John Walsh Walsh Registered Designs, 1851 – 1914

381704 – October 19, 1901. (Design for a centre flower holder)

381705 – October 19, 1901. Glass and metal. (flower stand)

386121 – January 23, 1902. (Designs for flower holders)

386122 – January 23, 1902. (Design for a basket)

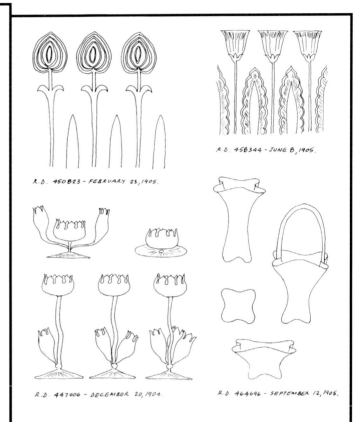

John Walsh Walsh Registered Designs, 1851 – 1914

409769 – May 9, 1903. Design for a set of flower holders to be made in metal and glass combined. The parts shown in yellow represents metalwork. The leaves and buds and flowers are made in glass which fit into metal sockets.

417965 – September 25, 1903. (Design for a flower holder)

John Walsh Walsh Registered Designs, 1851 – 1914

447006 – December 20, 1904. Design for a set of flower holders to be made in glass.

450823 – February 23, 1905. Design for decorating gas and electric light shades or vases to be made in Flint or coloured glass, the design can be moulded in semi-opaque or opalescent or it can be etched with acid.

458344 – June 8, 1905. Design for ornamenting glass shades in moulding and etching combined.

464696 – September 12, 1905. (Designs for a flower holder, basket, and small bowl)

John Walsh Walsh Registered Designs, 1851 – 1914

435651 – June 28, 1904. (Decorative pattern)

435652 – June 25, 1904. There is no illustration for this registration in the book of Representations, but it is recorded in that book, that a certificate was not issued for this registration.

435959 – July 1, 1904. (Design of a mold blown decorative motif)

436862 – July 13, 1904. (Design for a lamp shade)

436863 – July 13, 1904. (Design for a lamp shade)

440767 – September 9, 1904. (Design for a flower holder)

441666 – September 20, 1904. Design for a set of flower holders to be made in glass and metal combined.

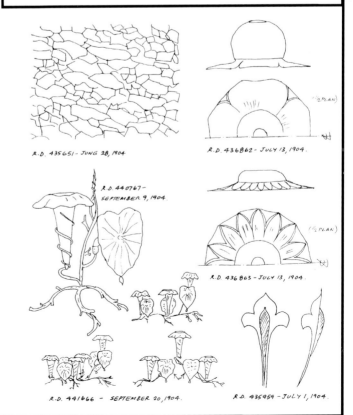

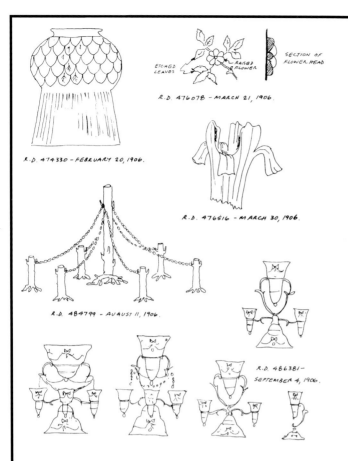

R.D. 474330 – FEBRUARY 20, 1906.

ETCHED LEAVES RAISED FLOWER SECTION OF FLOWER HEAD

R.D. 476078 – MARCH 21, 1906.

R.D. 476516 – MARCH 30, 1906.

R.D. 484799 – AUGUST 11, 1906.

R.D. 486381 – SEPTEMBER 4, 1906.

John Walsh Walsh Registered Designs, 1851 – 1914

474330 – February 20, 1906. (Design for a lamp shade)
476078 – March 21, 1906. (Design for a decorative floral pattern)
476516 – March 30, 1906. (Design for the rim of a flower holder)
484799 – August 11, 1906. Design for a set of flower holders to be made in glass or china
486381 – September 4, 1906. Design for a set of flower holders to be made in glass and mounted in metal

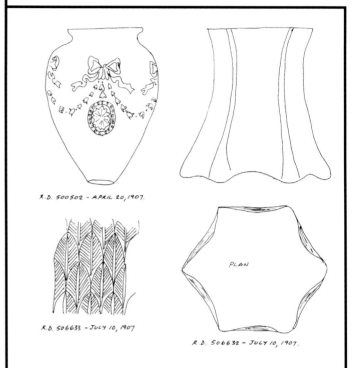

R.D. 500502 – APRIL 20, 1907.

PLAN

R.D. 506633 – JULY 10, 1907

R.D. 506632 – JULY 10, 1907.

John Walsh Walsh Registered Designs, 1851 – 1914

500502 – April 20, 1907. Gas, electric light shade.
506632 – July 10, 1907. Design for glass receptacle for table decoration purposes.
506633 – July 10, 1907. (Pattern for decoration)

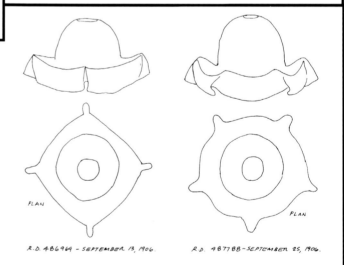

PLAN

PLAN

R.D. 486969 – SEPTEMBER 13, 1906.

R.D. 487788 – SEPTEMBER 25, 1906.

John Walsh Walsh Registered Designs, 1851 – 1914

486969 – September 13, 1906. (Design for lamp shade)
487788 – September 25, 1906. Design for shade for electric or other light to be made in glass.
492244 – November 30, 1906. Design for a set of flower holders to be made in glass or china, similar to Rd. 484799 above but using ribbons in lieu of chains.
493532 – January 2, 1907. (Design for a centre flower stand similar to 484799 above)

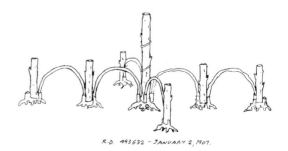

R.D. 493532 – JANUARY 2, 1907.

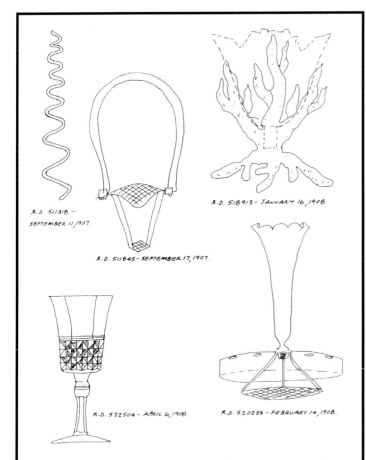

R.D. 51131B –
SEPTEMBER 11, 1907.

R.D. 51B913 – JANUARY 16, 190B.

R.D. 511B45 – SEPTEMBER 17, 1907.

R.D. 522504 – APRIL 6, 190B.

R.D. 520225 – FEBRUARY 14, 190B.

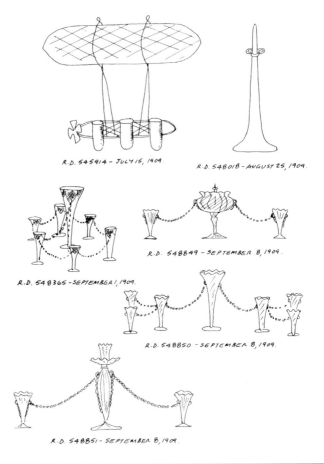

R.D. 545914 – JULY 15, 1909.

R.D. 54B01B – AUGUST 25, 1909.

R.D. 54B365 – SEPTEMBER 1, 1909.

R.D. 54BB49 – SEPTEMBER 8, 1909.

R.D. 54BB50 – SEPTEMBER 8, 1909.

R.D. 54BB51 – SEPTEMBER 8, 1909.

John Walsh Walsh Registered Designs, 1851 – 1914

511318 – September 11, 1907. Design for spiral to be made in glass to be used in vases as support for flowers or when inverted to be used to carry flowers.
511845 – September 17, 1907. (Design for a metal grid type flower support)
518913 – January 16, 1908. Design for glass support for glass vases and bowls. The support has a socket in centre into which the peg of vase or bowl fits as shown by dotted lines.
520225 – February 14, 1908. Design for glass cover and wire support for bowls.
522504 – April 6, 1908. (Design for a wine glass)

Top right:
John Walsh Walsh Registered Designs, 1851 – 1914

545914 – July 15, 1909. Design for flower holder to be made in glass and metal combined.
548018 – August 25, 1909. Design for flower support to be made in china or glass.
548365 – September 1, 1909. The novelty claimed is the manner in which the glass chains are connected to the vases.
548849 – September 8, 1909. Chains are attached
548850 – September 8, 1909. (Design for linked together flower holders)
548851 – September 8, 1909. Chains attached.
Right:
John Walsh Walsh Registered Designs, 1851 – 1914

528991 – August 19, 1908. Design for flower holder to be made in glass and metal. All pillars and rods to be made in glass. All other parts to be made in metal.
532581 – November 6, 1908. Design for a flower holder
536418 – January 30, 1909. Table glassware
540542 – April 15, 1909. Made in glass for separating services of tableware.
540934 – April 22, 1909. Design for menu holder in glass or china.

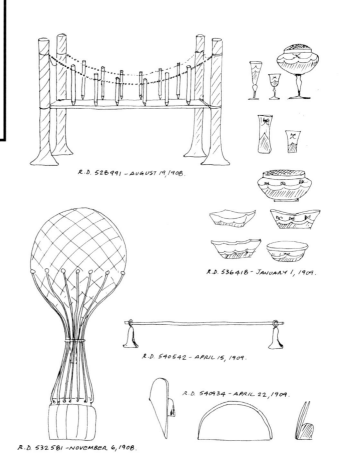

R.D. 52B991 – AUGUST 19, 190B.

R.D. 53641B – JANUARY 1, 1909.

R.D. 540542 – APRIL 15, 1909.

R.D. 540934 – APRIL 22, 1909.

R.D. 532 5B1 – NOVEMBER 6, 190B.

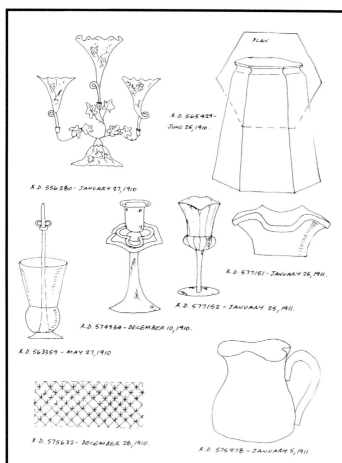

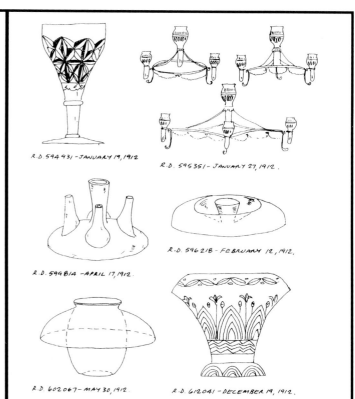

John Walsh Walsh Registered Designs, 1851 – 1914

556280 – January 27, 1910. Design for flower holders to be made in glass and metal combined, the predominating material being glass.
563359 – May 27, 1910. (Flower support in vase)
565429 – June 25, 1910. Design – gas or electric light having 6 or more sides, made in one piece to be made in glass
574934 – December 10, 1910. (Design for a combined candle holder and flower support)
575632 – December 28, 1910. Design for etching on flint or coloured glass.
575978 – January 5, 1911. Jug to be made in glass or porcelain.

John Walsh Walsh Registered Designs, 1851 – 1914

594931 – January 19, 1912. (Design for a wine glass)
595351 – January 27, 1912. The novelty is in the shape of the vases which are cut in the "Sheraton" style
596218 – February 12, 1912. (Design for a flower support device)
599814 – April 17, 1912. (Design for a flower support device)
602067 – May 30, 1912. (Design for a lamp shade)
612041 – December 19, 1912. (Design for a flower holder)

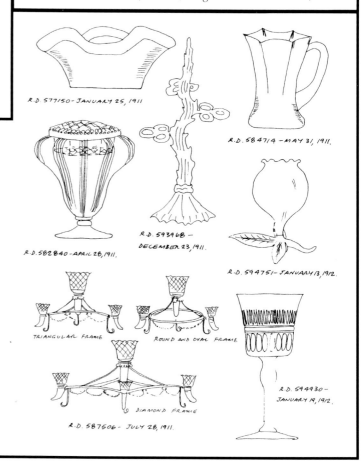

John Walsh Walsh Registered Designs, 1851 – 1914

577150 – January 25, 1911. Design for bowl for holding fruit, flowers or salad to be made in glass or porcelain
577151 – January 25, 1911. Design for bowl for holding fruit, flowers or salad to be made in glass or porcelain.
577152 - January 25, 1911. Design for wine glass to be made in flint glass.
582840 – April 28, 1911. (Design for a flower holder)
584714 – May 31, 1911. Design for jug to be made in glass or porcelain.
587506 – July 28, 1911. Novelty is the ornamental metalwork.
593968 – December 23, 1911. Design for flower support to be made in glass or china
594751 – January 13, 1912. (Design for a small flower holder)
594930 – January 19, 1912. (Design for a wine glass)

Brief Glossary Of Glass-Making Terms

Annealing process. To avoid the risk of cracking from internal stresses caused by uneven cooling of its various parts during its manufacture, the glass object was reheated to just below melting point, and allowed to cool slowly over a period of many hours or even days in a lehr, a long tunnel kiln lined with fire bricks. The temperature was graded from hot at its entrance to cool at its exit. The glass items were placed on steel pans and pulled along the complete length of the lehr. They were then removed, washed, and checked for damage.

Aqua regia. A mixture of nitric acid and hydrochloric acid, which will dissolve gold or platinum.

Aventurine. A dark coloured glass, usually green or brown, spangled with fine particles of gold, copper or other metallic material. Venetian glass makers are credited with inventing this type of glass, which attempts to imitate a naturally occurring mineral.

Blank. A completed glass item ready for decoration.

Blow pipe. A hollow iron tube, up to six feet in length, made wider and thicker at the end on which the molten glass is gathered.

Brilliant cutting. A style of cut glass with very deep, highly polished complex cut patterns, developed in America in the latter half of the nineteenth century.

Calcedonio. Variegated opaque glassware made in Venice in the late fifteenth century, to imitate Roman agate glass, which itself was intended to resemble the semi-precious stone.

Carnival glass. Pressed glass items given an iridescent surface by spraying a mixture of metallic salts over the hot glass and firing to produce a permanent finish.

Cire perdue. The object to be cast was first modelled in wax, and then coated with a ceramic paste. When the paste had hardened, the form was heated sufficiently for the wax to melt and run out. The ceramic mold now formed was filled with pulverized glass or molten glass, and placed in a kiln to fuse. When the article was formed and had sufficiently cooled, the ceramic mold was broken away, leaving a single copy of the original object that had been modelled in wax.

Cristallo. A type of soda glass made with the ashes of barilla, first developed in Venice in the fourteenth century, and which subsequently became the standard metal of the Venetian glass industry. Its softness in its molten state allowed the formation of elaborate shapes, and it was also suitable for diamond point engraving, but too brittle for cutting.

Cullet. Fragments of broken glass added to the glass pots to be remelted, and to act as a flux for the fresh ingredients of a new batch.

Diamond point engraving. A technique in which designs are scratched on the surface of glass with a diamond point.

Façon de Venise. High quality glassware in the Venetian style made throughout Europe in the sixteenth and seventeenth centuries, the techniques and designs of which were reproduced extensively in the last half of the nineteenth century, notably by Antonio Salviati.

Feldspar. A variety of minerals found in igneous rocks, consisting mainly of silicates of aluminium combined with some other minerals, so that they vary in their chemical composition, crystalline form and colour.

Flint glass. An old term for glass containing lead, dating from a period when calcined or ground flint was used as the source of silica in glass manufacture.

Fluorspar. This is a common name for calcium fluoride, a transparent, brittle mineral occuring in many colours.

Folded foot. The rim of a foot of a drinking glass or vase formed in thin glass which is folded over or under to give extra strength.

Flux. This comprises an alkaline substance, such as potash or soda, which is added to the batch to aid the fusion of the silica and other ingredients.

Frit. The mixture of silica, potash and metallic oxides heated in a separate furnace at a temperature low enough for the mixture to oxidise but not fuse. This is then added to the cullet in a clay pot in the working furnace and will eventually vitrify into glass.

Gather (or Paraison). The molten glass collected from the pot on the end of a blowing iron.

Glory hole. A small hole formed in a glass furnace through which a glass object can be reheated during the processes of manipulation and fire polishing.

Lamp work. Glassware formed from glass canes and tubes, heated, softened and shaped by hand tools, originally in the flame of an oil lamp, but later using a Bunsen burner.

Marver. A marble or polished metal slab on which a gather of molten glass is rolled, to smooth it or pick up other material.

Metal. A term used for glass in its molten and cold states.

Muffle kiln. A small kiln used to bring enamelled or gilded glass articles to the heat necessary for fritting or melting the applied decoration sufficiently to attach it permanently to the glass body.

Pate de verre. This technique comprises clear or colored glass, either transparent, translucent or opaque, ground into a very fine powder and mixed into a thick paste with an adhesive medium, usually just plain water. This paste was shaped either freehand, or on a pottery type wheel, or in a mould, and then fired. During the firing, the mixture fused sufficiently to preserve the shape of the article and keep it fit for use when it had cooled and hardened. The final surface has a matt, finely pitted finish.

Pellicle. A thin film or skin of acid resisting material, usually wax, gutta percha or powdered asphaltum.

Peloton. This technique comprises the application of short, random lengths of colored glass canes applied to the surface of an object in a random pattern. This method of decoration was patented by Wilhelm Kralik of Neuwelt, in Bohemia, on October 25, 1880.

Pontil. An iron rod to which a glass object is transferred after it has been blown, so that it can be brought to its final shape and decorated.

Prunt. A blob of glass applied to a glass object as a decoration, sometimes drawn to a point, impressed with a pattern, or a mask.

Rock crystal. A clear full lead glass, formed into thick walled blanks which are decorated by deep cutting with pillars or roundels, and by finer complementary cutting by copper wheel engraving, and by polishing.

Seed. A small particle of un-melted raw material or foreign matter found embedded in glass.

Soda glass. Glass in which the alkali is sodium carbonate, rather than potash.

Tazza. A shallow ornamental cup or dish on a stemmed foot, usually used to display food such as fruit and sweetmeats.

Vaseline glass. A transparent, yellow-green glass made with a quantity of uranium oxide. This type of glass will fluoresce under long wave ultra violet light.

White acid. A mixture of hydrofluoric acid with an alkali salt such as potassium carbonate or sodium carbonate which only attacks the surface of glass and produces a very fine textured, smooth obscured surface. This liquid was also used for producing a satin finish on the surface of coloured glassware.

Bibliography

Nineteenth Century Books and Documents

Pellatt, Apsley. *Curiosities of Glassmaking*, London: David Bogue, 1849.

Pattern and design books of the following manufacturers currently placed on loan with Dudley Archives and Local History Service at Cosely, West Midlands:

Boulton & Mills, Smart Brothers, Thomas Webb & Sons Ltd, Richardson family businesses, Stevens & Williams Limited
Archive material at Broadfield House Glass Museum.
Archive material at Stuart & Sons Limited factory at Stourbridge, West Midlands.

Registers and Books of Representations recording Registered Designs, in the custody of the Public Record Office, at Kew, London.

Periodical

Pottery Gazette and Glass Trade Review, 1877 to 1914

Nineteenth Century International Exhibition Catalogues

Great Exhibition of the Industry of All Nations, London, 1851.

The International Exhibition, London, 1862.

Universal Exhibition, Paris, 1878.

Twentieth Century Books

Arwas, Victor. *Glass; Art Nouveau to Art Deco*, London: Academy Editions, 1987.

Bosomworth, Dorothy, *The Victorian Catalogue of Household Goods*, London: Studio Editions, Limited, 1991. (This was originally published by Silber & Flemming, c.1883, as *Illustrated Catalogue of Furniture & Household Requisites c.1883*)

Brooks, John. *The Arthur Negus Guide to British Glass*, London: Hamlyn, 1981.

Evans,Wendy, Catherine Ross, and Alex Werner, *Whitefriars Glass, James Powell & Sons of London*, London: Museum of London, 1995.

Grover, Ray and Lee, *English Cameo Glass*, New York: Crown Publishers Inc., 1956.

Grover, Ray and Lee, *Art Glass Nouveau*, Rutland Vermont: Charles E. Tuttle Company, 1967.

Hajdamach, Charles R., *British Glass 1800-1914*, Woodbridge, Suffolk, England: Antique Collectors Club, 1991.

Heacock, William and Patricia Johnson, *5000 Open Salts*, Marietta, Ohio: Antique Publications, 1995.

Jackson, Lesley, *The Art of James Powell & Sons*, Shepton Beauchamp, Somerset: Richard Dennis,1996.

Klein, Dan and Lloyd Ward, *The History Of Glass*, London: OrbisPublishing Limited, 1984.

Manley, Cyril, *Decorative Victorian Glass*, London: Ward Lock, 1981.

Morris, Barbara, *Victorian Table Glass and Ornaments*, London: Barrie and Jenkins, 1978.

Revi, Albert Christian, *American Art Nouveau Glass*, Atglen, Pennsylvania: Schiffer Publishing Limited, 1968.

Revi, Albert Christian, *Nineteenth Century Glass*, Atglen, Pennsylvania: Schiffer Publishing 1967 (revised edition)

Reynolds, Eric, *The Glass of John Walsh Walsh*, Shepton Beauchamp, Somerset, England: Richard Dennis, 1999.

Ruf, Bob and Pat, *Fairy Lamps*, Atglen, Pennsylvania: Schiffer Publishing Limited, 1996.

Truitt, Robert and Deborah, *Collectible Bohemian Glass 1880 – 1940*, Kensington Maryland 20895: B + D Glass, 1995.

Thompson, Jenny, *The Identification of English Pressed Glass 1842 - 1908*, Cumbria, England: Jenny Thompson, 1989.

Thompson, Jenny, *Supplement to The Identification of English Pressed Glass 1842 – 1908*, Cumbria, England: Jenny Thompson, 1993.

Wakefield, Hugh, *Nineteenth Century British Glass*, London: Faber & Faber (second edition)1982.

Wills, Geoffrey, *Victorian Glass*, G.Bell & Sons, 1976.

Williams-Thomas, R.S., *The Crystal Years*, Brierley Hill, West Midlands, England: Stevens & Williams, 1983.

Woodward, H.W., *Art, Feat and Mystery – The Story of Thomas Webb & Sons*, Stourbridge, West Midlands, England: Mark + Moody Limited, 1978.